"If you're up for some life-rattling, world-shaking, head-turning, boat-rocking twists and turns in your life journey, then *Way to Live* is your global positioning device. This book will ratchet your faith up a notch (or 20) by inviting you into the ancient practices of faith, practices that may surprise you (and your friends) and challenge the world as we know it. You can't just read this book. You DO it."

KENDA CREASY DEAN
Co-author, *The Godbearing Life: The Art of Soul Tending for Youth Ministry* and *Starting Right: Thinking Theologically about Youth Ministry*

"*Way to Live* begins with real-life issues and real stories and then develops real faith! This is a wonderful collection of stories from the scriptures of young people's lives and anchored in the faith community's scriptures. And each chapter provides practical ways to live the Jesus Story."

ROBERT J. MCCARTY
Executive Director, National Federation for Catholic Youth Ministry

"*Way to Live* gets it! A vibrant, compelling, unique exploration of Christian practices written for today's youth by teen and adult authors. Practices that once may have been no more than a huge yawn during a Sunday-school lesson leap off the pages and connect with teen readers as dazzlingly real and relevant to their everyday lives."

PATRICIA HERSCH
Author, *A Tribe Apart: A Journey into the Heart of American Adolescence*

"There are dozens of approaches to youth ministry today, and yet the ones that make a difference in the lives of young people consistently draw them back into the practices of historic Christian faith. Dorothy Bass and Don Richter have done a masterful job at communicating many of the richest traditions we have to a new audience. There are no platitudes here, no condescending dismissal of teenagers' faith, but rather a warm invitation to a deeper, more complex relationship with God that makes sense in a postmodern adolescent's world. I am buying this for my own kids!"

Way,

EDITED BY **DOROTHY C. BASS** AND **DON C. RICHTER**

Christian
Practices
for Teens

UPPER
ROOM BOOKS®
NASHVILLE

Way to Live: Christian Practices for Teens
Copyright © 2002 by Dorothy C. Bass and Don C. Richter
All rights reserved.

The Upper Room® Web site: http://www.upperroom.org.

UPPER ROOM®, UPPER ROOM BOOKS®, and design logos are trademarks owned by The Upper Room®, a Ministry of the GBOD®, Nashville, Tennessee. All rights reserved.

Unless otherwise noted, scripture quotations are from the *New Revised Standard Version Bible,* copyright 1989, Division of Christian Education of the National Council of the Churches of Christ in the United States of America. Used by permission. All rights reserved.

"The Lord's Prayer" ecumenical text is used by permission of the International Consultation on English Texts (ICET).

The publisher gratefully acknowledges permission to reproduce copyrighted material appearing in this book. Additional credit lines appear on page 310.

Cover and interior design: My Tribe Communicates
Fourth Printing: 2008
At the time of publication all Web sites referenced in this book were valid. However, due to the fluid nature of the Internet, some addresses may have changed or the content may no longer be relevant.

Library of Congress Cataloging-in-Publication Data

Way to live : Christian practices for teens / edited by Dorothy C. Bass and Don C. Richter
        p. cm.
Includes bibliographical references.
ISBN 978-0-8358-0975-7
        1. Christian teenagers—Religious life. I. Bass, Dorothy C. II. Richter, Don C.

BV4531.3 .W39 2002
248.8'3—dc21   2002002492

Printed in the United States of America

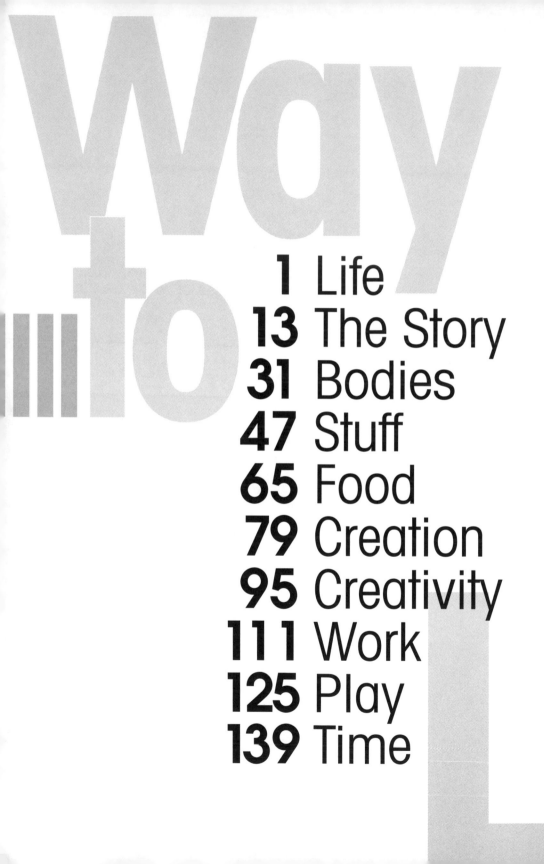

1	Life
13	The Story
31	Bodies
47	Stuff
65	Food
79	Creation
95	Creativity
111	Work
125	Play
139	Time

155 Truth
171 Choices
187 Friends
201 Welcome
217 Forgiveness
233 Justice
247 Grieving
261 Music
275 Prayer
291 Practice

299 The Authors
303 References
309 Acknowledgments

DOROTHY C. BASS
WITH JOHN SCHWEHN
AND MARTHA SCHWEHN

I||Life

I want a way to live that keeps me involved in what God is doing in me and in the world around me. Do you know a way to live that is like that? ■ ■ ■ ■ ■ ■ ■ ■ ■ ■ ■ ■ ■

—**Martha Schwehn, 15**

■ ■ ■ ■ **MARTHA:** I just got back from my first mission trip with my youth group. Fourteen youth plus four fairly cool adults piled into two vans and traveled to a town in Pennsylvania where lots of people are unemployed. We spent a week working with needy children and cleaning out a house that belongs to an elderly man who is sick. Both these jobs were hard, but we felt like we did them pretty well, partly because we learned to work together. We even had fun. It was kind of amazing.

Before work every morning, we had a quiet time to read a Bible story and think about it on our own. Then at night we gathered to talk about what we were doing and thinking. One morning we read the story about the good Samaritan who stopped to help a man who had been beaten up and left lying in the road (see Luke 10:25-37). I thought about the story several times that day, like when I was trying to show kindness to one of the little kids I was helping. That night I realized that sometimes I do respond to people in need, like the Samaritan did, but most times I am more like the two other characters in the story who walked by without helping.

As we repeated the routine of Bible study and work day after day, something awesome began to happen. I started to see a pattern. Here I was, way out of my comfort zone, far from home, sleeping on the floor every night and doing hard jobs every day—and amazingly, God was taking care of me and challenging me at the same time. But the coolest part of the pattern was this: I was getting involved in what God was doing. It was like God was working through me to care for those little kids, who usually don't get the kind of attention I was giving them. It was like I was becoming God's hands in that place.

Jeremy, our leader (he's 28), says the mission trip is his favorite part of every year. He thinks that's because on a mission trip he has a community that takes time to stop and talk together about how God is moving in our lives. Of course God is present no matter where we are, Jeremy says. But in our regular lives we miss out on some of the best parts of life with God, because we don't take time to notice how God is taking care of us and also stretching us through the challenges we face. It's like with the story of the good Samaritan. Most of us know the story, but we usually don't try to relate it to what happens to us.

Jeremy says the mission trip is also great because it's a time when we do what he calls "the dance." On each day, all the different practices that are part of a good life are right there. We eat, we pray, we work, we play, we sing. We don't worry about how we look or wish we had more stuff, because everyone is wearing work clothes and living out of a suitcase anyway. We are surrounded by a community of friends who discuss important issues. And somehow, all these practices fit together into a rhythm that feels right. You feel like you are moving to a beat that comes from someplace deep and true.

■ ■

Christ has no body now on earth but yours, no hands but yours, no feet but yours. Yours are the eyes through which Christ's compassion is to look out to the world. Yours are the feet with which Christ is to go about doing good. Yours are the hands with which Christ is to bless all people now.

—TERESA OF AVILA, a Spanish mystic who lived about 500 years ago

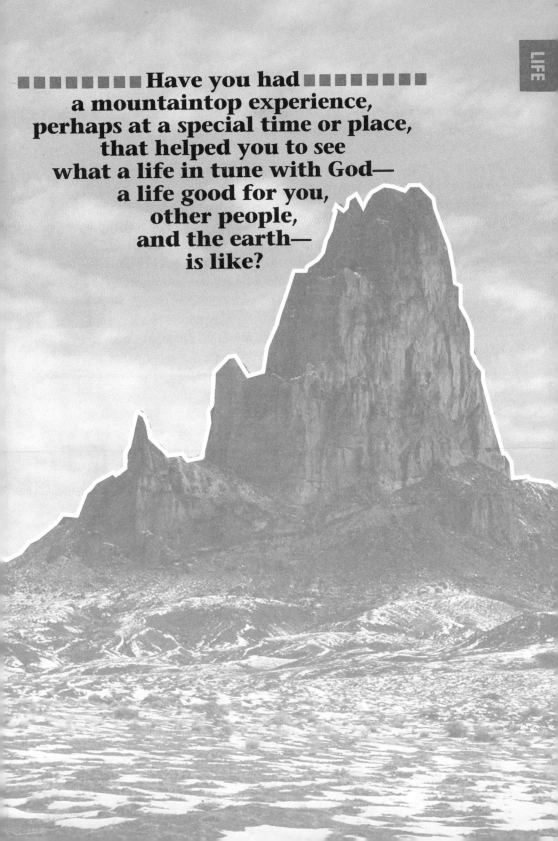

■■■■■■■■■ **Have you had** ■■■■■■■■
a mountaintop experience,
perhaps at a special time or place,
that helped you to see
what a life in tune with God—
a life good for you,
other people,
and the earth—
is like?

Some things came into focus for me on that trip. My pastor says it sounds like I had what's called a "mountaintop experience"—a time of special closeness with God that gets its name from Moses' meeting with God on top of Mount Sinai. But my pastor also insists that God is just as present in the valleys—and in the plains and the swamps and everywhere else. We are with God not only when we are being "religious" or doing extra-good things. We are also with God when we are doing the most ordinary activities you can imagine, things like taking a shower or playing a game. What's important is our everyday relationship with God, not just the special feelings we get on the mountaintop.

That's probably right, but it bothers me. The focus I had on the trip is already getting fuzzy. In the regular world it's harder to notice God. It's also harder to find a community where we talk about really important things. And it's harder to live out my faith—doing what I think is right can feel pretty risky. The dance Jeremy talked about gets jerky as I rush from one activity to another. And I feel like the different pieces of my life don't fit together neatly at all; there's not time for everything, and I get torn between different priorities.

I like my life at home, in the regular world. I love my friends, including the ones who don't go to church. It doesn't make sense to keep wearing work clothes every day and sleeping on the floor every night. But I do want to keep doing that dance. I want a way to live that keeps me involved in what God is doing in me and in the world around me.

Do you know a **way to live** that is like that? ■ ■ ■ ■

Searching for a way to live

You don't have to leave home to get in touch with a desire to figure out how to live in a way that is deeply, truly good. This longing can well up in you when you see someone at school put down an unpopular boy, when

■ ■ ■ ■ This is the last sentence of the Gospel of John:

"There are also many other things that Jesus did; if every one of them were written down, I suppose that the world itself could not contain the books that would be written." ■ ■ ■ ■

you feel bad after cheating on a test, when you haven't had a good talk with your mom or dad for weeks, when you learn about global warming in your science class. Your heart protests, but you don't know whom to share your feelings with or where to look for a better way. You just know that things aren't right.

You don't have to be a teenager to experience this deep desire either. But the teenage years are a great time to let the desire surface, a great time to think about what a "good life" would be like and to speak your hopes out loud. These are years when lots of people are encouraging you to think about how you are going to live. A teacher might ask what you plan to do after high school. Your big sister might keep a close eye on your social life, wondering where you are headed as you become an adult. You are getting used to being honest and reliable, or not. You are making choices today that will affect all your tomorrows. And besides, how you live matters right now. Life is not only something that lies ahead of you, after high school. You have talents and passions *today*. You have heart and mind and soul and strength *today*. You have the ability to help—or to hurt—other people and the earth *today*.

You do have the option of *not* thinking about how you live, of course. You could just go with the flow. Sit back and let other people tell you what to think and do. Some of the people who'd be glad to tell you are obvious: certain teachers, maybe your parents, even some of your friends. Others are not so obvious, like the "merchants of cool"—marketers who want your deepest desires to be for the things they sell, from clothes and makeup to CDs and cars. They'd like to cover your body with advertisements and clutter your mind with images of a "good life" that's pretty different from the one you deserve. Their "good life" is about great vacations, glamorous clothes, and the hottest cars—things few people possess and not what life is really about anyway.

Having a good life—God's life

This book invites you into a community of people who don't just go with the flow. This community's image of "the good life" is not about having lots of stuff or being more successful than other people. Instead, it's about getting involved in the loving, challenging life of God.

This community first gathered around a person who embodied the loving, challenging life of God. When Jesus healed the sick, invited himself to dinner at the house of an unpopular man, and taught those who followed him not to set their hearts on material things, his followers could see what God really intended for this world. Jesus taught his followers to pray; he washed their feet; and he told them to love one another.

A *way to live* started to come into focus. When Jesus was executed, this way seemed to be crushed and powerless. But when he rose from the dead, his followers soon realized that the world was changed forever, and so were their own lives. Trying to live as they had seen Jesus live no longer seemed beyond reach.

This community still exists today. Its members speak many languages and worship in many styles. Although they belong to what appear to be many separate communities—Catholic, Presbyterian, Evangelical, Lutheran, Methodist, and many more—at the heart of all these communities is Jesus. He promised always to be with them, and they experience his presence in many ways—in the faces of people in need, in the bread they share, in the music they sing, and even in the suffering they sometimes have to endure, just as he did. Sharing life with Jesus, they

Augustine of Hippo (d. 430) explored many paths to God before becoming a Christian. Looking back on his journey, he wrote to God that "our hearts are restless until they rest in You."

He believed that the restlessness in the human spirit, our yearning for truth and goodness, is a gift from God that keeps us from settling for unworthy ways of being.

Experience the challenge of living this way at www.waytolive.org.

are caught up into the loving, challenging life of God. Christians call this "life in the Holy Spirit."

Jesus said, "I came that [you] may have life, and have it abundantly" (John 10:10). The *life* he offers is not just a matter of existing. It's not just eating and breathing and going with the flow. It's *abundant* life. *Life* with a capital *L*. Life full of the kind of freedom and love and courage Jesus lived himself and gave to his community.

This is the bold, free life you can explore by reading this book. The authors of this book did not invent this way of living; it's thousands of years old. But we didn't find it in a museum either. People of all ages and many different cultures are living this life right now, in the fast-changing world of the 21st century.

Your challenge and privilege are to live it where *you* are—in *your* family, *your* neighborhood, *your* school, *your* world.

Dancing to the beat of God's heart

If you have a deep desire for a way to live that moves to a beat deep and true, the authors of this book invite you to spend time in these pages with us and with other members of the community with Jesus at its heart. We who have written this book, 18 teens and 18 adults from many different backgrounds, experience the same desire you do. We want to live life *abundantly* where we are. We come from cities, suburbs, and small towns all over the United States and from many different family situations. We are Protestants and Catholics, and we come from different ethnic heritages.

The dance will look a little different in the different places where we live. But all of us can learn to dance to the beat of God's heart, gaining wisdom from the experiences of the whole community of dancers across the years, while also doing some improvising that lets us express our own uniqueness.

The book focuses on 18 practices that ultimately blend together but are also different enough to talk about one at a time. One chapter is devoted to each practice. We could add a few more practices, but these seem like plenty for now.

You may read the chapters in any order. You can start by exploring something you feel pretty good at. Or start where you know you need help. Start at the end and read backward if you want to. Find a subject that grabs your attention and begin there. Flip through the pages until you find an illustration or quotation that catches you, and jump in at that point. Once you get into the book, you will find that every chapter is related to all the others anyway.

To really get into this way to live, though, you will need to do more than read. You will need to talk with other people who share your questions and passions so that you can face your doubts and speak your hopes out loud. And you will need to *do* some of the things you are reading about. We call these *practices* because they have to be *practiced*. Practices don't live on the pages of a book but in the bodies, hands, feet, eyes, and compassion of real people, and learning practices means doing them not just once but many times. So throughout this book we'll encourage you to try these

A faith community is very important to me as I work through doubts and try to live and act faithfully, truthfully, justly, compassionately.

—MAGGIE, 15

Gospel
the
Preach
at all times.

IF NECESSARY USE WORDS.

Attributed to
Saint Francis of Assisi

practices. Begin where you can. You're probably doing most of them already, at least a little. And you don't have to have everything figured out before you start practicing.

Take note: *Way to Live* includes no chapters on what not to do. Teens hear plenty of *don'ts* these days: don't drink, don't cheat, don't do drugs, don't have sex. We want to help you see the positive life that is open to you—not the prohibitions that assume you want to go in negative directions. For example, the chapter on eating and drinking does not criticize teens who drink alcohol, even though we believe that teens should not drink alcohol. Instead, that chapter invites you to share your food and your life around a table with your friends, your family, and other people you don't even yet know. The chapter on telling the truth does not include a lengthy condemnation of cheating, even though we know that cheating is wrong. Instead, it tries to show how satisfying a life lived with honesty and integrity can be, even when that way looks hard at first.

And notice this too: *Way to Live* is not a set of rules. Practicing life in the Holy Spirit certainly requires tough choices at times. It calls for the discipline of an athlete and the attentiveness of an artist. But it is not something you *have* to do to please someone else, not even to please God. Instead, this life is a gift you receive as you join hands with other people and walk with Jesus and his community toward the future God has promised, one step at a time.

We hope that these chapters will help you to see how your life matters—and how very much *you* matter—to God and to the world God loves. "Yours are the hands with which Christ is to bless all people now," a young woman named Teresa of Avila wrote to her friends half a millennium ago. Today the writers of this book address her words to you. Being a blessing to other people is a great joy. Being cherished yourself is a great joy too. And you are. We hope that you will see God's love for you personally shining through this book. We hope this book will help you see God's image in your own body as well as in the bodies of other people. We hope you will find here an invitation to enjoy your favorite foods and tell your favorite stories, surrounded by companions who share your deepest hopes for you and for the world.

This way to live gives you the chance to get involved in what God is doing in you and in the world around you. It's all about becoming part of the loving, challenging life of God. ■

SUSAN BRIEHL
MARY EMILY BRIEHL WELLS
MAGDALENA BRIEHL WELLS

▌▌▌The Story

The Bible tells the story of God's love for us and the whole creation. When we read and study, hear and tell this story, we meet Jesus. He invites us to join the story and share God's love. The more we "get into" this story, the more it gets into us and shapes the way we live every day. ■ ■ ■ ■

—Maggie Wells, 15

"Let's watch my movie!" called four-year-old Abby, the youngest of the three sisters I was baby-sitting for the evening. I expected an old Disney favorite when I said they could watch a movie before bed, but the girls had a different idea. They wanted to watch their family videos of the time when they were babies. Fine with me. I'd seen *The Little Mermaid* a few too many times anyway. The girls snuggled on the couch, and I sat down at the dining room table to finish my homework. I got nothing done. The girls weren't really interested in sitting quietly with the video; they just needed the pictures to jog their memories. They wanted to see and hear stories about themselves; but more than that, they wanted to tell the stories to me.

The Story according to Emily. **In the beginning God created the heavens and the earth. Where there was darkness, God spoke light. Where there was emptiness, God filled it with rock and water, bugs and berries, salt, sap, animals, and humankind. When the emptiness was filled, God loved it all, exclaiming, "This is good!" Creation was whole, unharmed, and buzzing with life.** ■ ■ ■ ■ ■ ■ ■ ■ ■

The older two told about seeing Abby for the first time and the day, a year later, when she took her first steps. They acted out the scene when Abby cut her own hair, including their mother's horror and their father's bold laughter. I joined in, adding stories about each of them and my own childhood. Abby delighted in it all. The video—the friends, family, and memories in it—reminded the children how deeply they were loved, even before they could remember.

For the same reason, people throughout time have told the stories about the beginning of the world and the human family. The Bible is our family story. It is the story of God's active and unending love for you and for the whole creation. Entering this story, we remember who we are and whose we are, how we got here and how to love one another. Telling and retelling these ancient narratives bring us closer to understanding our own part in God's love story. We may experience the story dramatized around a campfire, read with family and friends, studied in a youth group, or proclaimed during Sunday morning worship. God makes a home for us within the story, calls us to be changed by it, and gives us the voice to share it with others.

Getting lost in the story

Did you ever get lost in a book? The world falls away. Time stops. You forget to eat. The characters are as real as your friends. You are totally at home in the world of the story whether it's in the land of Narnia, Anne Frank's secret annex, or Maycomb, the tired Southern town that wakes up when Dill comes to live with Jem and Scout in *To Kill a Mockingbird*.

But soon things began to break.
The first people severed their relationship with God by eating the fruit of a forbidden tree. Later, families divided themselves by fighting and deceit. As whole civilizations formed, people worked for power and wealth, making slaves of others. God's heart broke with grief because hatred, fear, and pain now hid the beauty of creation.

The wildest dreams they'd ever had ▪▪▪ hadn't been half wild enough. ▪▪▪

—FREDERICK BUECHNER

Peculiar Treasures: A Biblical Who's Who

You wish such books wouldn't end, but they do; and you have to return to your so-called normal life. Sometimes, like a deep-sea diver, you surface *gradually* from the story world so you don't get the "bends." Other times, the shock of reentry blinds you, like walking out of a dark theater into the bright afternoon sun after a matinee. Once in a while we enter a story so thoroughly that the "real" world seems strange or altered. Or is it we who are changed?

I read Anne Frank's *The Diary of a Young Girl* when I was 13—the same age she was when she began writing it. I don't know which sandbox my head had been buried in, but I had never imagined children dying in concentration camps. Up to the very end of the book, I believed they all would leave their cozy hiding place after the war and live happily ever after. Anne's death in the concentration camp at Bergen-Belsen shattered that fairy tale.

A long night of crying followed. I wept for Anne, whom I had come to love, and for all the children who had died. The dawn brought many hard questions: Where was God? Why is evil so powerful? Could I believe in a God who didn't protect children? Am I safe? Am I evil?

Anne opened my eyes to a world more terrible and dangerous than I had imagined. But she also helped me see God weeping and suffering with us. I trembled when I gave Anne's *Diary* to Emily on her 13th birthday, anticipating her night of tears and dawn of doubts. I also gave thanks for Anne and the richer, more real life she opened to me and was about to open to my daughter.

Longing to mend creation, God chose Abraham and Sarah to be the parents of a new tribe, the Israelites. The Israelites' flocks multiplied and their families grew. When famine claimed the land, they fled, starving, to Egypt, where food abounded. Years passed and when they had grown strong again, they were enslaved as bricklayers by Pharaoh. Day and night God heard the groans of their ▪▪▪ ▪ ▪

Joining the story

I tremble and give thanks every time I read the Bible. God meets us on these pages and awakens us to a world more broken and more blessed than we imagined. If you love your life just as it is right now, forget about the Bible. Entering the biblical story, the story of God's self-giving love, and living among other people shaped by it, could be dangerous. When you get into this story, it will get into you and begin shaping how you live. When you think of yourself as part of this story, you will hear God speaking words of warning and comfort to you. Let yourself get lost in this story, and you will find yourself drawn into a new way to live.

You will see yourself in this story, but you won't always like what you see. Ask King David. The prophet Nathan told him about a rich man with many flocks who stole a poor man's only beloved lamb and killed it to prepare a meal for a guest. Hearing this, David cried, "That man must pay for his deed!" Nathan, as if holding up a mirror, said, "You are the man!" It was true. David had taken Bathsheba, Uriah's beloved wife, to his bed. Then he covered his deeds with a murder. Now the truth stares him in the face. Drawn into Nathan's parable, we see our own faces—and the policies of our rich nation—reflected in the mirror too.

Read more about it:
2 Samuel 11:1–12:15

Sometimes you'll see yourself in this story and be stunned by how beloved you are. Ask the woman of Samaria. Husbands had left her. Neighbors shunned her. Others called her unclean and unworthy. One day she comes to the well and meets Jesus. Listening in as she talks with Jesus, we feel as if we are standing beside her. Like this woman, we fear that if people knew the truth about us, they would reject us. So when Jesus, who knows everything this woman ever did, welcomes her, joy bubbles up in us too. Jesus is welcoming *us*, offering *us* abundant life.

Read more about it:
John 4

labor like prayers for freedom. God called a man named Moses, a herd of frogs, a swarm of insects, and an array of diseases to pester Pharaoh until he let the slaves go. As the Israelites escaped, Pharaoh's army chased them. At the Red Sea, God parted the waters, allowing the Israelites to cross on dry land. When the Egyptians followed, the water rushed back, swallowing the whole army. Led by the

The more you read this story, the more you feel at home in it. You think you are related to these characters—the whole mixed-up bunch of them—not by blood but by experience. Their history sounds like your life. One minute you like your family, the next you're ready to sell your little brother (see Genesis 37). One day you will follow Jesus anywhere, the next you deny ever meeting him (see Luke 22:54-62). Rebellious, faithful, generous, greedy, funny, sneaky, jealous, forgiven: We're related all right!

Soon you are so immersed in this story that you begin seeing people Jesus was forever seeing. They aren't characters in the Bible; they are kids at your school, people in your town. You read about Jesus blessing children (see Matthew 19:13-15), and then you see busy grown-ups brushing their children aside. You hear Jesus scolding his disciples for degrading a woman (see Matthew 26:6-13), then you listen to your classmates whispering about a girl behind her back. You see Jesus inviting poor and homeless people to a feast (see Luke 14:15-24), and then you notice the man who sleeps in the bus station. The story is changing how you see the world. Your heart breaks. It's another night of weeping, another dawn of doubts. How are you going to live now that your eyes are opened?

Eventually your dreams change; you start dreaming of a world made new by this story. You see what Isaiah saw: weapons beaten down and transformed into farming tools (see Isaiah 2:2-4). You hear what the psalmist heard: hills singing, rivers clapping, and all creation humming with joy (Psalms 96 and 98). You envision every child going to bed with a full tummy. You feel the angry knot inside your heart loosening and know you can forgive the one who hurt you. Then you realize that even your wildest dreams haven't been half wild enough. Your hopes, your goals, your plans make sense only if they serve the vision of God's mending the entire universe with mercy, the vision announced by prophets, fulfilled in Jesus, and continuing to unfold (see Revelation 21:1-6). You tremble. You're lost in

prophet Miriam, the Israelites sang and danced, celebrating their freedom and God's love for them. God gave the Israelites everything they needed: bread falling like rain from the sky, water pouring from rocks, freedom, ten commandments by which to live, and eventually a land to call home. ■ ■ ■ □

this story. Where is it taking you? To life, richer and more real than you imagined, thanks to God.

Opening the library

Maybe the Bible is new to you, and you have no clue what it's all about; or maybe you are like I am and feel that after years of Sunday school you might explode if you hear about the animals walking two-by-two, Jonah in that enormous fish, or Daniel and his docile lions one more time. Often we think of the Bible as a dusty old book, out of date and too daunting to read, or as a collection of happy animal stories from Sunday school. As I prepared to write this chapter, I looked at several books about scripture and thumbed through the thin, delicate pages of my own Bible. I was excited (and relieved) to discover how diverse the Bible is and how much I *can* understand. You can too, whether you are reading it for the first time or viewing familiar passages in a new way.

Imagine a varied and intriguing library (or an awesome page of Web links). You walk in, it smells like paper and paste, and you start browsing. You find all sorts of books—novels, poetry, massive volumes of obscure laws, a set of pioneer-day diaries, world history books, colorful collections of mythology, fairy tales you know by heart, songbooks (for camp, church, the car), and a hardcover atlas. This is the Bible: a compact, portable library. For instance, Leviticus is a collection of laws; Joshua, Judges, 1 and 2 Samuel, and other books tell Israel's history; the Book of Psalms is the songbook for

Over the years, some generations thanked God for these gifts, while others forgot their Creator. So God sent poets, prophets, and judges to remind them. In different words and melodies, in forceful and gentle tones, King David, Isaiah, Joel, Deborah, and all of the others tried to say the same thing: "Do justice, love kindness, and walk humbly with God" (Micah 6:8, paraphrase).

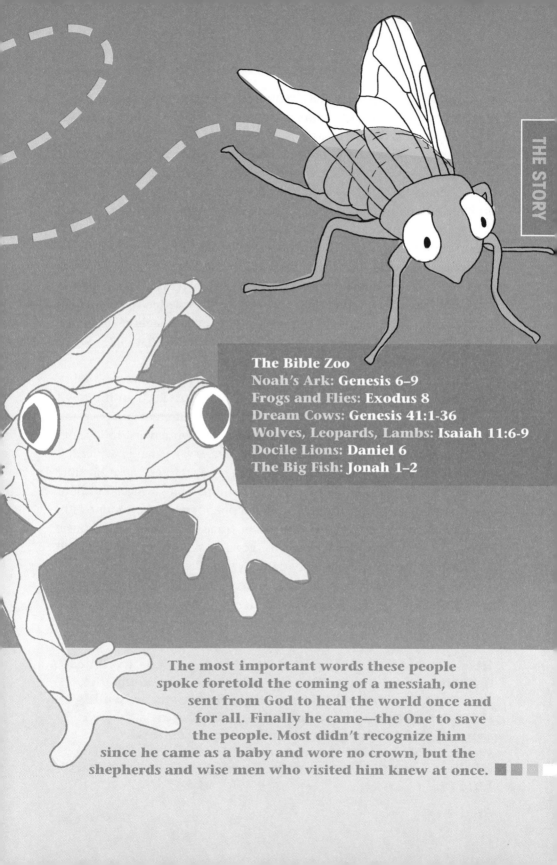

The Bible Zoo
Noah's Ark: Genesis 6–9
Frogs and Flies: Exodus 8
Dream Cows: Genesis 41:1-36
Wolves, Leopards, Lambs: Isaiah 11:6-9
Docile Lions: Daniel 6
The Big Fish: Jonah 1–2

The most important words these people
spoke foretold the coming of a messiah, one
sent from God to heal the world once and
for all. Finally he came—the One to save
the people. Most didn't recognize him
since he came as a baby and wore no crown, but the
shepherds and wise men who visited him knew at once. ■ ■ ■

both Jews and Christians; Acts includes a journal of Luke's and Paul's travels; and Revelation is a vision of hope written to suffering Christians.

The Bible is divided into two sections, the Old and New "Testaments" or "covenants." The Old Testament (sometimes referred to as the Hebrew Scriptures) is the story of God's work in the world before Jesus. This is the Bible Jesus knew. The New Testament is the story of Jesus' life and death and the birth of the church after his resurrection. A follower of Jesus named Paul started many of the first Christian communities. He wrote letters to these young churches, letters that became books in the New Testament. His letter to all who "belong to Christ" living in Rome became Romans; the letter he wrote from prison to Philemon is known as Philemon, and so on. If you listen closely, these books really sound like letters meant to help faraway friends live faithfully. Some even end with familiar lines. In his letter to the Romans, Paul writes, "Greet Prisca and Aquila." It's like "Say hi to Dad for me!"

The Bible has four Gospels called Matthew, Mark, Luke, and John. They basically tell the same story, the story of Jesus. Each author has a unique take on the story because each wrote for a different audience and with a different focus. *Mark*, the shortest Gospel, was written first and focuses on the suffering of Jesus and his followers. *Matthew*, written in a community of Jewish Christians, presents Jesus as the "new Moses." *Luke*, possibly written by a physician, tells many stories and parables, especially about Jesus' healing people. Written last and in a poetic style, *John* contains stories and characters not found in the other three. If you want to read the Bible, start with a Gospel, which means "good news." Any one of them will get you into the heart of the story right away.

Like any good library, the Bible is easier to understand and appreciate if you know some basic stuff before stepping inside. Nothing says you have to understand every book or even take everything off the shelf right

His mother, Mary, named him Jesus, though some would call him Emmanuel (God-with-us), Prince of Peace, Redeemer, and Lord. He revealed God's love for the world by healing the sick and raising the dead, eating with outcasts, forgiving sinners, and teaching about God's mercy and justice. Powerful and satisfied people hated Jesus for threatening their way of life. Hoping to silence his teaching, they killed him.

away. Many people have been studying this ancient library for years, and a community of believers waits to help you explore the shelves and corners.

Speaking to the heart

Maggie read the whole Bible when she was six. OK, so it was *The Beginner's Bible* and fanciful cartoon characters surrounded a few simple sentences on each page, but she did it. When she finished, she wrote her name in that Bible in big, black letters: MAGGIE. Then she read it again. That book belonged to Maggie, but Maggie also belonged to the book. Told in words and pictures that she understood, the epic story of God's love for the whole world became her story. God knew her by name and loved *her*.

Tom has never heard the story, but he has seen it! He sees the story every Sunday as images and ideas rise from the fingers and facial expressions of his pastor, Beth Lockard. Both Tom and Beth are profoundly deaf. While they can read the texts in English, the story springs to life in their faith community through American Sign Language. The Word enters their hearts through their eyes.

The Bible originally was written in Hebrew and Greek and later translated into Latin. By the Middle Ages, only highly educated people read Latin, so average folk depended upon their priest to tell them what the Bible said and meant. In the 16th century, Martin Luther began what he called his most important work, translating the Bible into German. He visited with the very people he hoped would read his translation: his barber, the milkmaid, mothers and their children, farmers and their families. He wanted to choose words that would speak to their hearts so they would hear the good news of this story spoken to them, God's promises made to them.

The Word comes from God's heart and is spoken into ours, joining us to the story of God's saving love. A six-year-old reads a picture-book Bible

This story is no tragedy; when Jesus died, the brokenness of creation and the sins of all people died with him. Three days later Jesus was raised from the dead. Appearing to his astonished followers, he breathed on them the Holy Spirit and told them to share the good news: What was broken is now mended; in God life is stronger than death. The followers went out, telling everyone they met about Jesus' ■ ■ ■

and knows God loves her. A deaf man watches the Sunday readings rise from the hands and face of an interpreter and knows he is set free to serve others. In order to let the Word enter *your* heart, choose a Bible written in language you can understand. Write your name in it. Claim it as your own. Read it and discuss it with others. And trust that you belong to God and to this story.

Twisting the story

One day in the summer after ninth grade, some friends and I gathered at a park to toss a Frisbee, eat drippy ice-cream cones, and talk. We quickly tired of playing, but none of us wanted to part and go home. So we began a discussion that drifted from topic to topic and finally settled on politics. Our debate was heated. Three people in the group strongly supported one side, and two were arguing adamantly for the other. People generally talked politely and openly at the beginning, but toward the end harsh words were flying.

Some of the words were what my mom calls "Bible bullets"—one-liners from the Bible hurled at someone on the other side of a disagreement. Quotations and examples flew at rocket speed, hitting me as if to say I was betraying my religion by having a particular opinion. This upset me because I knew my views were largely based on my faith. But my friends' views were based on their faith too. I admit that if I had memorized more Bible passages, I would have shot back; but my collection was limited and irrelevant, so I lay back on the grass and waited for the cease-fire. That afternoon my friends and I joined a long line of people who have abused the Bible's message and purpose.

Throughout history the gospel of welcome and freedom has been twisted to exclude some while lifting up others. For example, in his

being raised from the dead. Some stayed close to home, while others, like Paul, traveled far and wide. He stopped in towns and villages reminding people to live as followers of Jesus. Though some followers were killed and many were rebuked for their beliefs, they held fast both to Jesus' promise to remain with them and to the vision of a world made new by God.

"Lord"

Touch the left shoulder with the pointed thumb of the right "L" hand, palm slanted downward. Now move the hand down in a semicurve across the chest to the right side of the thumb touching the waist.

■■■■■■■■■■■■■
While they can read
the texts in English,
the story springs to
life in their faith
community through
American Sign
Language. The Word
enters their hearts
through their eyes.
■■■■■■■■■■■■■■■

letter to the Romans, Paul calls for people to share the good news of Christ's love so others can hear it. This is a good thing. However, in the past, some people read this passage very narrowly. They interpreted Paul's words "Faith comes from what is heard" (Romans 10:14-17) to mean that because deaf people cannot hear, they cannot have faith or be saved. Isn't that crazy! Paul wanted to invite more people in, but his words were used to exclude the deaf. In the same way, other passages were and are used to justify keeping slaves, beating women, killing millions of Jews in the Holocaust, exploiting creation, and shunning gays and lesbians.

I live in Spokane, Washington, near a place in northern Idaho that for years was the home of the Aryan Nations. Members of this group use the Bible to support their claim that they belong to a superior race and are responsible for saving America from people of other ethnicities. However, by speaking of extremes, it's easy to brush off our own "Bible abuses" as small and harmless. You might consider ways that you have used the Bible to hurt another or a passage you have quoted out of context. For instance, it's easy to find passages in the Bible saying women are "unclean" or lesser than men, but by looking at these passages in the context of the time and in light of Jesus' words and actions, it's clear that men and women are equal in God's eyes.

My mom grew up with a girl who believed it was physically impossible to burn a Bible. My mom was so eager to prove this girl wrong that she scorched a few pages of her own Bible. Like my mom, we often disrespect the Bible, using it to "prove" a point. And like that girl, we often treat the book as if it were magical. We want the Bible to give us easy answers to big questions, save us from difficult situations, or show us a map of our future—magically. When we use scripture to "prove" ideas we already hold or to hurt others or to protect ourselves from the messiness of life, we are misusing it.

Here's good news: The Bible was written for more than just individuals. We interpret and understand it best in the company of others, including those we don't agree with. Maybe those people with whom we disagree challenge and stretch us the most. I'm sure my friends and I have not had our last heated debate, but if we can avoid getting too defensive, we're going to learn a lot from one another.

Cracking the Book

You can read the Bible anytime, anywhere, alone or with others. It's a *portable* library after all. Read a psalm each night before going to sleep. Read it slowly; let the poetry sink in. Pack your Bible when you hike and read Genesis 1 at sunrise. Then at night, under the stars, tell the creation story in your own words. Meet your friends at a coffee shop on Saturday to study the scripture lessons that will be read at your church on Sunday. Read a Gospel with a faraway friend, one chapter a week. E-mail your reactions and questions to each other. Before you crack the book, pray for the Holy Spirit to guide you and give you understanding. Below are three ways to read Scripture that my mom, my sister, and I have found helpful, especially in small groups. We'll use Jesus' teaching on nonviolence to illustrate.

1. The Västerås method

Developed in Sweden for small groups, this method needs no leader. One person reads the chosen passage aloud. Then everyone reads it again silently, using the following symbols to mark insights, ideas, and questions in the margins. Don't be afraid to make notes in your Bible!

¡ Make this candle marking beside phrases that give you a new insight.

∧ Make this mark by phrases that tell you about God or come to you as good news.

∨ Make this mark by phrases that point out a need you have or a challenge you face.

? Make a question mark by anything you don't understand.

After an agreed-upon length of time, the participants share their markings, beginning with the candles, followed by the

> But I say to you that listen ∧, Love your enemies ¡, do good to those who hate you, bless those who curse you, pray for those who abuse you ∨. If anyone strikes you on the cheek ?, offer the other also; and from anyone who takes away your coat do not withhold even your shirt. Give to everyone who begs from you; and if anyone takes away your goods, do not ask for them again ∨. Do to others as you would have them do to you.
> —LUKE 6: 27-31

arrows pointing up, then the arrows pointing down. As members of the group share their insights, many of the questions others raised may be addressed and answered. If questions remain, the group may decide to consult a reference book, a pastor, or a teacher. Don't be afraid to ask questions. No doubt or discovery can "undo" the power and meaning of this story for you. In fact, sometimes studying the Bible raises more questions than it answers!

Emily's notes on the passage: A candle marks "love your enemies" since it alters the way I view my relationships. An upward arrow marks "I say to you that listen," showing God's persistence in teaching us. Downward arrows mark "pray for those who abuse you" and "if anyone takes away your goods, do not ask for them again." These lines contradict my inclinations to hold grudges and live by fairness, not grace. "If anyone strikes you on the cheek, offer the other also" gets a question mark. I need help seeing how that advice would get me anywhere but bruised.

2. Ignatian deep reflection

Saint Ignatius of Loyola invited the members of his order, the Society of Jesus, to join the biblical story by using their imagination. Try this: Choose a scene from one of the Gospels. Imagine yourself being in it. Become one of the characters mentioned in the story or make up a new character to be. Don't watch the scene like a TV show. Participate in it! This method takes practice. Mom says she tried it for weeks before she could stop analyzing everything and let the more creative part of her brain lead her. Below are steps with Mom's reflections.

1. Read the story slowly, either silently or aloud (Luke 6:12-19, 27-31).
2. Close your eyes and breathe deeply, slowly, until you are relaxed and calm.
3. Picture the scene. Begin with details in the text. Let your imagination fill in the blanks. *(We are outside . . . daylight. Jesus prayed on the mountain all night. He and his disciples come to a level place . . . far from town . . . an open field . . . dry, prickly grass . . . one tree . . . soft, warm air.)*
4. Let the scene come alive. Who is there? What's happening? What are the sounds? smells? actions? *(Excitement . . . many people . . .*

Come, Holy Spirit, open our eyes, enter our hearts, and shape our lives by your Word. Amen.

Meet your friends at a coffee shop on Saturday to study the scripture lessons that will be read at your church on Sunday.

young, old . . . many skin colors . . . noisy, many languages . . . lots of children . . . some very sick . . . Jesus sits beneath the tree. He speaks, "Come. Sit down.")

5. Place yourself in the scene. Where are you? Why? What are you doing? feeling? *(I am in the crowd but alone. I am not sick . . . curious . . . I sit on the prickly grass near a child who speaks Spanish. He smiles at me . . . sweet. I am happy, hopeful, and a little nervous.)*

6. Focus on Jesus. Watch him carefully. What is he doing? saying? How is he feeling? *(Jesus is calm . . . he looks at the crowd . . . but not directly at me . . . he blesses us with his eyes. I feel welcomed . . . children crawl up on his lap . . . a soft breeze . . . he speaks, "Blessed are you.")*

7. Choose a sentence to dwell on—something Jesus says or does. See him turn toward you. *("Love your enemies. Pray for those who abuse you." Jesus comes to the little boy next to me . . . he is from El Salvador. "Bless her," Jesus says to the boy. "Pray for her." He means me! I am this child's enemy! My nation has abused his people, harmed his family. I feel sick, sad. "I'm so sorry," I say, but I can't speak Spanish. The boy takes my hand. I am crying. Jesus holds me, rocks me.)*

8. Rest in the company of Jesus. Breathe slowly, deeply. Let this be your prayer.

9. If you are with others, you may share your reflections with one another.

3. Explore and discover

This method is a treasure hunt! The Bible was written two thousand years ago in a setting very different from ours. Some words and ideas don't translate easily into English. Some ancient customs don't translate easily into the 21st century. What did these stories mean to the original audiences? How can we join this old, old story? You'll need tools: a Bible with cross-references (if you are in a group, use several translations among you), biblical maps, a Bible dictionary, a concordance (this book locates any word in the Bible). Explore each clue. Follow every lead. You are seeking God's Word to you. Jesus is the treasure. Below, Maggie shares her exploration and discovery.

- Explore how the passage fits into the whole chapter, the whole book, even the entire biblical story. Luke 6:27-31 is part of the Sermon on the Plain (Luke 6:17-49). Jesus has just chosen his twelve disciples. People have come from all over to hear him and to be healed. He seems to be introducing his beliefs and inviting people into his way of life. He's getting them ready to follow him.

- Search for parallels and cross-references to the passage; discover similarities and differences. For instance, Matthew 5–7 is a longer sermon with many of the same sayings, but it is set on a mountain.

- Find words or phrases you don't understand in a Bible dictionary. Locate places on a map. I found the phrase "strike the cheek" from this passage in several places in the Old Testament and wondered what it meant exactly. A Bible dictionary explained the act as a common way to humiliate someone, not beat up the person! And "turn the other cheek" didn't mean "let someone keep hitting you."

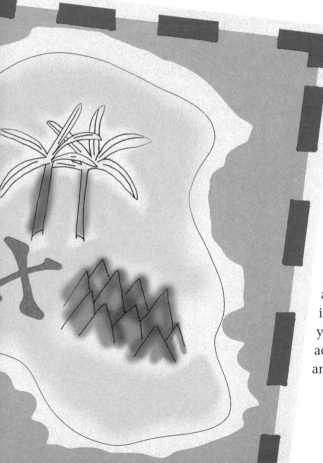

Turning the other cheek surprised the person who struck, throwing him or her off-balance. Jesus isn't telling you to stay in abusive relationships. He isn't telling you to strike back. He is showing you another way to live: Keep your dignity. Expose acts of violence and disrespect as powerless. All the ways our culture puts people down—name calling, pranks, taunting—can't take away your worth. That worth is a gift from God. However, you can creatively reveal such actions for what they are: silly and useless.

Way to live!

The Bible is often called God's Word. We listen for God to speak through this story. When God wanted to speak directly to our hearts in language we could understand, God spoke Jesus. Or as the Gospel of John puts it, "The Word became flesh and lived among us" (John 1:14). We meet Jesus, God's living Word, when we read scripture. The Bible has been described as the swaddling clothes wrapped around the Christ child and as the manger in which he is laid. When we come to the Bible, it is as if we are coming to the manger and unwrapping those clothes, eager to see Jesus.

We never come to the manger alone; we come in the company of others. Even when we read scripture by ourselves, a "great cloud of witnesses" surrounds us, all those people who were joined to this story before us. Their struggles and doubts and deeds of mercy tell the ongoing story of God's love. We can consider them our reading companions.

The Bible's story continues in our own lives too. Whenever we declare God's love to the world by caring for the earth, welcoming a stranger, living truthfully, or seeking justice, we help others see Jesus. Each of these practices and all the others in this book are rooted in scripture. When we crack the Book, we come to the side of the manger. Jesus meets us, welcoming us into a way to live that brings life—God's life—to the whole world. ∎

KAY BESSLER NORTHCUTT
WITH CLINTON TRENCH

⫼Bodies

A *practice* is what you do to get better at something like playing the cello or basketball. With enough practice, you become a musician or an athlete. The same thing is true about the body. The body is God's great gift to us. It's something we can practice caring for. Eventually we'll get really good at taking care of it. ■ ■ ■ ■ ■ ■ ■ ■ ■

—Clinton Trench, 15

Between the sixth and seventh grades I grew six inches. As my height increased, so did my clumsiness. After I'd broken a lot of dishes (I couldn't carry them from the dining room to the kitchen sink without tripping), Mom said, "Enough, Kay! I'm signing you up for modeling lessons!" Mom hoped modeling school could teach me how to walk "gracefully" again.

It worked. No more broken dishes. And at the end of the lessons, I was invited to work for the modeling agency. I modeled for ramp shows and trunk shows and did some TV commercials. When I was 18 years old, I represented my state, Oklahoma, in America's Junior Miss Pageant. Eileen Ford saw me on the nationally televised pageant. She wrote me a letter inviting me to come to New York City to become one of her models. I couldn't believe it!

I flew to New York, moved into the Barbizon Hotel for Women, and began building my portfolio of photographs. It was awesome being in New York. I loved the Empire State Building and the New York Public Library. I loved bagels with cream cheese and the Statue of Liberty. I totally loved Bloomingdale's and New York pizza by the slice. I loved being 18 years old living on my own in New York City!

After I'd been there a couple of weeks, Ms. Ford sent me to a casting call for a television commercial. The casting agent took one look at me and shook his head with contempt. "No," he said, dismissing me. When he noticed my dumbfounded expression, he explained, "Your nose spreads when you smile."

My face burned a bright, hot red. I hadn't been this embarrassed since Matt Oney called me "Queen of the Cooties" in front of the whole fourth grade. I walked back to the Barbizon, stuck my nose—yes, the same nose that spread when I smiled—into a 400-page novel and consoled myself with a 48-hour readathon. I needed a vacation from my humiliation. I needed time to figure out what to tell my family and friends. How on earth could I tell them that my perky but spreading nose had eliminated me from the world of rich and famous models? I needed help, and I knew it.

My pastor, Jerry Johnson, could always make me laugh—even at myself—and he was very wise. So I called him. I poured out my heart to him, telling him all about my goofy nose and my humiliation. Jerry listened while I blurted out my hurt feelings. Then he told me that I was "much more than meets the eye."

The casting agent took one look at me and shook his head with contempt. "No," he said, dismissing me. When he noticed my dumbfounded look, he explained, "Your nose spreads when you smile." ■■■■

Jerry told me that I was made in God's image, which made me—including my imperfect nose—"holy and awesome"! He rushed on quickly to emphasize that I wasn't the only one created in God's image. *Everyone is.* In the story of creation (the first chapter in the Bible), we are told that human beings were made in God's image.

As Jerry talked, I stopped for a minute to think about his body. Nine days after graduating from seminary, when he was just 23 years old, Jerry contracted polio. He changed from a strapping six-foot-five young man who played basketball to a paraplegic who relied on a wheelchair for mobility. His right arm and hand were paralyzed too. And he was told to forget his future in the ministry because "no church would ever call a paralyzed pastor." But a church did—*my* church.

I remember bringing a friend to church after Jerry's arrival. She was—well, sort of horrified when the deacon wheeled Jerry up to the pulpit. She'd never seen a paralyzed person (much less a paralyzed pastor), and she leaned over to me whispering, "Why didn't you tell me that your minister was paralyzed?" I was shocked! I actually had *forgotten* that Jerry was in a wheelchair; it had never occurred to me to tell my friend about it.

This same paralyzed man was now talking to me on the telephone—telling me that *all* bodies are "holy and awesome" because they are formed in God's image. Jerry—perhaps better than anyone else—knew what he was talking about. Gripped by the fact that I had complained to Jerry about something so insignificant as my nose, I tuned back in to what he was saying.

Jerry reminded me that I could play the piano and that I was a good student. He kept telling me about all the things I'd done that really mattered—playing piano for our church, directing our children's choirs, being a good friend to all the kids in our youth group.

Then Jerry told me to go to a mirror. I dragged the telephone over to the hotel room mirror. Jerry told me to stare at my reflection and to practice saying "made in God's image" while I stared. He asked me to imagine what being made in God's image might mean, for me and for every other child of God. Consoled, I told him I'd see him soon and hung up the phone.

"Mirror, mirror, on the wall . . ."

Over the next couple of months an amazing change took place. When I went to the mirror searching for God's image, I found something new. I saw God in me. My self-image slowly began to change. I started to see other people differently too.

Twenty years later I had a "back-to-the-future" moment with another mirror. But it wasn't *my* face in the mirror. It was another girl's face. I was in a hurry to get to a rehearsal in a huge Methodist church, and I popped into the rest room. As I pushed the door open fast and hard, I startled a 14-year-old girl staring at herself, daydreaming in front of a full-length mirror. She had just brushed her hand through her hair then tilted her head to just the right angle for examining the results of her hair-toss experiment. My abrupt entry into the bathroom surprised her. Embarrassed, she blushed a bright pink as she leaped away from the mirror and hurried out.

As the girl disappeared through the door I could hear Jerry's voice saying "there's something holy and awesome" about every body. I was frustrated that I hadn't been able to tell this girl what Jerry had told me. I wanted to encourage her! I wanted her to know that it was so *right* for her to be watching herself in the mirror! It was the face of God she was wearing after all—and greatly to be admired.

I later learned that this same girl was hospitalized for anorexia nervosa a couple of weeks after I had seen her. Apparently when she looked in the mirror she saw a distorted view of herself—not a wonderful child of God created in God's very own image. Many of us experience such distortion to varying degrees. The steady pressure to have the "right" look can backfire, leading to an endless hunger for perfection.

When we admire God's image within our own faces and bodies, they become something to celebrate—whether we are paralyzed, able-bodied, large, fat, small, or lean! Believing our bodies are good and claiming them as "holy and awesome" motivate us to cherish and care for our bodies. What we do with these bodies of ours really matters!

Looking good?

Fifteen-year-old Matt got to the heart of the matter when he asked, "If we are made in God's image, does that mean we should treat our bodies the same way we would treat God?" It's a great question to explore, but first, a reality check about the kinds of bodies our popular culture values.

Watching TV or glancing through a teen-oriented clothes catalog reveals why so many teens have insecurities about their bodies and faces. Most of the images from TV and magazines emphasize highly idealized bodies that typically do *not* closely resemble the bodies teens actually have!

> # You just want to look like everyone else and above all not be noticed— the main thing is not to stick out!
> —BETH, 15 ■ ■ ■ ■ ■ ■ ■ ■

Guys get these messages as much as girls do. The "right" kind of male body is athletic, lean, and tall with well-developed muscles. The skin is free of acne, the teeth are perfectly straight, and the hair sticks out only where it is supposed to.

It's easy to give in to the temptation of measuring yourself by the perfect images on TV and billboards. In high schools from Paris to San Diego, body image is self-image. My goddaughter, Emma, says, "The ninth-grade world is a place where definitely the most important thing is how you look." It's a place where she has to be hyperalert to her looks and everyone else's—especially what is cool and what is not. It's easy to feel vulnerable. Exposed. What if you don't look "right"?

Even Olympic athletes, who have the strongest, best, most beautiful bodies out there, feel vulnerable to the pressure for perfection. Every four years when the Olympics get under way, some athletes are caught taking steroids. Even world-class athletes are under terrible pressure to enhance their bodies beyond what is natural. They too feel stressed to attain an "ideal" level of strength and speed.

If Olympians are vulnerable to such pressure, none of us are immune. Distortions easily creep into how we see our bodies and how we think about them. Wishing for what we think is missing—the right breasts, a perfect nose, a "six-pack" abdomen, blemish-free skin—is pretty common. Our opinions about the way we look matter because they influence the way we feel about our bodies. And the way we *feel* about our bodies influences how we care for them.

Some of us feel pretty great about our bodies. Lots of guys aren't comfortable talking about the "beauty" of the body, but they can feel that something beautiful is happening when they make a great catch in a game or run a personal best time in a track meet. Seventeen-year-old Liz knows this feeling too. She's a gymnast who feels physically powerful. "I know my body really well from working so much with it. I feel really strong. I *like* feeling strong!" Nancy too knows the beautiful power of her body. "I learned my own beauty through ballet," she says.

Liz, Nancy, and lots of other teens have confidence in and respect for their bodies. They learned the power of their bodies through working hard, sweating, and performing under pressure. They know their own bodies like they know their own minds. Strong and in great shape, they feel at home in their own skin.

Bodies matter. Choices matter.

Christians believe the body is God's gift to each person—an amazing gift. The wonder of our bodies puts the Internet and all technologies in their place as latecomers and fairly unsophisticated by comparison!

"That healthy body is the greatest gift God gave you!" my mom constantly told me. But she *always* followed the "body as greatest gift" lecture by extracting a promise. "Promise me that you will never, ever smoke a cigarette!" she'd say. That's how I figured out that my body was healthy and strong but also vulnerable. When Mom asked me to promise "never, ever" to smoke a cigarette, I understood that my body could be easily damaged by the things I chose to do or not to do, like smoking.

Advice for taking care of our vulnerable bodies can end up sounding like a long preachy list of "don'ts." "Don't drink and drive." "Don't have sex." "Don't smoke or chew." Or as Matt said to me, "Taking care of my body means not giving in to temptation." The laundry list of "don'ts" and temptations can blur the bigger truth: Our bodies are fragile. We can damage them.

Taking care of my body means not giving in to temptation.

—MATT, 15

Our bodies are fragile and at the same time incredibly strong! It's so easy to feel *invincible*. My friend Elizabeth, now in her 30s, recalls: "When I was a teenager I drove fast. I smoked. I drank and then I drove. I was convinced nothing really bad could happen to me."

I praise you,
for I am fearfully
and wonderfully made.

—PSALM 139:14

BODIES

■ ■ ■ ■ ■ ■ ■ **Suddenly you walk into ninth grade and there's all this boundary- and limit-setting to do. You have to decide what's OK and what's not OK. The Jesus boys say they won't even kiss until they're practically engaged, but I think their ■ ■ ■ boundaries are weird!**

—KEN, 15

But we all have friends or family who have died in tragic car wrecks. We also know people like my pastor Jerry who contract life-threatening diseases such as polio or cancer through no fault of their own. We know victims of random violence, killed or wounded by guns in accidents or crimes. The bottom line is that we are *not* invincible. Events beyond our control can alter our lives and our bodies forever. But choices within our control can also change our lives permanently. Our future depends both on things that happen to us and the choices we make. That truth means what we do with our bodies really matters.

There's pressure everywhere, coming from all directions. Here's what 14-year-old Jessica told me: "It's really hard because everyone markets straight toward us teenagers—chips, sodas, smokes—because *they know we feel strong.* They know we have young, healthy bodies, and we don't think anything bad can happen to us. We end up eating what we want as if it doesn't matter."

Eating. Drinking. Driving. Smoking. Working out. Playing. They all matter. What we do with our "holy and awesome" bodies *matters.* It matters if we keep them safe or not. If we keep them clean or not. If we exercise to make them strong or not. If we damage them through neglect or nurture them with an apple a day and enough sleep.

Our bodies have a lot of power. What we do with our bodies, how we treat them, who we share them with—all these actions shape who we will become in the future. The choices we make about caring for our bodies can determine our future.

To share or not to share? How much to share?

The goodness of God's creation includes physical pleasure, so the physical pleasure that our "holy and awesome" bodies can experience is "holy and awesome" too. Pleasure includes physical desire and sex. But pleasure comes to us in many more varieties. There's the pleasure of food. And play. The pleasure of laughter. The pleasure of music and hospitality. And the pleasure of sharing our lives. And of making and keeping promises.

Our souls are thirsty for connection. We long to know others and to be known by them. Consider intimacy. Everyone has a deep need to be touched and held. It's as if our skin is thirsty for human contact. Sometimes a group of teenagers can look like a Twister game in *very* slow motion—sitting together on sofas or the floor, draped all over one another, legs thrown over one another's, arms intertwined. That tangle of teenagers is a powerful picture of connecting, making contact, nurturing our touch-hungry skin. But touching skin to skin is not the same thing as intimacy. It won't fulfill our deep hunger for intimacy.

Intimacy means experiencing emotional closeness with another person. Hugging, hand-holding, patting, or a tender caress can be caring expressions of intimacy. Intimacy thrives in trust, and many teenagers are great at trusting. Intimacy includes caring and sharing, laughing and crying. Intimacy encompasses both caring for our bodies, souls, and emotions and caring for the bodies, souls, and emotions of others.

Understanding the meaning of intimacy is an important part of becoming a healthy sexual adult. The confidence we gain through intimacy and trust gives us the capacity to touch and be touched in ways that honor God's image in both individuals of a couple. This confidence helps build backbone to say no if someone touches us inappropriately or if we don't want to be touched at all.

What do adults know?

Honest discussions about sex with trustworthy adults are also significant steps in becoming healthy sexual adults. It's hard to get reliable information about sex and bodies. I remember the day I asked my mom about masturbation. I guess I trusted her a lot. She answered all my questions and didn't seem one bit embarrassed. Maybe she could do this because she was so comfortable with her own body. I learned a lot about my body that day—and I also learned that it is possible to talk about things related to sex in an open and honest way.

One day in the fourth grade I was reading a *Newsweek* magazine article that referred to oral sex. I asked Mom what that meant. It just so happened that at the moment I asked her, she and four church ladies were at our kitchen table addressing envelopes for a wedding shower. Stunned

■■■ **We don't touch much at school.** ■■■ **Maybe a couple of boys will "high-five." But mainly we don't touch. My youth minister, Marlene, gives us sideways hugs, and a lot of times the adults at church hug us. I like it when they hug me.** —CLINTON, 15

LIMIT-SETTING STATEMENTS
"I am not comfortable doing this."
"This is not part of God's plan for my life at this time."
"This is not honoring me (or you) as a child of God."

■ ■

silence filled the room. Mom said, "Oral sex is something we will talk about later." I realized then that Mom's openness about sex was private in the sense that it was limited to the family circle. It was a good thing to know.

Mom said that being a teenager was a time for growing into myself. She warned me that if I merged with someone sexually as a teen, I would short-circuit the process of becoming a whole adult. She told me that God made sex so there couldn't be anything dirty or nasty about it—contrary to what I heard kids saying about it at school. She said God made sex as a gift to humans and that it was the "most beautiful, pleasurable, holy thing imaginable between two loving, committed adults." She emphasized that God made sex for adults who had made a covenant with each other.

The adults I knew who loved and cared about kids agreed with my mom that it's best for teens to postpone sex—both intercourse and oral sex. But all the *teens* I knew were at least thinking about sex. Every movie, every TV show, every novel I read focused on sex, and the people having sex were *not* married to each other. According to MTV, sex was *not* about God and adults and holiness. Did my mom know what was going on in the world? Whom could I trust—my friends? movies? novels? my teachers?

I went to Jerry. "When's the last time you heard me do a wedding?" he asked. I couldn't remember. Jerry laughed and then reminded me of a vow every bride and groom say to each other: "for better and for worse, for richer and for poorer, in sickness and in health, to love and to cherish, until death do us part." It sounded boring and ancient to me. Then Jerry totally surprised me. "Kay, it's a biological fact that teens are capable of sex, but the real question is whether teens have the capacity to covenant with another person 'to love and to cherish, until death do us part.'" Jerry said the difficult road that might ultimately lead to this kind of covenant lies in learning to practice pleasure through kissing and touching a-little-bit-along-the-way without merging sexually.

That practice of pleasure can be done, but it involves developing a kind of compass. Setting that compass means determining your limits *before* getting into a situation where those limits may be tested. Setting that compass requires talking to God about your limits and asking for God's help in holding to them. Some teens set their touching-a-little-bit-along-the-way compass according to whether or not what they're doing would disappoint their parents. One teen said she measured how far to go with physical intimacy this way: "I don't want to cross a bridge I can't go back over." Some people choose not to kiss at all during dating.

Jerry advised me to set my moral compass by that wedding vow. He said that when I had grown into the capacity to love and to cherish another human being in that way *and* had found the one to whom I could make that promise, it would be time to be married *and* to have sex.

Meanwhile, my mom became totally preachy about teenage pregnancy. All my friends had heard her speechette: "Intercourse = Sex, and Sex = Baby." One evening at the dinner table, Mom said, "Please pass the butter . . . girls, if you have sex, you will get pregnant." My sister and I burst into uncontrollable laughter, and so did Mom. She knew she'd crossed the line. But Mom wanted to make sure we knew that if we thought birth control would make sex safe, we were wrong. When teenagers have sex, pregnancies can result. AIDS is also a risk, along with a multitude of sexually transmitted diseases. Abstaining from sex is a responsible choice for teens.

Sexuality is a holy and awesome dimension of your body. As you slowly grow into your sexuality, you can learn to honor your body. At the same time, you will be growing in the capacity to be truly intimate—and to be pleased with the person in the mirror. Eventually you'll be ready for sex—when you can promise "to love and to cherish, until death do us part."

What are you going to wear?

John told me his "identity was pretty fragile" when he was 14. The relentless questions of *How do I fit?* and *Where do I belong?* were never far below the surface. His classmate Joan confirmed John's insight, noting that one of the biggest problems for her in the ninth grade was being accepted.

Surviving within such a state of heightened self-consciousness escalates the importance of fitting in and knowing that you belong. Smack-dab

42

14. I was so caught up with "fitting in" and think of anything else. —JOHN, 15 ■■■■■■■■■■

in the middle of the identity crisis that comes with being a teen, teenagers have created brilliant ways of camouflaging self-consciousness. Like clothing. Clothing functions as a protective cover. It provides a good way to "not stick out," says Beth, 15. If in doubt about what's "in," step into The Gap or whatever fashion spot is popular *this* year.

"What are you going to wear?" is a hot topic on cell phones and e-mail screens. Whether going to a school dance, a football game, or a party at a friend's house, most teens want to be dressed "right." Wearing the "right" clothes is a way to practice belonging, to practice identity.

But some teens don't have access or money that enables them to look like everyone else. These students may feel especially vulnerable. And there are still others who decide they don't want to give in to the pressure to dress a certain way. Some teens feel manipulated by corporations that constantly throw advertisements at them—even putting ads (labels and logos) all over the clothing they charge teens money to buy. A few decide for this reason to wear only clothing from thrift stores. "It's a political decision," 15-year-old Abby said. "I buy only secondhand clothes now, usually from Salvation Army. Otherwise I'm giving in to corporate pressure to look 'right.'"

Clothed with compassion

Susan, 15, told me about the day her period began unexpectedly. When she stood up to leave class, her jeans were visibly stained, unbeknownst to her. But several girls saw her predicament and quickly formed a circle around Susan, walking her to the bathroom to protect her from embarrassment, clothing her with a human shield.

In the letter to the Colossians, we read about clothing ourselves with compassion. *Compassion* means, according to Webster's, "sympathetic consciousness of others' distress." But in the Christian tradition it means more. It means "suffering with," feeling what others feel. Having *compassion* removes the pressure of *where do I belong* and *how do I fit in* and puts the emphasis on relationship.

Compassion. It means clothing one another with garments of acceptance. It means making sure no one feels the naked vulnerability of being left out or left alone. Compassion means looking beyond the styles that are "in" and learning to clothe other people's bodies with our care for them. It's what Jesus did. He clothed people with care, especially care for their bodies.

Jesus paid a lot of attention to bodies. He delighted in sharing food and wine with others. He washed the dust-covered feet of his disciples. Jostling his way down a crowded street, he noticed when a woman touched the hem of his clothing (see Luke 8:43-48). He also knew that getting rest was important. After the disciples' first preaching tour, Jesus immediately took them away to "rest for a while" (Mark 6:31). And he was moved to compassion again and again by the broken bodies of the people who came to him for help. Once he made mud using his own saliva and put it on the eyes of a blind man (see John 9:1-11). Another man was so crazed that he lived naked in a cemetery, but Jesus recognized that even this person was made in the image of God and drove the demons from his body. Jesus clothed this man in compassion, and soon the man was wearing clothes made of cloth as well (see Luke 8:26-39).

Our bodies are holy and awesome—yours, mine, *everyone's*. Made in God's image—yes! And then wrapped in the clothing of compassion. By following Jesus, we see that life with God is not just a spiritual thing. Life with God involves our whole being, including our body—whatever the shape of our nose or the condition of our skin or the firmness of our muscles.

The body of Christ

One time when my youth group went on retreat together we decided to plan all the worship services by ourselves with no adult supervision. We sent the sponsors to take a nap while we planned the closing Communion service. After lengthy discussion, we decided to have Communion in the swimming pool at midnight, beginning with a foot-washing ceremony.

As people entered the pool area, we asked them to sit on the side of the pool with their legs dangling in the water. Slowly Randy Nixon and Sherie McNutt, youth group members, went from person to person, scrubbing our submerged feet with a camp towel. The underwater lights made

■ ■ ■ ■ ■ ■ **Read stories of Jesus' care for bodies in Luke 8: 43-48;**

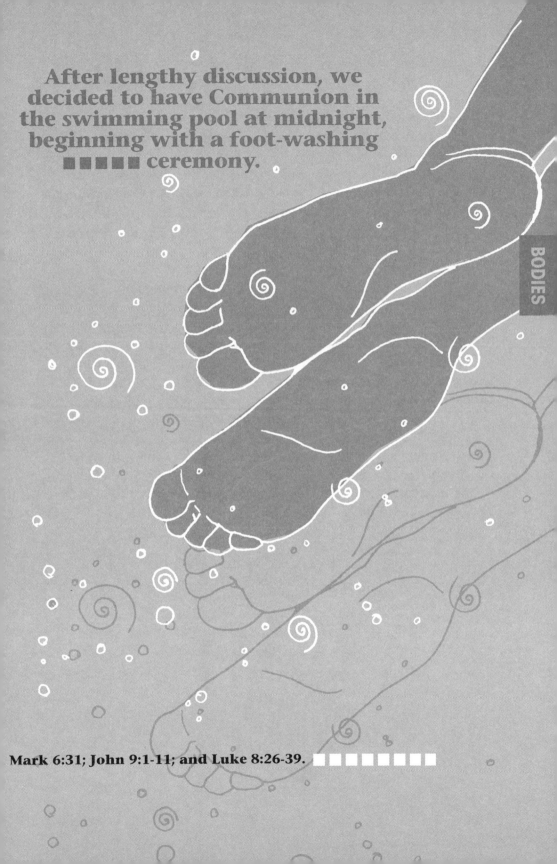

After lengthy discussion, we decided to have Communion in the swimming pool at midnight, beginning with a foot-washing ■ ■ ■ ■ ■ ceremony.

BODIES

Mark 6:31; John 9:1-11; and Luke 8:26-39. ■ ■ ■ ■ ■ ■ ■ ■ ■

the water glow a turquoise blue. The stars were bright overhead. As Randy and Sherie made their way around the pool, everyone grew silent, surprised by the pleasure of having our feet washed—at midnight, with the crickets singing and the water lapping.

When it was time for Communion, we rolled our pastor, Jerry—wheelchair and all—down into the shallow end of the pool on a plywood ramp we'd built that afternoon. When Jerry's body entered the water, he could move. He became buoyant, and his healthy left arm grew stronger. He served Communion to us that night, for the first time in our lives. In the warm embrace of the water, Jerry was strong enough to hold a cup of grape juice and the Twinkies we'd decided to use for Communion bread.

Jerry said that probably the best way to have Communion is in water because the water reminds us of our baptism. He told us that in the waters of baptism, everyone becomes the same. There is no longer popular or unpopular, paralyzed or able-bodied. There is no longer even male or female. Jerry said that baptism represents the greatest belonging. Because of our baptism, we would always be in the pool together, forever changed—even when driving our car on dry land to high school the next Monday morning.

Youth group was never the same after that watery midnight Communion service. From then on, the members of our group belonged to one another. We fit. We became a body—a holy and awesome body. The body of Christ. ■

MARK YACONELLI
WITH ALEXX CAMPBELL

|||Stuff

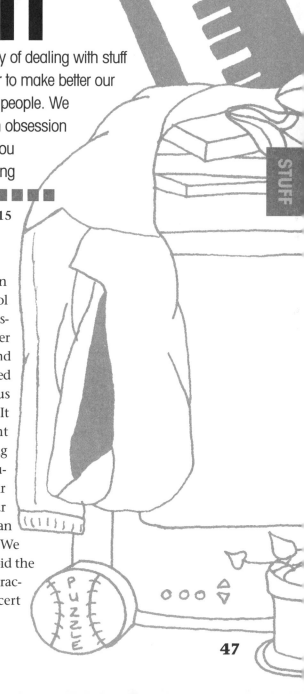

We tried to find a practice, a way of dealing with stuff (material possessions), in order to make better our relationship with God and other people. We realized that Americans have an obsession with stuff, and we tried to help you reflect on your own way of dealing with stuff. We hope this helps. ■ ■ ■ ■

—**Alexx Campbell, 15**

The Assignment

It was only as the bus stopped in front of Saint Francis High School that Alexx Campbell began to question the Assignment. As the other students pushed into the aisle and filed out of the bus, Alexx remained seated, gripping his Optimus Concert-Mate electric keyboard. It was a large, awkward instrument given to him by his parents during one of their many parental hallucinations. He could still hear their voices from three years ago, "Your mom and I never learned to play an instrument, and we regret it. We thought this would help you avoid the mistakes we made. With a little practice you might become a concert pianist."

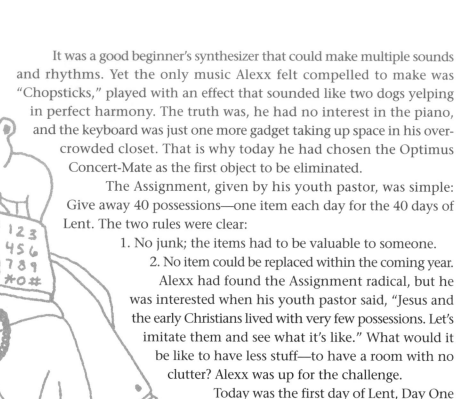

It was a good beginner's synthesizer that could make multiple sounds and rhythms. Yet the only music Alexx felt compelled to make was "Chopsticks," played with an effect that sounded like two dogs yelping in perfect harmony. The truth was, he had no interest in the piano, and the keyboard was just one more gadget taking up space in his over-crowded closet. That is why today he had chosen the Optimus Concert-Mate as the first object to be eliminated.

The Assignment, given by his youth pastor, was simple: Give away 40 possessions—one item each day for the 40 days of Lent. The two rules were clear:

1. No junk; the items had to be valuable to someone.

2. No item could be replaced within the coming year.

Alexx had found the Assignment radical, but he was interested when his youth pastor said, "Jesus and the early Christians lived with very few possessions. Let's imitate them and see what it's like." What would it be like to have less stuff—to have a room with no clutter? Alexx was up for the challenge.

Today was the first day of Lent, Day One of the Assignment. Selecting the first item to give away had been simple, and he had no worries about someone's wanting the keyboard. It was in perfect condition, and many of his classmates played piano. Alexx con-sidered himself a new Christian; giving away stuff was an experiment, a test to see if Jesus and the early Christians were right about living with less. But did this really make life better? He didn't know.

"You can't hide in here." The bus driver interrupted his thoughts. "Off to class, young man."

Alexx walked off the bus, stepped up to the front doors of the school, and went in. Within minutes he encountered Kyle Grossmont, a fellow player from the freshman

You shall not make for yourself an idol, whether in the form of anything that is in heaven above, or that is on the earth beneath, or that is in the water under the earth. You shall not bow down to them or worship them. . . .

—DEUTERONOMY 5:8-9*a*

baseball team. Alexx paused, gathered his thoughts, and then said casually, "Hey Kyle, check this out." Kyle stopped, stepped out of the stream of hurrying students, and faced Alexx. "I'm getting rid of this keyboard. It works perfectly. I even have the manual. It's like a regular synthesizer, with different sound controls, samplers, and effects. Here, I'll show you. . . . " Alexx paused; he noticed Kyle was standing still with a perplexed look on his face—as if Alexx were speaking some ancient form of Pig Latin. Alexx got to the point, "You want it?"

Kyle stood perfectly still, his face suspicious. His eyes began to search, darting back and forth between the keyboard and Alexx's face, looking for a sign that would help him interpret these words. Reading his thoughts, Alexx spoke up, "This isn't a trick. It works perfectly. I just don't want it anymore. I'm doing an experiment with my pastor. We're trying to live with less stuff . . ." Alexx trailed off, suddenly realizing this explanation was only causing greater confusion. Kyle continued to stand still at the edge of the rushing stream of students in the hallway. Slowly Kyle's face began to shift—his eyebrows lowering, his eyes squinting, as he said almost angrily, "What are you talking about?"

Alexx spoke slowly, as if speaking to a first-year student of English, "I'm trying to get rid of stuff. I don't want this keyboard. So I brought it to school to see if anyone wants it. It's in perfect condition. Do you want it?"

Still confused and seeking to make sense of it all, Kyle asked carefully, "How much?"

"Free," replied Alexx. " I'm not trying to make any money. I just want to get rid of it."

An awkward pause. "Free" was not an appropriate answer. Now in addition to his squinting eyes and furrowed brow, Kyle began slowly shaking his head and walking backward as if stepping away from a crazy person. "You're up to something—or you're nuts." And with his head shaking back and forth, Kyle turned and entered the flow of students.

Alexx received a similar response from his locker mate, the kids in first-period English, and his friends in the lunchroom. Nobody could understand why someone would give away something valuable. It didn't make sense. All day he faced confused faces and questions, "Is it stolen?" "Is it your sister's?" "Is it broken?" "Are you getting back at your parents?" "Do you expect a favor in return?" Alexx tried to explain what he and his pastor were up to, but no one understood. Why give away something that worked, something that wasn't junk, and something that was fun to play? Why give away perfectly good stuff?

At 5:00 P.M. Alexx stepped back on the number 14 bus headed for home. In his arms he held the Optimus Concert-Mate. He felt dejected and confused. No one understood his attempt to live with fewer possessions.

Walking into his room that night, Alexx looked around at all his belongings. So much of it was unnecessary—stuff he didn't use, didn't need. He went to his desk, took out a piece of paper and pencil, and made a list of the perfectly good things he could live without. See the actual list on the next page.

Over the next 40 days, Alexx Campbell boxed up each of the items on this list to be given away. His room became more simple: a bed, a desk, a chair, some clothes, some books, some sports equipment, and a few other items. His friends still don't understand.

Stuff is everywhere

It's hard to imagine life without stuff. Think of people living completely without material items—no clothes, no entertainment devices. No-thing. Cities would be nudist camps—without the group volleyball. With no musical instruments, rock and roll would be replaced with "rock and stick."

STUFF TO GIVE AWAY

IMUS CONCERT-MATE ELECTRIC KEYBOARD
MINIATURE BLACK STONE BEAR STATUE
RMONICA
INESE FINGER HANDCUFFS
UCH-TONE PHONE
QUISHY PEA-POD TOY
AD OF DRAWING PAPER AND SET OF CHARCOALS
RAMED DRAWING
TWO PAIRS OF PANTS AND SOME SHIRTS
BOOK ON THE CIVIL WAR
STRATEGO BOARD GAME
REMOTE-CONTROL TRUCK
RAINCOAT
3-D CHESS BOARD GAME
JEWEL CD
RED HOT CHILI PEPPERS CD
TELEVISION SET
SOCCER SHORTS
BASEBALL PUZZLE
BOOK ENTITLED THE 11TH HOUR
MINIATURE SPEAKERS FOR CD PLAYER
A BOOK ENTITLED DINOTOPIA
ED EMBERLEY'S THUMBPRINT BOOK
MICHAEL CRICHTON BOOKS SPHERE AND ANDROM
FAR SIDE PREHISTORY BOOK
RD GAME

CLIMBING PANTS
A MOBILE
RABBIT FUR CHAIR COVER
PHOTO MOSAIC PUZZLE
FLOWERPOT
ANTIQUE THAI CARRYING STICK
CLASSIC BOOKS COLLECTION
NERF FOOTBALL
NIKE JACKET
LAMP NEXT TO BED
MICHAEL CRICHTON BOOKS JURASSIC PARK AN
MONO: THE PROMISED LAND
BANANAS AT LARGE 1 CD
TAHITIAN CARVING

PUZZLE

No hospitals, refrigerators, heaters, and cooking utensils would make life one big *Survivor* game without the cash prize, free car, and product endorsements.

The truth is, nobody lives without stuff. Wherever you find people, you find stuff. Try to picture your life without the stuff. It's difficult. Five years old: Life was my banana-yellow bicycle, popgun, and hiking boots with the two-inch soles. Twelve years old: Life was basketballs, music on my clock radio, and stovepipe pants with the big comb in the back pocket.

Try to picture your room when you were five years old, 10 years old, and now. What was the stuff of your life then, and what is it now? On page 54, make a list of the stuff you valued in your life at five years old, 10 years old, and at this time in your life. Now make a list of the stuff you think you'll value when you are 20, 40, and 60 years old. (Really, write it down!) What do you notice about your lists? As you look them over, what stuff is (or has been) necessary for you to have a good and fulfilling life? What hasn't?

What is stuff?

Stuff refers to the material items created, collected, used, or displayed by human beings. All the things that surround our lives can be considered stuff. Everybody has stuff, although not everybody values, owns, or has access to the same stuff. Compare your own list of valuables to that of a Native American from the Pacific Northwest in the year 1400. A young man from the coastal Makah tribe might have listed cedar-bark raincoat, redwood canoe, bearskin blanket, whaling spear. A young woman from the United States in 1800 might have listed weaving loom, quilt, washbasin, woodstove. Different stuff

STUFF OF VALUE AT DIFFERENT AGES
    5
    10
    20
    40
    60

RULES TO LIVE BY

RANDOM THINGS I OWN

GOOD STUFF?	BAD STUFF?

enables different ways of life. Unlike Alexx Campbell and most people living in developed countries, neither the young brave nor the prairie home-maker owned enough to participate in the 40-day Lenten giveaway.

Our stuff actually affects how we think, act, and live. For example, compare life with the car versus life with the horse as the primary mode of transportation. In horsey days travel was serious. Travel took a lot of time and could be risky. People were much more vulnerable to nature. They smelled the land, experienced changes in the weather, and had to watch out for dangerous animals.

The car makes life different. Living with cars, we perceive the space between two points as shorter. In a car people rarely feel rain, heat, cold, or other weather on their skin. Wild animals are almost never a concern, unless they splatter across the front grille. The car has changed the way people live. Consider the other 1,001 everyday things added to life since 1800 (planes, television, cell phones, microwave ovens, and so on), and you begin to realize how life has changed. *Stuff changes you.*

Not only the stuff itself changes how we live; what we believe and how we act with stuff can make one way of life different from another. My friend Paul believes you should never buy stuff new if you can get it used. Paul almost always shops at thrift stores. On weekends he goes "Dumpster diving"—looking for useful items that other people have thrown out. He has furnished his home with nice furniture that other people considered junk. His clothes, again mostly from thrift stores, cost him less than $100 a year. For his wedding he even found a used tux for less than $20.

Paul's belief and practices result in no debts, less need for money, and a good feeling about using fewer environmental resources. Paul lives under a rule different from most people's, which makes his life as a whole different from that of most North Americans.

When people in the United States want something, generally they go to a store where they can get the item brand-new. When a toaster breaks, a shirt goes out of style, or a dresser drawer falls apart, usually they chuck the apparently "useless" item in the trash bin. Different rules about stuff create different ways of living.

What are the basic practices regarding stuff in your family? Do you have your own ideas or practices about how you relate to stuff? Take a minute and add to the list on page 54 a couple of the rules you live by when it comes to purchasing, owning, or relating to stuff.

The good stuff

Think about these questions: How do you know which stuff is good—not clutter or junk? Which stuff is worth keeping? For most human beings throughout history, answering would be easy: All stuff is worth keeping. Up until a hundred years or so ago, not much stuff was available, and most of it was necessary: cooking utensils, tools for work, clothes, and some decorative items. There were no large department stores, no catalogs, no eBay, and no other sources for an endless supply of things. Because stuff used to be scarce, people lost control when they faced 25 different kinds of toilet seat covers, 55 different styles of Barney the Dinosaur, and thousands of different styles of shoes. Over time shopping has shifted from small corner stores to department stores to malls to warehouses. In North America, people have gone nuts. They build larger and larger houses with more closet space, double garages, and storage sheds in the backyard—all designed to provide more room for stuff.

Now we have places like the enormous storage warehouse in Freemont, California—four stories high and as long as a city block. When you walk in, it looks like a space-jet hangar from *Star Wars*. Inside the warehouse, workers in orange suits and yellow hard hats drive forklifts with bulging plastic-wrapped pallets filled with stuff that ordinary families are paying to store. Paperback books, stuffed animals, sweaters, and Power Rangers press against shrink-wrap as they're lifted and stacked four stories high. In the back another five workers stoke a gigantic incinerator where all the stuff that has been forgotten or left is burned. Ten percent of the stuff in this warehouse will end up in the incinerator.

How can we tell the good stuff from the bad? A basic proposition: *The good stuff includes those things needed to increase health, love, joy, peace, hope, creative expression, faithfulness, and relationships with people and other living organisms.* Stuff is good when it helps you and the people around you become fully alive, the people God created us to be. This is the rule Jesus lived by. Jesus enjoyed and approved of all the stuff that brought life to people: fishing nets, boats, perfume, homes, eating utensils, clothing, and cushions. Jesus appreciated those material items that deepened people's love for God, others, and themselves.

If I test the stuff in my home according to the proposition above, I see that a lot of my stuff can be considered good: refrigerator—keeps food edible, brings greater health; phone—allows greater connection with family and friends; art supplies—encourage creative expression.

However, some stuff makes me question whether it's good for my life or not, for example: alligator backscratcher, sports jacket I never wear, a shelf of books I've already read. Good stuff is "needed," which means it's useful in our quest to live the good life God offers us. If an object has no particular use, it becomes clutter. A good hat might be a form of expression and protect the eyes from the sun. Four hats are too many—useless clutter, distracting from the simple life Jesus calls us to live.

On page 54 write five random things you own. Now ask yourself, *Is this stuff good?* Do these things bring greater joy, freedom, and love—do they create greater connections between myself and others?

When I was 15 years old, my grandmother bought a children's guitar for five dollars at a garage sale and mailed it to me. It was a cheap wooden, nylon-string guitar with cracked tuning pegs and peeling varnish, what most musicians would call a "beater." Although that guitar was twangy and ugly, it was the only possession I would have rushed in to save had our house caught on fire. I loved that guitar. That guitar helped me stay in touch with my heart. I learned how to make music—music that made me want to write down my thoughts and feelings, music that made me want to sing about my life. That guitar helped me create deep friendships with other kids who wanted to make music. That five-dollar guitar changed how I live, how I see and experience life. It was good stuff.

The bad stuff

For seven years I've taken high-school kids from the West Coast of the United States across the border into Mexico to build houses for poor families. Every year, as we cross the border, I slow down and ask the young people to look at all the factories lined up just one mile into Mexican territory. Immediately the young people notice the names of stylish clothing labels, car companies, and toy manufacturers. These are the factories that produce stuff for the people in the United States.

Mexican factory workers—and workers in other developing countries—have few rights. They are often fired for voicing concerns about safety, sickness, or tending to family emergencies. Many of the people working in these factories are teenagers who are paid only two dollars an hour for difficult and tedious work. These young workers often are exposed to dangerous chemicals outlawed in U.S. factories. Why do these factories exist? So that North Americans can have more and cheaper stuff.

A proposition: *Stuff is bad when it diminishes health, love, joy, peace, hope, creative expression, faithfulness, and relationships among people and other living organisms.* If I buy tennis shoes made by a 12-year-old who was paid two bucks an hour and was exposed to dangerous chemicals in the process, I've bought bad stuff. When my two sons and I collect action figures from fast-food meals—toys with lots of packaging and little plastic gadgets that use up great amounts of natural resources and create greater waste for landfills—we've got bad stuff. When I buy an extra jacket just because I want two different styles, especially when others are in need of warm clothing, I've got bad stuff.

The truth is that a lot of stuff is bad for us and for the planet. Forests are decimated, wildlife made extinct, people overworked, families split apart—all because of stuff. Facing this truth is difficult. Although we know that lots of stuff is bad, there is also really cool stuff that would be fun to have, stuff that would make us feel good for a while. The truth is that stuff is seductive.

Worse news is that even good stuff can turn bad. For example, consider the Walkman. The Walkman is a cool gadget. You can play the music you want to hear when and where you want to hear it. You can create your own little sound track wherever you are—just stick in a tape or CD, slap on the headphones, and you have your favorite tunes lifting you to another plane. The Walkman seems to be good stuff; it makes the joy of music available at any moment.

When I played sports in high school my freshman year, the team would travel to games on a bus. The Walkman was not readily available then. Bus trips were very noisy—filled with 60 other students and me talking, telling stories, sharing jokes, singing, and playing games. During my junior year, the Walkman came out for mass purchase, and soon most students were trying to get one. Then all you could hear on our bus trips was music leaking out of multiple headphones. We didn't talk very much; I didn't get to know the younger students; nobody sang. Kids who couldn't afford individual tape recorders felt like outsiders and often sat alone.

At home, the effect of the Walkman was even greater. My brother, my two sisters, and I each received a Walkman and other personal music devices the same Christmas. Although they added musical pleasure to our lives, we no longer spent evenings interacting with one another. As soon as we came home, we often popped in tapes and drifted into our own worlds. These music machines diminished my relationship with my own siblings. They were bad stuff.

Stuff-ing

Set this book down and look around—notice how many advertisements surround you. Do you notice the logos? the names of companies pressed on T-shirts, shoes, and almost every manufactured object? North American culture spends most of its time and energy on buying and selling stuff. Finding a place where you don't encounter an advertisement is almost impossible. Even when you hike up into the mountains, your shoes, backpack, and T-shirt labels remind you of companies and their stuff.

If you think about how North Americans relate to stuff, you will discover some unhealthy beliefs and compulsions:

Stuff makes you happy. Feeling sad? How about a new outfit! Feeling left out and unnoticed? Get one of these trendy gadgets and you'll be a new person! For every problem there is a product. Watch enough commercials and you'll believe that the happiest people on earth are those who have purchased the right stuff.

Stuff is who you are. Advertisers tell you that you are what you own. Do you want to be a Mercedes-Benz–and–Ralph-Lauren-sweater person or a new-Volkswagen-Bug–and–Gap person? If you want to change your identity, you only need to buy different stuff, wear different labels, and be seen with different gadgets. You can be like those you admire if you just own the same stuff they do. Buy the jacket that Britney Spears wears—you'll be more like her! Get the tennis shoes like Michael Jordan's, and you'll

■ ■ ■ ■ In third-century Egypt a teenager named Anthony was on his way to church thinking about how the first followers of Jesus gave up all their possessions. As he walked into church he heard the following verse being read: "Sell all that you own and distribute the money to the poor, and you will have treasure in heaven" (Luke 18:22). He sold all his possessions and spent the rest of his life living simply in the desert, praying and counseling people who traveled to the desert to seek his advice. ■ ■ ■ ■ ■ ■

be a part of his club. Wear those expensive jeans made in Europe, and people will know you have class and power. The most admired people in American culture are those who have *become* stuff. Clothes have their names on them; cologne and jewelry carry their signatures; action figures are modeled after them. They are hot stuff.

Stuff is God. Understanding why many people worship stuff is not hard when you know they've been trained to believe *(a)* "stuff equals happiness," and *(b)* "you are your stuff." People who could work fewer hours, have more time off, and do more creative things decide instead to spend a lifetime at the office so they can buy more expensive stuff.

We watch television admiring and worshiping the material items we see. We take our sadness, hurt, anger, and low self-worth to the shopping temples. We hand over our offerings—symbols of our labor—in order to receive designer shoes or a new CD. We leave feeling like a new person; our item has blessed us with a new beginning; we look to it to provide us with joy, freedom, life. When stuff is God, holidays (holy days) are only about things. Christmas ceases to be a day for gratitude, family time, and reflecting on the life of One who shows us how to live. Instead, Christmas becomes a time of great stress and disappointment as we seek to purchase, exchange, and return—stuff.

God stuff

Even though the ways we live with and think about stuff can be damaging, God still wants us to have stuff. God gives us life and the elements in nature with which to create, enjoy, and share stuff. After all, Jesus was a carpenter, and he made stuff, so stuff can't be bad. How people relate to stuff is the problem. Focusing on material things as central to life is a constant temptation. Jesus clearly knew this when he told his followers

"You cannot serve God and wealth" (Luke 16:13). Jesus believed that love of God must come first, before all our other loves—especially our love of stuff.

Since the time of Jesus, Christians have struggled to keep the desire for stuff in balance with life in God. Sometimes they blow it. But sometimes they succeed, because they are guided by the following beliefs:

Stuff belongs to God. No one really *owns* anything. Christians have always believed that the earth and all that is created from it come from and return to God. That's why it's ridiculous to store stuff for yourself when it's not yours and, ultimately, you can't keep it. The ancient Israelites learned this lesson when God provided them with daily bread—*manna*—during their 40 years of wandering in the desert. Those who tried to store up and hoard the manna instead of sharing and trusting God found that "it bred worms and became foul" (see Exodus 16).

Stuff is for sharing. If our stuff belongs to God, the question arises, What does God want us to do with God's stuff? The answer is that we are to use our stuff to spread love. Stuff should be used to continue the work of Jesus, to alleviate suffering, and to make life full of love, relationship, joy, peace. Early Christians took to heart this rule of sharing their stuff. They met in homes and shared all their possessions. In the Book of Acts we read, "All who believed were together and had all things in common; they would sell their possessions and goods and distribute the proceeds to all, as any had need" (2:44-45). A well-to-do couple named Ananias and Sapphira literally dropped dead when their community learned the two had sold property and secretly conspired *not* to share the proceeds with their brothers and sisters in faith (Acts 5:1-11). Sometimes what seems like more is less.

When considering a purchase, use these questions from the "Buy Nothing Day" campaign sponsored by the Media Foundation: ■ ■ ■ ■ ■

1. **Do I need it?**
2. **How much will I use it?**
3. **Could I borrow it from a friend or family member?**
4. **Can I do without it?**
5. **Is it made of recycled materials, and is it recyclable?**
6. **Is there anything I already own that I could substitute for it?**

God will provide the stuff. Look on any coin minted in the United States and you'll find the phrase "IN GOD WE TRUST." Do we really live as if we believed that today? Throughout history some Christians have lived simply, with few possessions, and have trusted God to provide enough food, clothing, and shelter to live a satisfied life. In trusting God to give us what we need, Christians experience a new freedom. We don't have to worry about debts, making great amounts of money, keeping storage units, or being tied to a job. We are free to go wherever God leads us, to live the life we long to live.

Keep stuff in perspective. Few of us *decide* to make stuff the center of our lives. Instead, bit by bit stuff begins to take up our lives: We get a television; we want a new DVD player; we upgrade our computer; we decide on a new car. Soon most of our waking time is spent thinking about, maintaining, and interacting with stuff. Jesus advised, "Where your treasure is, there your heart will be also" (Matthew 6:21). In other words, whatever you think about, worry about, spend time with, and long for will become the focus of your life. Christians believe that stuff easily can get in the way of our true focus, loving God and loving others. Because stuff presents this danger, many Christians in history and today have greatly reduced their possessions. Staying clearly focused by yourself is hard though. Christian friends need to rely on one another to keep stuff in perspective, so it won't distract them from God.

What stuff distracts you from enjoying the life God has given you? Like Alexx, make a list (on page 64) of the stuff you could give away in order to have a more simple and God-focused life.

Completing the Assignment

Alexx and I contributed some of our stuff to "The Clothes Closet" at the seminary where I work. Since completing the Assignment, I've seen a few of the items Alexx and I gave away. I saw a teenager from Korea, whose family came to campus with almost no funds and no possessions, wearing my sports jacket. I watched two grade-school boys, whose parents wait tables to pay tuition bills, laughing and chasing Alexx's remote control truck. I watched a middle-aged woman smiling and coasting effortlessly down a side street on the bike I had previously owned.

One night as I walked past the cramped, cinder-block apartments that house many international students on tight budgets, I heard music. It was the muffled sound of an electric keyboard gently playing "Twinkle, twinkle . . . little star. . . ." The notes were hesitant. A child was practicing, learning to make music.

I stood there and wondered if it was the Optimus Concert-Mate electric keyboard that Alexx had given away. I imagined the amazed expressions on the faces of the parents who saw this expensive instrument sitting free and available to whoever needed it. I wondered how life would change for the little child who was learning to play. I wondered if one day this child would tell someone that if there were a fire in her house, the Optimus electric piano would be the one item she would want to save. I thought about all the ways we are connected through stuff, all the ways in which we love one another through our possessions, and all the stuff God has given us just to bring us pleasure.

And then I sat on the curb and listened to the child play. I thought of Alexx in his uncluttered room. And I smiled. ■

MY STUFF TO GIVE AWAY

SUSAN BRIEHL
MARY EMILY BRIEHL WELLS
MAGDALENA BRIEHL WELLS

III Food

We all need to eat and drink every day. But food is more than body fuel. It is a gift from God that connects us to the earth and to the needs of others. At the table we share food and our lives. We also thank God, welcome strangers, receive friends, and meet Jesus. Eating together, we become companions for life. ■ ■ ■ ■ ■ ■ ■ ■ ■ ■ ■ ■ ■

—Emily Wells, 18

FOOD

"You eat first with your eyes." That's my dad talking. He's big on "presentation," paying attention to the color and shape of the food on the plate. He loves to cook for his family and friends, and he wants them to enjoy with all their senses the meals he serves.

"Remember the food pyramid!" That's Mrs. Potter, my eighth-grade life skills teacher. She wanted us to get in the habit of eating foods low in fat, high in fiber, and full of vitamins, minerals, and protein.

"How was your day?" You guessed it—that's Mom. Conversation at the table is as important to her as food, building relationships as crucial as building strong bones.

"I'll have a veggie burger and fries, please." That's my older sister, Emily. She has been a vegetarian since she was in eighth grade. Her concern for hungry people and for the environment led her to make this change in her diet. I admire her for that.

These are some of the people who influence what I eat and how I serve and share food. There are others trying to influence me too. You've heard them in ads for soda pop, snacks, and fast-food places. If we listened only to them, we'd be gobbling grease and sugar on the go all of the time. Mrs. Potter wouldn't like that.

Everyone has to eat. But when we follow the way of Jesus, food is for more than survival. Food is a gift of creation, a sign of God's love. To share food is to share God's goodness. Meals are a way to welcome and serve others, just as Jesus welcomes and serves us. In fact, when we welcome others, we welcome Jesus (see the "Practice" chapter). He said when we give food and drink to those who are hungry and thirsty, we are giving these things to him. For Christians, eating and drinking aren't finally about good nutrition or table manners. How we eat and drink shapes a way to live—receiving and sharing God's gifts with grateful, joyful, and generous hearts.

Saying thank-you

When our daughters, Emily and Maggie, were very small, suppertime was hectic, messy, and funny. Inevitably something was dropped or spilled or rejected as unsuitable for consumption. The first time Emily tasted creamed spinach, she screwed up her face as if I were trying to poison her, and then she spit the entire mouthful in my eye. Maggie, on the other hand, delighted in her food. She once reached into her bowl of scrambled eggs with both hands and squeezed until eggs squished through her fingers. Thrilled, she laughed and squeezed again. We all ended up laughing.

Sharing a meal with the girls became much more pleasant once they learned to use a fork and spoon and a few basic table manners. Like lots of parents, my husband and I taught our children to say those "magic" words—*please, thank you,* and *no thank you.* But even before they could speak, we began teaching them another way to say thank-you. We taught them to fold their hands while we prayed, giving thanks to God for the gift of the food before us. Soon they could say the words with us, "Come, Lord Jesus, be our guest, and let these gifts to us be blessed. Amen."

If the only prayer you say in your entire

By teaching them to give thanks before meals, we welcomed our daughters into a deep, rich faith practice. Jesus too was taught by his parents and his community of faith to give God thanks before eating. Before Jesus fed the hungry multitude on the hillside, when he gathered for supper with his disciples for the last time before he died, and on that first Easter when he ate with the friends he met on the road to Emmaus, Jesus said thank-you to God for the gifts of food and drink. Every time we pray at the table, we join Jesus, and many others, in seeing God's grace in our food and giving thanks.

As the girls grew, so did our repertoire of table prayers. Some were memorized, some spontaneous, some sung. When the girls were in grade school, we added a second line to the "Come, Lord Jesus" prayer: "Let there be a goodly share on every table, everywhere." These words call to mind a whole world of people, those we know and those we never will meet. The prayer reminds us that gratitude is the seedbed of generosity and that God's will is not only that we be fed but also that none be hungry.

Seeing connections

We are driving home, east across the state of Washington, after visiting my grandparents. My sister and I are in the backseat looking out the windows. We leave the chaos of the city, climb the pass through the Cascade Mountains, and watch in awe as the mountains give way to the rolling fields of the Columbia River Basin. As far as I can see, the land is covered in green and gold. On the side of the road are signs bearing the names of the crops: wheat, alfalfa, corn, potatoes, peas, beans, sweet onions. We count 22 crops, and those are just the ones that border the highway.

I roll down my window. The hot July air rushes in, smelling of warm soil and pungent grasses. Mom passes out lunch: sandwiches and juice.

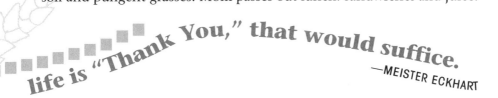

life is "Thank You," that would suffice.

—MEISTER ECKHART

Perhaps the wheat for this bread was grown in these very fields, I think as I take a bite. How amazing that from this land, not far from my house, comes a bounty great enough to provide bread for thousands of people. More amazing yet, the contents of my sandwich come from all over the country, maybe from around the world. The tomato came from a California hothouse, the cheese from a Midwestern creamery, and the grapefruit juice from trees in Arizona or Florida. This meal, basic in content, simple in presentation, and eaten en route, not only satisfies my hunger but also connects me to many places, people, and seasons.

Being so interwoven with the whole world is one of the wonders of living in this century. However, the old saying "With rights, come responsibilities" is still true, especially with regard to food. My lunch may connect me to fields warm with sun and rich with rain, to farmers, pickers, bakers, and vendors paid well and treated fairly, and to people around the world feasting on the same goodness. But it also connects me to gross injustice and abuse: land laden with pesticides, children laboring in fields, elders weak with hunger. The daily, necessary acts of eating and drinking bind us to both the beautiful and the broken. How do we respond to this truth as we live as God's people?

Our first response is gratitude. We thank God for such generous and nourishing gifts. Giving thanks opens our eyes to our connections to others. We see that we cannot thank God for the food we have and then turn our backs on people who are hungry. We cannot praise God for the bounty of the land and sea and close our eyes to the ways we abuse and pollute the soil and water.

So, our second response is to extend God's generosity to all people. Extending God's generosity means actively working to restore honor

■■■■Com • pan • ion
Latin: *com-*, together + *panis*, bread =
"one who eats bread with another."

and life to those people and that land burdened with the work of providing food. It means sharing our food with those who have none, being advocates for the poor, and working to change policies and systems that keep some people hungry while others have more than enough to eat. In short, giving thanks to God is more than saying grace at the table; it is living lives that reflect God's justice and love.

Making choices

Gathering the bread crumbs from my lap, I roll down my window and send them back to the fields, back to the land from which they came. Making choices about the food we eat begins with reconnecting ourselves to its source. Start by tracing a food you eat regularly—including everything involved in its production—back to its ultimate source. This exercise is like drawing a family tree backward (only it will look more like a tangled shrub). Then ask yourself whether the people who worked to produce or move the food each step along the way were well paid, treated fairly, given time off, and able to work in safe conditions. And don't forget the land. Was it respected, replenished, and rested? Most foods won't pass this test. In fact, were we to eat only food we could guarantee was brought to us by hands working under just conditions, our diet might consist of potatoes grown in our own backyards and rainwater caught on our tongues.

This little exercise can be discouraging because it shows how complicated the issue is. When we face our participation in unjust systems, we realize we can't escape them. Perfection is not an option. When I get discouraged, I remember the prayer Jesus taught. At my church each Sunday, just before we share the bread and wine of Holy Communion, we say the Lord's Prayer. The line that catches my attention is "Your will be done on earth as in heaven." Praying this, we commit ourselves to knowing and doing God's will here on earth, every day, in every aspect of our lives. And we pray with a global community of people who also long for a world shaped by God's love. With me they are willing to work to make that happen.

Looking out the car window as we enter our hometown, my mind drifts back to the fields. I think of all who work to bring us food: the harvesters, those who invented and built the equipment, the miners, the sowers, the earth that bore the golden grain, the rain that nourished it, the seasons and the light. Light— it all comes back to light, the first day of the created world, the first ingredient for life, the first gift from God. As it was in the beginning, everything finds its source in God.

A place at the table

You probably know Harry Potter, the central character of J. K. Rowling's books. Harry attends Hogwarts, a wizardry school. When the school was established, four wizards each formed his own house, gathering students with traits and qualities in common with him and one another. On the first day of school, new students, one by one, put on the Sorting Hat. The hat magically discerns the gifts and traits of the student and tells that individual which house he or she will belong to for the next seven years. Students in each house share not only some basic characteristics but also a common room, quidditch teams, classes, and a table in the Great Hall where everyone gathers for daily meals and special feasts. While eating around this table, students tell stories from the day, make plans, discuss homework, and joke around.

The summer before I entered eighth grade, my family moved from Holden Village, a small community in the Cascade Mountains of Washington, to Spokane, the second largest city in the state. On the first day of school, I told myself I would be fine as long as I stayed in my seat and focused on my teachers and work. But lunch frightened me. I walked into the cafeteria where

■ ■ ■ ■ ■ ■
Six things to do:
1. Learn where your food comes from.
2. Find out which food companies are committed to caring for creation.
3. Write letters supporting just labor laws and humane food policies.
4. Tithe. Give 10 % of your own money to help feed people or prevent hunger.
5. Volunteer in a soup kitchen, hospitality house, or community garden.
6. Join or start a Bread for the World chapter (see www.bread.org).

Maggie

hundreds of kids sat. I didn't see an open place. No one looked up to greet me. I couldn't tell where I should sit, where I might find friends or at least people I had things in common with. I wanted the Sorting Hat! I wanted someone to tell me where I belonged and who my companions should be. I didn't need the students to cheer when I walked to their table like they did at Hogwarts when a new student was placed in their house, but a smile or a kind word would have been nice.

Before that day in eighth grade I hadn't realized how much I enjoy—and take for granted—eating with friends and family. Even eating peanut butter sandwiches in the cafeteria with friends makes a big difference in the day. I talk with people, laugh with them, and rest in the company of familiar faces. Meals with my family are also important. Even when the food isn't fancy, I look forward to suppertime. Sometimes we tell stories, jumping up from the table to act out parts. Other times we have heated discussions about politics or hard conversations about family matters. When we are too tired or distracted to say much, it's good to be together anyway. At school and at home, those I eat with help me know who I am and where I belong. I think that's true for lots of people.

Where do you eat? With whom do you eat?

One day, during that first hard year in a new town, my sister was sitting on the floor in her school's hallway eating her lunch alone, feeling forgotten and ignored, when suddenly a boy threw his backpack down in front of her and plopped next to it. They didn't know each other. He was a freshman and she was a junior; she read poetry, he imitated Jim Carrey; she lived at home with us, he was a resident of "the institution," a home for psychiatric patients, and hadn't seen his parents in years. They couldn't have been more different.

FOOD

Yet from that day on they ate lunch together, sharing stories and cookies. Two people without friends, two people who felt out of place, became unlikely companions.

■■■■■■■■■■■

Jesus ate with the most unlikely people. He didn't look for folks who shared certain traits or gifts or values with him. He invited everyone. Jesus looked up in the tree where short Zacchaeus—a despised and dishonest tax collector—sat, and he said, "Come down. Let's eat lunch at your house." At that meal, Zacchaeus and Jesus became companions. And Zacchaeus's whole life changed! (See Luke 19:1-10.)

Jesus ate with his close friends Mary and Martha. He also ate with strangers—5,000 of them—outside in the middle of nowhere. He shared meals with sinners, which got him into trouble, and with "religious" people who tried to get him into big trouble. For Jesus, eating and drinking with others was more than a way to fuel up for the day. Meals connected people to one another, bound them together. At the table, outsiders found a place to belong. Strangers became companions and enemies became friends.

Jesus told a story about a man who gave a feast for his rich friends (see Luke 14:16-24). They all had excuses for not coming. "Go out to the streets and alleys," the man told his servants. "Bring in the poor, the homeless, and those who aren't welcome anywhere else." This is how God sets the table. Everyone is welcomed because everyone belongs. All who are hungry and thirsty eat, drink, and rejoice. No Sorting Hat. No magic. Just a wide welcome. How would our lives change if we practiced setting the table like God does?

Fasting

My cousin Nick is a wrestler. He is very careful about how much he eats, especially when he's "making weight." My best friend dances and, like Nick, she works to keep her weight consistent. Both my sister and I worry about friends who are always dieting or who almost never eat because they want to be thinner. Voices all around them seem to tell them they must look like the models in magazines, the actors in movies, or the athletes on television. These voices say, "You aren't good enough. You are not worthy of love unless you are thin, pretty or handsome, sexy or athletic." Such voices can turn our minds against our bodies. They can warp our image of ourselves and distort our understanding of God. When such distorted perspectives take over, our bodies become objects to perfect; food becomes an enemy; and eating becomes an obsession or a secret burden rather than a time of companionship and joy.

Sometimes Christians fast, refraining from certain or all food and drink for a day or a season. There is a huge difference, however, between dieting and fasting. Fasting is not a means to lose weight, make a sacrifice, or prove how worthy or self-disciplined we are. Fasting is a way to say yes to life, together. Ancient communities conserved food during the winter when animals were hibernating and fields lay barren. They restricted their eating so that they all could live until the next harvest. Then they feasted! For Christians too fasting is not primarily a solitary discipline any more than feasting is a private event. We fast with others: our Bible study or youth group, our family or congregation. Fasting with others helps focus our attention on the community and God rather than on ourselves.

Last spring our youth group joined others from neighboring churches in a 24-hour fast. We hoped to raise awareness of and money for those in our city who are hungry. John Cassian, a monk who lived in the fourth century, fasted another way: He did not eat between meals. He thought snacking at every little twinge of hunger kept his mind too focused on his stomach and his desires, instead of the needs of others. Eat enough, he

FOOD

■■■■■ **I want a fast from gluttony**
■■ **of nations, systems, policies**
■■■■■■■■■ **that feed some well**
■■■ **while others starve for grain,**
■■■■ **for bread, for dreams, for peace.**

—JAN RICHARDSON, *Sacred Journeys*

taught, not too much or too little. And avoid grazing throughout the day. Wait until mealtime. Then you will be truly hungry when you sit at the table with others, and you will be more thankful for the food in front of you.

Fasting can make us more aware that we are human, fragile, and utterly dependent upon God. You might try a simple fast with your family or friends, perhaps one day a week during Lent, the five weeks before Easter. Decide on a very simple meal: a baked potato, a bowl of rice, or a plate of pasta. No one would need to spend much time preparing for or cleaning up after such a meal. You could give the money you save on those meals to a food bank or a homeless shelter. Or you could spend the time you save not cooking and doing dishes working at such a place. But most importantly, you and your table companions could pray for awareness of your neighbors' needs and the goodness of God. Together you would be saying Yes! to life.

Feasting

The scent of ham fills the air. There's a pop as a jar of home-canned dill beans is opened. Little kids scuttle around, nearly tripping everyone they pass. Someone sets the table with the holly plates. Someone else gets the beverages from the old refrigerator in the basement. John Denver and the Muppets sing carols from the tape player. The music is so corny that no one can resist singing along. Once the busy preparation is over, everyone sits and a familiar voice prays a prayer, thanking God for the meal, those who worked to bring it to the table, and the group gathered. This is Christmas dinner at Grandma's. It's a feast and celebration. I can't think of a time when I am happier.

■ ■ ■ ■ ■ ■ ■ ■ ■ ■

I love Maggie's description of Christmas dinner at her grandma's house, the house where I grew up. Reading her words, I can smell my mother's ham, see those "holly" plates on the table, and hear her grandpa, my father, praying in his strong, kind voice. The scene is full of joy, and Maggie is right in the middle of it, smiling. But our family, like yours, isn't perfect, and

How might feasting—
eating with others to
celebrate God's love—
help mend a
relationship in
your life?

neither are our memories. We often gloss over the painful times, remembering only what was lovely. Maybe you have sad memories of family gatherings—holidays when you were shuttled from your mom's house to your dad's, a Christmas heavy with grief over one who wasn't there, celebrations with too much alcohol or a forced hilarity that tried to mask deep divisions, old wounds.

For Christians, feasting isn't about making a Hallmark-perfect memory or putting on a Martha Stewart–style extravaganza. Nor is a feast a time to harm our bodies by overeating or drinking too much. A feast is a sign of God's abundant mercy and extravagant grace. In the middle of our failings and our many kinds of poverty, we gather to revel in God's kindness and generosity. Around the table, we rejoice that Jesus has come to bring us hope and new life. We celebrate that relationships, once torn to shreds by angry deeds and hurtful words, are now mended. We say Yes! to God's life in us. Even you, when your life is a total mess, are welcomed to this table, to the feast of God's love.

Once there was a young man who made a total mess of his life. "I don't want to be part of this family anymore!" he said, leaving home. He took all the money his dad had saved for his future and spent it doing stupid things. One day he woke up broke, hungry, and alone. He felt as good as dead. He thought his dad might give him work and a place to stay, even though he knew he didn't deserve it. Imagine his surprise when he neared home and saw his dad running to welcome him. He felt like he'd been given a new life. "Let's party!" his dad cried. "You were lost and are found. You were dead and are alive." (See Luke 15:11-32.)

Breaking bread with Jesus

I was sitting on the edge of the sandbox at recess during second grade, talking to my best friend, Melissa. We went to different churches so we were curious about what Sunday morning was like for each other. This time we were talking about Holy Communion. She'd never had it, and I had every week for as long as I could remember. "Do the pastors change the bread into Jesus?"

> **Compassion is the keen awareness that all living beings are part of one another and involved in one another.**
>
> —THOMAS MERTON

she asked me, because my parents are pastors. I didn't know. I told her I'd find out on Sunday.

Since I was about five years old, I have had two "church" jobs: to help Mom bake the Communion bread on Saturday night and to carry it up to the altar just before the meal. On this particular Sunday I watched the bread very closely, but I never saw "it" happen. That is what I told Melissa at school the next day. I told her how everyone sang as I carried the bread to the table. I told her how Mom said a prayer of thanksgiving over it, just like we do at home before dinner. I told her how people stood in a big circle as Mom and Dad gave them pieces of bread, saying "the body of Christ," and the people said, "Amen!" Then the people went back to their seats and others took their place in the circle. After everyone had eaten, we sang one more song. Though I couldn't explain it to Melissa, I knew that Jesus was there—in the singing and the praying, in the unending circle of people, and in the bread we shared.

■■■■■■■■■■■

The meal Emily describes is the meal followers of Jesus have shared for two thousand years. It is known by several names, including the Lord's Supper, Holy Communion, and the Eucharist. The earliest Christians called it "the breaking of the bread." As they did, we share the bread and the cup, remembering Jesus and his life given for us. We hear his words: "I love you. I forgive you. I am with you and will never leave you." In this meal we are deeply connected to Jesus. We also are connected to one another, to the unending circle of baptized people, and to the whole creation.

When we break the bread of the Lord's Table we taste and see God's future, that day when God's will is done on earth as in heaven. Then all who hunger will be fed. All who thirst will be satisfied. The walls that divide us will be broken down. Creation will be cherished and tended. Every person around the table will sing of God's goodness. And heaven and earth will join the song.

This meal, where Jesus gives himself to us, shapes every other meal we eat. Whenever we eat and drink Jesus calls us to live as if God's future were already here. Whether the menu is roast turkey and all the trimmings or microwave mac and cheese, our eyes are opened to see our food as a gift from God. Whether we are at home or at school, at a ball game or a birthday party, our hands are opened to share these gifts. Alone or with others, we practice God's hospitality, justice, and mercy each time we break bread with glad and generous hearts. ■

■■■■Taste and see that the LORD is good.
—PSALM 34:8

▮▮**Creation**

This chapter is about a practice that helps people realize how passionate you should be toward creation. The practice of caring for creation helps you understand that creation is not just scenery. You are living in creation, and your outlook on life will affect not only how you feel about creation but how you treat it. ▪ ▪ ▪ ▪ ▪ ▪ ▪

—**Tim Frazier, 14**

As a boy, I knew my dad less by sight than by sound. As far back as I can remember, he held down two jobs to keep afloat. A foreman carpenter by day, he nursed a fledgling construction company at night. He was always working. And his presence at home was evidenced not so much by his hulking frame as by the noise he made from a distance. A constant din drifted under doors and along hallways like the smell of baking bread and hovered teasingly at the edge of my awareness.

At dinnertime, in between lunging after meat loaf leftovers and bickering over peas, I tingled at the high-pitched wail of his circular saw slicing through lumber in the garage. After bath, as I built my own houses out of wooden blocks in my bedroom, I kept time to the staccato tapping of his electric typewriter snapping out purchase orders in the den. And while I lay in bed, burrowed under my covers yet unable to sleep, I was soothed by his soft six-pack snore harmonizing with the dull drone of the family room TV.

CREATION

I did not so much see my dad in those early years; I overheard him.

Like the backdrop of ocean waves in a seaside home, the constant ebb and flow of his sounds both comforted me with their ever-present rhythm and called me with their promise of rich adventure in deeper waters. They anchored me, yet they also set the star toward which I sailed. Because I knew that one day, when I was big enough, I would be standing proud as my dad's pint-size partner and making noise right alongside him, grabbing bites of a sandwich between passes on the table saw, filing carbon copies as he peeled them out of the typewriter, or sitting back on the couch, tossing back a couple of cold ones while watching Red Skelton reruns on TV. Those sounds of his may have been coarse. But they were my lullabies. They sustained the dreams I sought in my sleep.

One night, when I was no more than seven or eight years old, sunk deep within the darkness of a child's sleep, a distant voice enticed me into foggy consciousness.

"Frank, you awake? Frank, 're you awake?"

Suddenly I popped up, eyes blinking wide like a puppy dog bobbing out of the water.

"Dad!" I cried. "What's the matter?"

"Nothing," he whispered with hushed excitement as he placed a fist-ful of clothes on my bed, his eyes sparkling in scheming mischievous-ness. "Here. Get dressed. I need your help. We got a job to do."

If I had not yet shaken off the warm drippings of sleep, these anomalous words finished the job as I jolted to attention. A job? Me and Dad? Just the two of us? In the middle of the night?

"I can get dressed in 50 seconds! Watch."

"You do that. I gotta get some things. Meet me out in the truck as soon as you're ready." Then his voice dropped to a barely audible though exaggerated enunciation. "And. Be. Qui-et." He grinned, then hulked a tip-

Then there is the sea, with its vast expanses creatures both great and Leviathan whom you

toe toward the door, tossing his head and whispering, "And don't forget your coat. It's gonna be chilly."

Beside myself with curiosity, I slid out of bed, careful not to rouse my younger brother in the bottom bunk. I dashed into my clothes, snagged a slicker and stocking cap, and rushed out the front door.

When I rounded the corner of the porch, I was stunned into stillness. Backed onto the driveway and already idling puffs of white smoke into the midnight sky was my dad's pickup truck. But the source of my astonishment was directly behind it. Hitched to the back of the truck, like a train car all ready for a nighttime trek to an exotic land, was my dad's sailboat, a scruffy-looking 14-foot West Wight Potter he had found deteriorating in back of a job site and for which he had promptly swapped his services. My dad used it mostly for rare fishing trips with friends. Occasionally, on a festive Sunday afternoon, the family enjoyed a leisurely sail across the local lagoons. But a maritime adventure, just the two of us, in the lonely middle of the night? I was soaring in the heady sphere of fantasy.

A slap on the back broke my bewildered spell as my dad, giddy with conspiracy, bounced down the porch and shuffled past me.

"C'mon, Tiger. We're going on an adventure."

Not wanting to get left in the wake of Dad's enthusiasm, I scrambled to the passenger side, heaved the door open, and hauled myself up into the toasty warmth of the cab. My dad dropped a few things in the boat, then leaped behind the wheel and in a single motion slipped the truck into drive while swinging the door shut, checking it at the last moment to make as little sound as possible. Quietly we slid into the deserted street, my dad flashing on the headlights only as we glided by the neighbor's house.

"How 'bout you pouring me a cup of coffee?" my dad asked, his words laced with excitement.

"Sure, but . . . Dad, where are we going?"

teeming with countless creatures, and small; there ships pass to and fro, made to sport with. —PSALM 104:25-26

"Well, see, it's like this. I was in the den getting caught up on some paperwork when the first mate of an oil tanker radioed the Coast Guard." Some part of my dad fancied himself a sailor, and he often worked to the staticky backdrop of the sea-traffic channel on his shortwave radio set.

"They had set off from Oakland and were headed for the Golden Gate when they spotted a humpback whale straying somewhere near Alcatraz. Ya know they're migrating south about now, and one musta got separated from his pod and slipped into the bay by mistake. The tanker crew watched him surface a few times, figuring he didn't know how to get back out o' the bay, but they lost track of him near Treasure Island.

"Well, the Coast Guard started radioing patrols all along the East Bay, figuring he's headin' straight toward Oakland or will follow the deeper water toward Richmond. But the way I figure it, they got it all wrong." My dad was contagiously intoxicated with scheming excitement. "The way I look at it, that poor thing's separated from its family and scared, and he's going to want to get back to them. Sure, he'll try to double back the way he came, but he's probably disoriented and, with all that tanker traffic at this hour, he'll get flustered. He'll have two choices—go north where the water's deeper, like the Coast Guard think, or go south.

"Now at a time like this, an animal relies on instinct. He's going to try to catch up with his family. And his family's migrating south. He doesn't know he's in a bay, so he'll head the same way as his family. Now, he'll have to slip under the Bay Bridge, but the water's deep there and the patrols are all east. So he'll have no problem there. Then it's open waters all the way 'til he runs right smack-dab into the San Mateo Bridge. And, Tiger, that's right where we're gonna be. Ready to greet him and lead him home."

My dad flashed me a look of unadulterated self-certainty and pride, his monologue serving as much to double-check and confirm the logic of his deductions as it was to catch me up on the mission. But catch me up

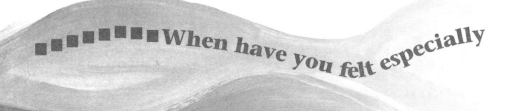
■■■■■■■■■When have you felt especially

he did—converting me both to the humanitarian necessity of this rescue operation and to the certainty of his seemingly self-evident conclusions. As Dad turned his head back to the road and leaned forward in renewed determination, I soaked in the enormity of our mission and allowed it to capture my own inebriated allegiance.

Wow, I thought. *My dad and me. We're going to save a whale!* I could see it all. This huge creature with sad, mournful eyes lost in the vast dark waters of the San Francisco Bay, swimming around in circles, trying in vain to find the channel that would take him back to sea and home. And we were on our way, my dad and me, like Saint Francis in a motorboat with his seafaring sidekick Brother Leo, and we were going to save that lost soul. We would spy the whale trapped at the shallow end of the bay and, puttering ever so cautiously in our West Wight Potter, we'd nudge up along his side. He'd see that we meant to help, and he'd brush up close to the boat while I stroked his hump. Then, together, we would sail in tandem toward the Golden Gate Bridge, me with a hand on a fin, my dad at the helm, the traffic of ships parting, giving way to the whale and his rescuers leading him back to the sea. It was gonna be great.

I too sat up high in the seat and, with all the resolve of an animal rights activist and a lot of the tenderness of a puppy dog lover, I prepared for my part.

"Now, when we get to the marina," my dad ran through the detail, "I'll back the boat into the water. You jump out and grab the towline and tie it to the dock. Then stay with the boat 'til I get back. Think ya can handle it?"

"No sweat, Dad," I retorted confidently.

"Good. I'll park the trailer and we'll be off."

Like a well-drilled naval unit, we set the boat into the water, I manning the lines while my dad drove off with the skeletal trailer. In moments,

close to nature?

he dashed back from the darkness with a thermos stuffed under one arm and rolled-up nautical maps splaying from the other. He jumped onto the boat and revved up the motor while I untied the lines, first from the back cleat, then from the front. I gave the bow a shove and hopped aboard. We were off, easing straight into the choppy starlit darkness that separated us from the distant lights studding the San Mateo Bridge.

Dad poured himself a cup of coffee while I laced up my life jacket, grabbed a searchlight, and took my post at the tip of the boat's bow. Standing tall with coffee in hand, he jockeyed the tiller while I, balancing the searchlight on my shoulder like a sailor on watch, made wide, sweeping arcs of light over the waters in front of us, the back-and-forth semicircles flashing into every shadowy crevice jostling in the waves.

The tension was palpable. Both Dad and I were certain that at any second the spout from a whale's blowhole would pierce through the water's surface.

"There, Dad! I saw something go under water. Go that way." And my dad jerked the boat in the direction of my light. But it was only the bedeviling play of the moon's light on the waves.

"Wait!" my dad yelled. "Shine the light over that way." And the boat was redirected toward another promising sight or sound slipping away into the elusive mystery of the sea.

"No! Over there!"

Like two kids on Christmas Eve, seeing Santa behind every rooftop chimney, we chased phantom shadows and fleeting glimpses and distant slurpy splashes all the way across the bay, convinced that somewhere, lurking in the vast waters underneath us, a lost creature was in need of our help. We circled back and repeated our jagging search in the waters bound by the bridge, reached the near side, and circled again. For several hours we crisscrossed and zigzagged and looped and circled our way through those waters, a swirling spaghetti noodle of a search, ever poised on the edge of discovery. But that lonely whale eluded us, hovering just beyond our search's reach. So we put about and puttered along the length of pilings beside the bridge. Still we found nothing. We hugged the shore by Coyote Point and peered into the coves. Still nothing. So back to deeper waters and our relentless, aimless roaming.

Just where in the world could he be?

And then, Dad had an inspiration.

"Wait a minute," he gushed as if the answer were right under our noses all along. "We're going about this all wrong."

He sat up, straight-backed and silent, and scoped out the situation.

"Yeah, there we go."

He spied what he wanted and piloted the boat out toward the darkest point in the bay, the place most distant from the horizon of city lights and bridge traffic that surrounded us. Once there, he slowed the boat to a crawl, then cut the engine altogether.

"Yeah," he exhaled with satisfaction. Then he mouthed, "Cut the light" and motioned with a slit across his throat.

I switched off the searchlight.

In that instant everything changed.

"Yeah," my dad intoned again, almost reverentially. And I felt it too.

It was as if the whole vast universe—the boundless waters below us and the night sky above us and the mountains' silhouettes stretching into the distance—suddenly revealed itself to us, allowing us to stumble into its still and phosphorescent center. The night sky enveloping us from above was a canopy of swelling, pulsating lights held in a blanket of darkness. The waves of the bay encircling us frolicked in gentle, playful reverie. And the quiet. The quiet itself seemed a palpable presence. Seeping up out of the sea, it held every hushed sound on the planet—every breath, every heartbeat, every wave lapping on the hull—wrapped them all in the pregnant stillness into which every sound dissolves. All of it—the waves, the quiet, the stars above and the hills in the distance—seemed joined in a vast conspiracy of grace, which reached out from every direction and wrapped us both, two longing souls seemingly alone in a depthless sea, as tiny and insignificant as a pair of corks bobbing in the bay, in a compassionate and intimate embrace. Here in this place in this moment, the face of creation bore the gentle smile of a Madonna holding her infant close to her breast.

For several moments we sat there.

Then, silent as the night, I shuffled my way to my dad's side at the boat's stern and sat next to him. He put his muscled carpenter's arm around me and, together, we rested silently in the tiny boat, cradled by creation.

Some Aborigines believe that there are places in the world so sacred that if one dwells there long enough and still enough, one can hear the sacred music that plays deep in the womb of the world as steady as a mother's heartbeat pumping life into the planet. This was one of those places.

It was some time before my dad breathed words into the moment. "Isn't this something?"

Dear God, I never thought that purple and
Until I saw your sunset

"Yeah, Dad," I assented. "But what about the whale?"

He bent low to whisper near my ear, his voice as hushed and his gaze as awestruck as if we were inside an ancient cathedral.

"Well, I don't know why I didn't think of this sooner, but if you were a frightened whale, the last place in the world you would come near is some noisy sailboat slicing up the sea with a searchlight. No, you'd turn and head for the deepest, darkest place you could find, and you would hide down there until all that noise went away. And only when you thought that it was altogether safe would you creep up real slow like and poke your head out. And if you were all alone" (his voice got even softer) "and it was all safe, only then would you cry out for help—for the ones you miss most. Whales do that you know; they cry out to one another. It's like a wolf's howl, only deeper. You'll know it when you hear it. Oh, we're going to find him all right. Not by looking though. By sitting here real quiet. And listening for him."

And listen we did. I was sure my dad was right. That lonely whale was down below us resting in the same bay we were. And if we waited long enough, it would slide to the surface to issue a lonely cry for his own mom and dad. I listened that night. Oh, how I listened, straining my ears in every direction for the sound of that whale's cry, yearning to rescue that lonely, fragile beast. For a long time, I listened.

After a while though, my listening gave way to resting, resting in the quiet, resting in the luminescent play of starlight on the water, resting in the gentle rock of the boat in the waves. The misty air grew chilly, and I nestled deeper into my dad's chest, his Papa Bear arm reaching farther around me, while his gaze fixed on the distant waters. I might still have thought about the whale, spending the lonely night away from his family, but I stopped listening for the sound of his cry. The wash of the waves lapping against the boat and the gentle purr of my dad's breathing were all

orange really went together. last night. That was cool!

—EUGENE, 6, in *Children's Letters to God*

the sounds I needed. As far as I was concerned, the rescue effort was done. I drifted off to sleep.

We never did find the whale that night. In fact, my only other memory of the evening is the sound of my dad's work boots thumping dully on the slate floor of our entryway when he carried me to my room and put me in my bed, still fully clothed.

The next day we read in the paper how some marine biologists found the whale near San Pablo Bay, some 50 miles north of our patrol, and safely led it to sea. My dad's and my services were no longer needed, which was just as well. Dad had a deadline to meet, and he moved back to the garage, reanimating the sounds of his hammers and saw blades.

Before a great deal longer, Dad moved out altogether.

On a sunny Sunday afternoon, I stood on the driveway and watched him drive his loaded truck around the corner without so much as a glance, his dejection so severely contained. He took a lot of himself with him when he left. He took his tools and his files. He took his clothes and his desk. He took his books about sailing and the chair he read them in. He even took his boat, towed timidly on its trailer like a dragging but docile hound dog.

He took all his stuff. But he did not take the sounds. I could still overhear them from every room in the house—the searing screech of his saw blade in the garage, the staccato typing in the study, that staticky buzz of his shortwave radio. Like ghostly trails of smoke, the sounds hovered throughout the house and haunted me as I moved about.

But mostly I could overhear him as I lay in bed at night. I dove down deep into the sea of my covers and strained my ears until I could swear that I could hear him—the soft purr of his pickup idling out front, the dull thump of his work boots in the slate hall, the latch of my door receding as the knob turned, the squeak of the door as it eased open ever so clandestinely, and those words, whispering forth in his husky voice, "Frank, you awake? Frank, 're you awake?"

Yeah, Dad. I am.

"Did you ever see your dad again?"

Tim and I were sitting in the grass of a park looking up at the San Bernardino mountains. The southern California sky was pleasantly blue above us, but the rocky peaks of the mountains were barely recognizable through the smoky haze of afternoon smog. As we had been every Friday afternoon for several weeks, we were sitting in the park next to Tim's high school talking about our assignment for this book: caring for creation. Today we were sharing times in our lives when we felt especially close to nature.

Tim's List

I don't know what to do about the big stuff. But I know how we can start with some of the little stuff. (1) Recycle. Take the time to put the can into the recycling bin. And complete the cycle—only buy things that come in recycled containers. (2) Save gas. Walk, ride a bike, rollerblade, whatever. But cut down on the gas. (3) Cut down on paper use. Use both sides of binder paper, photocopy back-to-back, and take a canvas bag to the store for carrying your groceries. (4) Get outside. Ask to have Sunday school, youth group, even worship outdoors somewhere. And let people share their stories about being close to nature. (5) Be 60 Minutes. Choose one company to research how it treats the earth, then tell people the facts—like your friends, your parents, even your congressperson. Tell the press while you're at it. And let the company know that you're telling the press. That ought to get some attention. So, five things. They don't stop global warming or fill in the hole in the ozone, but they are a start. Who knows? Maybe if everybody starts doing some of this little stuff, the big stuff will take care of itself.

Tim described an early morning at a camp in the Berkshire hills of Massachusetts. He woke up at dawn and took a solitary walk through the woods. He came upon a meadow and sat down. The woods were so still and quiet he actually felt like he was a part of them, that the trees and the shrubs breathed the same air and shared the same ground as he. He felt reverent, as if God were present in that very moment at that very place, and he wanted to pray. But he didn't need to find a prayer to say. The silent sense of being at one with the woods was prayer itself.

"Yeah," I told Tim. "I know exactly what you mean—a moment so close to creation it feels like prayer." That's when I told him the story about looking for the whale with my dad. I described the prayerful moment we shared in the middle of the moonlit bay.

"I saw my dad again," I finally answered Tim. "He came by on Sundays and took my siblings and me for ice cream. Sometimes he even took us camping. But we never had another moment like that one, just the two of us, on such a memorable adventure."

"Did you really stay awake at night and listen for him?"

"Yes. I really did. I wished that he and I could go back to that midnight moment and live there forever. But it wasn't just feeling close to my dad that was so special. It was the whole experience: the adventure and the sense of purpose we had trying to help this wounded creature that so needed our care—and the way creation gave back. In that mystical moment of stillness at the center of the dark bay, with the stars and the waves and the quiet, I felt profound grace and peace. It was weird. I felt so insignificant before that infinite beauty, and yet I felt absolutely significant at the same time—I felt somehow an indispensable part of the whole thing. I sensed in that moment of caring for creation that creation cared back for me."

The woods were so still and quiet he actually felt like he was a part of them, that the trees and the shrubs breathed the same air and shared the same ground as he.

"I can see that. When I was in those woods, I felt as loved as at any time in my life. So how did it affect you, that moment?" Tim wanted to know.

"I don't know exactly. That moment was a seed that lodged deep within me, and it has yearned to grow and bear fruit. I can feel it inviting me to grow into a sensitivity for lost and wandering creatures of all kinds, to grow into a desire to pause and appreciate the beauty of starry nights and moonlit waters, even to grow into a stirring passion to notice the ways creation is wounded and needs us to respond with acts of care and healing. I hardly live like that much of the time. But I can feel the yearning inside of me. And remembering that story reminds me of how I want to be. Is it like that for you?"

"Yeah. When I remember that morning at camp, it makes me feel that this whole world is precious. It makes sense that God called it 'good' when God created it."

"I love that part of the creation story. In fact, the word God uses when God calls creation 'good' also means 'beautiful.' God is like an artist making this fantastic painting or sculpture, and God keeps stepping back and saying, 'Wow, isn't that beautiful."

"But it's not always beautiful, Frank. I mean, just look at the smog in front of us. And that's nothing. Think of all the mountains blasted away for minerals and the forests stripped of trees and the animals mistreated in laboratories and the toxic waste dumps that poison poor neighborhoods. It's not beautiful at all. A lot of creation's pretty messed up."

"It is. In fact, the Bible talks about that too. Something about all of creation groaning in pain, waiting for the healing and flourishing promised through Jesus. Jesus didn't come just to save humanity; he came to save the planet, the universe."

God saw everything that [God] had made,

"Yeah, but we can't wait for Jesus to come back. What do we do about it now?" Tim demanded, sitting up straight. "I mean, most adults I know think of creation as scenery, as something you just look at while you're driving down the road. Sometimes it's pretty, sometimes it's ugly; but it's just scenery. It's not something you have any relationship to. Or do something about."

"Maybe that's a place to start right there—nurturing a relationship with creation. How do you feel close to the earth?" I asked Tim.

"Well, I don't see any way to be close to it without being out there in it. Just spending time outside, walking in the hills, noticing the animals, working in gardens. That's a start. And stories—remembering the stories of the times when we felt close to nature. Just talking today reminds me how important that is. But we shouldn't just spend time with the pretty side. We've got to notice the ugly parts too. You told me about taking a class to see the industrial waste site in south-central L.A. right next door to the elementary school where a lot of kids just happened to get cancer. Maybe if people noticed that kind of stuff, they would be moved to do something about it."

"But do what, Tim? Let me put it back to you."

"Well, maybe that's just it. We're too quick to do things. You know, all day at school or on TV we hear about the things we're supposed to be doing to save the planet—recycle, cut down on gas, turn off the lights. All that's important; don't get me wrong. I mean, I could come up with my own list. [And he did!] But something seems to be missing from all of those lists. It's like, you gotta do things, but you gotta care first. There's this group in L.A. that takes inner-city kids to the mountains for a week. Those teens have never been in nature before. I mean, I know nature's everywhere, but they've never even heard the sounds of a mountain stream or wind in

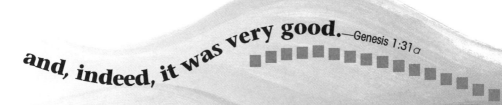

and, indeed, it was very good.—Genesis 1:31a

the trees when they're not muffled by traffic. And they love it up there. They love it so much that when they get back they cannot stand all the garbage in the empty lots and on the streets of their neighborhood. So they organize cleanup drives and plant gardens and take kids up to the mountains the next summer. And now, they've started like 15 Earth groups of those kids in L.A. alone. They're doing things, but it's because they've learned to care first."

"You know, Tim, there's a traditional Jewish saying that if you kill a single tree, it's like silencing a thousand songs, and if you save a single soul, it's like saving all of humanity. Maybe taking care of creation works the same way. Every little act, whether it's cleaning up an empty lot or recycling one can, is like my trying to save a single whale. It's only one act, but it's caring for one creature whose presence gives God infinite delight. And that's enough by itself."

"I don't know. Maybe. What I do know is that things are pretty messed up. And it's time to do something about it—to live out our prayers and what the scriptures say. It's time to actually care for Earth. And who knows? Maybe when you're out there caring, and really doing things, maybe that's when you're praying in the way that's most important." ■

We are not likely to fight to save what we do not love.

—DAVID ORR, *Earth in Mind*

CAROL LAKEY HESS **AND** MARIE HESS

III**Creativity**

Creativity began with God and is central to the nature of God. In the beginning, God created . . . and set in motion further creativity. Like God, everyone has it in them to be creative, whether by painting a room, building a model, or simply playing in the mud. Creativity doesn't come just from special talents; it comes from inside each and every person. It's something we can all practice. Get your creativity juices flowing by appreciating the world around you. Smell the beautiful flowers, take a walk on a sunny day, sink your toes in cool mud, listen to the birds chirping. Realize you're creative! ■ ■ ■ ■ ■

—**Marie Hess, 16**

Think of a time in your life when you did something creative. What did you do? Did you dance or paint or sing or do something else? Carol's memory belongs in the "something else" category:

I was five years old. I had been eyeing the trench at the end of our street for several days, and I yearned for the fun it would allow me. I can't remember why the trench had been dug, possibly for laying pipeline. But I *do* remember my mother's telling me it was off-limits to the likes of me. Maybe because it was too dangerous, maybe because the trench diggers had made it clear that kids were to keep out, maybe because it was black dirt that would leave one filthy. I went out of my short-legged way to walk several feet around the trench each day to avoid temptation.

But then it rained.

A dry trench was enticing enough, but a muddy one was irresistible—not just to me but to some other neighborhood kids. I can't remember if I was the leader or the follower. All I remember is that a half dozen or so of

CREATIVITY

Did you know that "cleanliness is next to godliness" is not in the Bible? ■ ■ ■ ■ ■

us kids were knee-deep in glorious, wondrous mud before I knew it. We slithered, we sloshed, we slid. We danced our lives in the earth; we painted our world (well, mostly ourselves) in rich, dark silt. We probably proved the value of whatever reason the rule-makers had in forbidding this activity. Our fun was dangerous; it undoubtedly wrecked the intended shape of the trench; we all looked like creatures from the Black Lagoon by the time we were finished. Yet we were living in the moment, and the fact that this was forbidden activity was lost to that moment. Or maybe the forbiddenness added to the sweetness of it. If you could have seen our cheeks beneath the mud—which of course you couldn't—you would have seen the rosiness of earthy joy.

Then it grew dark. It was time to go home, and suddenly I was jolted back into a world outside the magic of the trench. Here I was, hair hanging in mud-caked *dread*locks (pun intended!), white shirt unrecognizable. The many layers of mud on my sneakers gave them the appearance of hobnailed boots—the creature from the Black Lagoon with Frankenstein's cobbler. Every rebel has to pay the piper, and my time had come. I panicked. How could I face my mother? "I can't go home," I told my friend.

"I'll walk you," she answered.

We got to the end of my sidewalk, and I lost heart. I stood and sobbed.

"Come on." My friend pulled my arm, causing clods of dirt to drop to the ground. The brave rebel of the hour before was literally falling apart. Every step closer left a muddy piece of me on the sidewalk. I bawled louder and louder. My friend went to the door and got my mother.

My mother came running toward the sound of her sobbing child, wondering what horrendous injury would produce such melodrama. Then she saw, then she knew, then she was relieved rather than angry. A dirty rebel was easier to face than a hit-and-run victim. She plucked me up, made me remove my clothes, and plopped me into the bubbliest bath—and I got just about clean again, not counting the residue silt in my hair, which left traces on my pillowcase each morning and took several washings to finally remove.

Up from the bed of the river God scooped

OK, we know what you're thinking: *Cute story, but what's that got to do with creativity?* When you think of creativity, you probably don't think of little girls in dirty ditches. You probably think of colorful paintings or heartfelt poetry. To be sure, paintings and poetry are fine types of creative expression. But we want to pay some attention to ordinary creativity too, the kind of creativity possible for everyone, whether or not they think they are "creative."

The little girl dancing in the muddy ditch is a metaphor. Creativity is getting dirty with gusto, plunging into the depths of life and this world with all our human imagination and inventiveness. Often friends invite one another into the practice of creativity, as my group of little friends did. Sometimes creativity works against orderliness and leads to pressure against the limits of our lives—limits like a mother's rules about cleanliness. Creativity comes in many forms. But whenever we allow ourselves to get involved creatively with our world, we are taking part in a practice that can help us to wake up and open our senses, minds, and feelings to God, the world, and other people.

God got dirty first

Consider the lilies of the field, how they grow: they neither toil nor spin, yet I tell you, even Solomon in all his glory was not clothed like one of these (Matthew 6:28-29).

Creativity began with God, and it is central to the nature of God. In the beginning, God created . . . and set in motion further creativity. God was extravagant, creating creatures and plants galore—many that seem to have no purpose other than to give delight or amusement. Was it divine fun or what when God created the giraffe? Don't you love a God who didn't stop with lilies but also flung about lilacs and daisies and roses and mums and flowers whose names we don't even know? (What's with us *buying* so much stuff when the really great stuff is already around us and inside us? Speaking of "stuff," have you seen that chapter yet?)

In our tradition, everything begins with God playing in the mud. In the earthy story of Genesis 2, God forms humankind as a potter forms clay, shaping Adam (the Hebrew word *'adam* literally means "earth-creature")

the clay; And by the bank of the river

**epiphany:
a sudden
illuminating
perception**

from the dust of the ground (Hebrew *'adamah*, clay). The biblical story is not about a God who waves a magic wand from behind a protected and uncontaminated heavenly chamber while creation puts on a show outside! God got divinely down and dirty. And if that wasn't enough, God got even dirtier when God became a human being in Jesus of Nazareth, tromping in the rich muckiness of life on earth—at times dancing in the dirt, at times grieving in the grime.

God got dirty first, and God invites us to push up our sleeves as well.

Getting dirty with gusto

We all have a need to be creative and express ourselves, whether or not as a recognized artist such as a painter, musician, poet, or dancer. We believe that God made us with this need and loves the creativity we express, however we do it.

Creativity usually means the ability to discover or produce something that is new: new solutions to problems, new inventions, new works of art. Yet creativity also can refer to the activity of God's Spirit within each of us. When you express what is authentic to God's creative Spirit within you, you bring a unique gift to the world, because no one else can say or do or see the world exactly the way you can.

Marie knows well that creativity is more than being an artist, a musician, a poet, a dancer, a writer. Creativity can be expressed in an act as simple as repainting a bedroom. She writes this account:

As a child I moved around every three or four years. My location always changed, but one thing remained constant: My room was always rather large. It wasn't until I moved to my current house that I faced a problem: My room was just too small. To make matters worse, at the time we moved I was beginning to enter that tomboyish stage, so I painted the walls a near colorless color, bought a very dark comforter to match my very dark rug, and soon wondered why my room just didn't have that cheery, homey

He kneeled him down; And there the great

Consider the lilies of the field, how they grow; they neither toil nor spin, yet I tell you, even Solomon in all his glory was not clothed like one of these.
—Matthew 6:28-29

God Almighty Who lit the sun

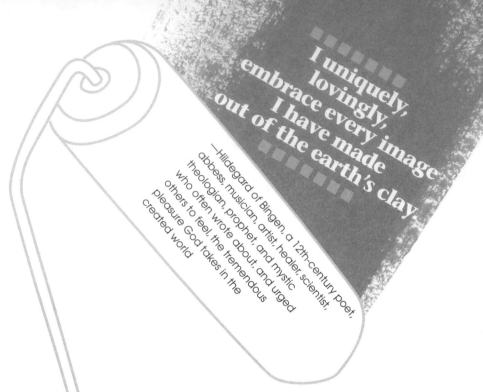

feeling. I complained constantly to my mother that my room was just too small. How could I live happily in such a small room? I was convinced it just wasn't possible; I was doomed to a life of misery!

The summer before my junior year, my dad painted our upstairs bathroom a very pretty blue color to cover the light-seaweed shade that had irked us for years. Every day after that, showering just seemed much more pleasant. The new paint shade made such a difference, not just in the appearance of the room but also in the attitudes of those who used it. When I realized this, I had an epiphany! I finally discovered how I could improve my "nonlivable" room: Give it some color! I informed my mother of my idea, and she loved it.

Days later, we marched into a hardware store and went straight to the paint section—as if we knew what we were doing! After purchasing all the necessary items (eventually—it took us a couple of trips), we prepared my room. We put drop cloths on the floor (we finally found a use for those hideous flowered sheets my parents got when they were first married), taped the ceiling so we'd paint a straight line, and stole two of my

and fixed it in the sky, Who flung the

CREATIVITY

dad's T-shirts (also old and hideous) to serve as smocks. Then we spackled the holes left by old posters. Finally we were ready.

We rolled and rolled and rolled and rolled paint on the walls until we got so tired and giddy we started painting each other (if you look closely, you can still see the bright yellow spots in my mom's hair). Except for some smudges on the ceiling, which we decided to cover with glow-in-the-dark stars, we did an awesome job. (It's now a joke with us when we make a mistake: "Oops, we need another star!") Within a week, my room was completely redone. We painted the walls bright yellow, bought a set of bed linens with a blue background and yellow stars scattered all over, hung beautiful prints on the walls (Van Gogh's *Starry Night* and one of Monet's lily pond paintings), and bought frames for pictures of my friends and family. My room finally reflected who I really was. It finally felt like home to me.

My creativity didn't come from any special talents. It came as a gift (the epiphany), an invitation to express my true self. Most people wouldn't consider simply painting a room a form of creativity, but most people would be wrong. Everyone can be creative, because God's creative Spirit is within each of us. For me all it took was a bucket of paint and a little heart. What'll it take for you?

Now maybe you are still having trouble considering yourself to be creative, or maybe you are looking for a way to express yourself. There's one good way to get your creativity flowing: Start paying attention to the world around you. Emily Dickinson, a poet who started writing when she was a teenager, once said that Jesus' statement "Consider the lilies of the field" was the only commandment she never broke. That's my kind of commandment!

Warning from Marie: *The "To-Doodle" stuff coming next—my mom's idea— is kind of corny, but I think it's still a good idea.*

stars to the most far corner of the night,

To-Doodle: Before you continue reading, please find an object from nature. It can be a leaf, a branch, a flower, a bug. Use your senses: Look at it, touch it, wonder about it, and write down what you notice. The promptings below are only suggestions. Don't worry if you can't fit your "noticings" into these categories.

1. I see _____

2. I feel _____

3. I smell _____

4. I thank God because _____

5. I wonder about _____

Paying attention to the world around us is the beginning of creativity. Paying attention to the world inside us takes us a step deeper.

Dancing in the trench of deep feelings

As we sat down to revise this chapter, Carol's father, Marie's grandfather, lay in a coma in California, in his last days. He'd had a hard, unhappy life, and it seemed at first that the last thing we could think about at this time was creativity. Who feels creative in the face of death, especially a death following a tragic life? Creativity is life-affirming, and death makes us face the end of it. We wondered, *Can we do this?* Carol tells what happened:

On the morning after I had spent a day and a good part of the night on the phone contacting long-lost relatives, I woke up to a pink sky. And I thought about how much my father loved the created world; how, if he could see the sky at that moment, he'd probably pause and notice it. I started jotting down words that might someday turn into a poem.

Who rounded the earth in the middle of

If you were here
If you were here, Dad
Would you point and say, "Look!"
Like you did when I was little?
Or maybe
I am looking now
Because you told me to look then
The gift you left me

Not great poetry but a creative response to a pain-filled situation. Creativity, in fact, often either emerges from or leads us into painful places. In her book *A Sense of Wonder: On Reading and Writing Books for Children*, Katherine Paterson relates that a friend of hers thought that the two creatures most to be pitied were the spider and the novelist—their lives hang by a thread spun out of their own guts. Good stories, as well as songs and paintings and dances, often come from emotions and wounds.

It is also important to mention that authentic creativity may never receive wide public circulation or approval—or may receive it late. Though we all can walk into a bookstore and find volumes of Emily Dickinson's poetry today, only seven of her poems were published in her lifetime. In recent years, one of Vincent van Gogh's paintings (not any of his versions of *Starry Night*, which In Our Humble Opinions are some of *the* greatest paintings) sold for the largest amount ever offered for a painting up to that time, yet Van Gogh sold only one painting during his pain-filled life.

Creativity can also be spun from threads of joy. Marie was inspired by this quote from Plato: "Music gives a soul to the universe, wings to the mind, flight to the imagination, a charm to sadness, gaiety and life to everything." Marie reflects:

Music has been a great influence on my life, especially in the past few years. Throughout my early years, my music tastes mirrored those of my older brother, Nate. He and I used to pretend we were music critics and

his hand; This Great God,

create a "Top 20 Songs" list weekly. It was his introduction that led me to my fascination with music. Listening to music brought "the spark" to my day. My friends' comments, "Marie, do you always have to sing to the music?" and the famous "Who sings this song? Keep it that way," failed to thwart my love for music. Ironically, my love grew stronger. (For more on music, see the "Music" chapter.)

Not only did I love to sing along to music, I began to enjoy creating my own music. Writing songs provided me an opportunity to express my true self. Recently I wrote music and lyrics to my first complete song and recorded it for my boyfriend on the occasion of our six-month anniversary. The guitar beat was slightly off at times; my voice failed to hit every note right on; and the lyrics occasionally were mumbled, so the recording was far from perfect. But knowing that I was possibly offering a soul to the universe or wings to a mind or even a charm to cure someone's sadness left me with an amazing feeling.

To-Doodle: Think about something in your life that draws on deep (sad or happy) feelings. In the "trench" on the next page: (1) Doodle, sketch, or draw whatever those feelings suggest, or (2) Write down a few words that you associate with those feelings, and, if you wish, turn those words into a rough poem or story.

Complaint from Marie: Cornball rating is getting pretty high, Mom. I can't keep defending your "to-doodle" activities! Oops, maybe you need a star to cover this one.

The gifts of creativity can become a burden as well. Because art is spun out of our own gut, because (returning to the opening metaphor) creativity is getting dirty in the rich but gritty trenches of life, creativity and its results may take people where they would rather not go.

My youngest son, Paul (Marie's brother), had an assignment to write an essay on a real event in his life. My husband, at Paul's request, had taken him and our older son to Woodstock '99, and Paul chose to write about his experience there. His essay was displayed on parents' night. My husband

Like a mammy bending over her baby,

CREATIVITY

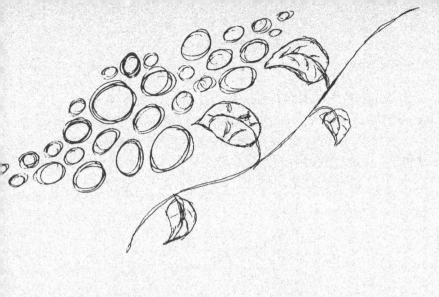

Kneeled down in the dust

This is not a black and white world to be alive I say the colors must swirl and I believe that maybe today we will all get to appreciate the beauty of gray.

—ED KOWALCZYK, "THE BEAUTY OF GRAY" (LIVE)

and I read the essay and we thought it was rather flat compared to Paul's usual style. As a writer myself, I couldn't help but feel disappointed.

My husband and I mentioned to Paul that we had seen his essay, and, God forgive me, I finally blurted out, "I'm surprised you didn't mention more details." He then reported, "Oh, the teacher made me take out the parts about the people with nose rings and tattoos, the pot we smelled everywhere, and the fact that some of the women took their tops off in the mosh pit. Good thing I didn't even mention that Flea played naked." Paul laughed. Then he showed me the copy of the essay he had handed in, which his teacher had highlighted with a yellow marker. What was yellow was allowed to stay in; what was not highlighted had to go. All the sensual details that Paul had carefully attended to stood before me, as naked as Flea, without the required yellow raiment.

In censoring Paul's essay of the sensual details, the details that would have made us see, smell, and hear the actual event of Woodstock, the teacher was trying to avoid offending people.

Have you ever created something that offended others? Have you ever had your creativity "plunked in a bubble bath," so to speak? That is, have you been asked to change something to avoid offending others? Have you ever found—perhaps like Paul's avoiding any mention of Flea's lack of attire—that you *yourself* have censored what you noticed in order to avoid offending someone? Do you ever see artwork or hear music that you find offensive?

Interestingly, similar controversies have arisen over parts of the Bible. For instance, the psalms include some of the most creative and beautiful portions of biblical literature. But take a look at Psalm 137 (on the next page). Read it all the way through.

Toiling over a lump of clay Till he shaped

Psalm 137

By the rivers of Babylon—
    there we sat down and there we wept
    when we remembered Zion.
On the willows there
    we hung up our harps.
For there our captors
    asked us for songs,
and our tormentors asked for mirth, saying,
    "Sing us one of the songs of Zion!"

How could we sing the LORD's song
    in a foreign land?
If I forget you, O Jerusalem,
    let my right hand wither!
Let my tongue cling to the roof of my mouth,
    if I do not remember you,
if I do not set Jerusalem
    above my highest joy.

Remember, O LORD, against the Edomites
    the day of Jerusalem's fall,
how they said, "Tear it down! Tear it down!
    Down to its foundations!"
O daughter Babylon, you devastator!
    Happy shall they be who pay you back
    what you have done to us!
Happy shall they be who take your little ones
    and dash them against the rock!

it in his own image; Then into it

Did you read all the way down? Starts off beautifully, and then— *WHOA!* we get chin-deep in a muddy trench of feelings! Would you read this in worship? the whole thing? part of it? Would you read it to little kids? If you were asked to preach a Youth Sunday sermon on this psalm, what would you ask yourself about the last two lines as you prepared your sermon?

On the one hand, this Bible passage describes in heartfelt terms a people's feelings about horrible mistreatment. We can all appreciate the beautiful lament of the opening. We know what it's like to lose something and to sit down and weep as we remember what we once had. We probably know what it's like to be forbidden to sing songs that remind us of past times. But then the psalm goes deep, deep into the emotions generated by facing the evil and pain of injustice. Those deep feelings are raw, violent; they tromp dangerously close to evil themselves.

While we can value the poem's honesty and even identify with the desire for revenge, we probably would not want to condone or promote those feelings and the actions connected with them. Yet the pious people of faith who gathered these psalms for the people of God did not "yellow highlight" the acceptable stuff; they included the dirty, offensive stuff. Perhaps if we find a creative outlet for our deep and muddy feelings, we will channel the anger and hurt and violence rather than fuel it.

How we use deeply honest artwork can become an important issue for communities of faith. For instance, Psalm 137 is helpful in illustrating how it feels to be mistreated, and it may even be useful as a guide to naming and expressing our own ugly feelings. This psalm is not helpful in suggesting how to act in response to those ugly feelings. And so we, as people of faith, are left with both a gift and a burden, calling us to wisdom.

Do you have any ugly feelings like the ones expressed at the end of Psalm 137? How might you express them in an artistic form? How does such expression help channel the pain?

Trench-tromping with others

When the authors of this book were together in North Carolina, Frank Rogers (cowriter of the "Creation" chapter) led a nature walk. He asked

he blew the breath of life, And man

■ ■ ■ ■ This is salvation: When we marvel at the beauty of created things and praise the beautiful providence of their Creator. ■ ■ ■ ■ ■ ■ ■

—MEISTER ECKHART, a spiritual teacher and writer who lived about 700 years ago

us to remember a time when we felt close to creation, and he then instructed us to pick up something from the earth that reminded us of the connection we had felt. I (Carol) immediately thought of the story that begins this chapter, and I strode over to the mountain creek and scooped up a handful of mud. We told our stories to one another, and I rolled and squeezed the mud pie in my hand while listening. Then Frank said it was time to pray, and he asked us to hold hands. I turned to Emily Wells (who was standing on the side of my mud-filled hand) and told her she did not have to touch my very dirty hand! With a smile and a shrug, Emily boldly grabbed and held on to my muddy palm as we all prayed together.

Emily's gesture is symbolic of many things: accepting persons in their messiness, being willing to share in another person's connection to the world, not breaking the chain of community because one gets a little dirty in the process. Surely there are limits to all these gracious practices, but Emily didn't set hers too tight. In fact, I felt I had come full circle in retelling my muddy trench story, with a blessed twist: I got to play with mud, and nobody made me clean up right away! (Thanks, Emily!)

To-Doodle:
Censure from Marie: *Mom, I know where you wanna go with this one, but puh-leez! DON'T EVEN THINK ABOUT asking us to make mud pies together!*

—or not to To-Doodle . . .
OK. Anyway . . . creativity is connected with expressing our uniqueness, including our particular feelings and perspectives. Creativity also implies

CREATIVITY

became a living soul. Amen. Amen. ■
—FROM "THE CREATION" BY JAMES WELDON JOHNSON

openness to the uniqueness of others and willingness to see how their particular gifts might contribute to a community. Sometimes creativity calls for getting muddy together . . . [or not]. Always, it is cocreating with God, who got dirty first and who tromps in trenches with us still.

Painting our world—"Oops, we need another star"

We started with our feet deep in the earth's mud, but we want to end with our eyes glimpsing stars in the heavens. Remember our experience painting the room? Whenever we (actually it was mostly me, Carol) smudged the ceiling, we covered the spots with stars. We thought that was a good image for life sometimes. Creativity, in fact, is a practice in hope. When things go wrong, if we can make something from it or if we can imagine a day when God will make things better, then we have hope that sorrow is not the last word. Now neither of us is a Pollyanna (sickeningly optimistic)—far from it! We know that sometimes life is just plain horrible (like when your father dies). And yet, we believe in a God who both dances in mud and paints the night with stars. God can sometimes make sparkle what seem like smudges. ■

NANCY PINEDA-MADRID
WITH ANGELA FERNÁNDEZ

⦀Work

What is the first thing that comes to mind when you hear the word *job*? Are you consumed with negative thoughts? Many teenagers find their jobs to be tiring and boring. It's easy to get in a rut, to feel negative internal and external forces. It is important not to settle for a job but to search for our work. Our work will have the characteristics that bring us happiness and fulfillment. ■ ■ ■ ■ ■ ■ ■ ■ ■ ■ ■ ■ ■

—**Angela Fernández, 15**

The class bell at Saint John's had rung, but the students were still talking. Cathy and Paloma were catching up on Rachel's most recent crush when Sister Mary Margaret cleared her throat and began.

On the blackboard Sister Mary Margaret wrote a word the girls didn't know: *VOCARE.* "Quiet down," she said. "Can any of you tell me what this word means?"

"I thought this was math class," Cathy whispered to Paloma. "We're supposed to get equations, not words. . . ."

She hushed as the teacher turned to face the class. "Anyone?" Silence. The teacher continued: "*VOCARE* is the Latin root for the word *vocation.*" Now the girls understood: This was going to be a pitch about becoming a nun.

"Many of you might think that I am going to talk about religious life," the teacher said, smiling knowingly in their direction. "And religious life is indeed one way of thinking about vocation. *Vocation* means *calling,* which implies that someone is calling. For Christians, the Caller is God. All of us are *called* by God to love God and to love our neighbors as ourselves; some of us do it by making promises like the ones I and the women in my community have made; others do it within other kinds of relationships. But that's not my point today. The word *vocation* also refers to *work.* Did you ever wonder if God might be calling you to do a certain kind of work?

WORK

"When I was a sophomore in high school, I discovered how much I enjoyed math, especially algebra. Math taught me how to think, how to concentrate, and how to stay focused. I could get lost in a wonderful sort of way when I was trying to work out an algebra problem. Perhaps algebra is not your thing. But I like to tell my sophomores this story every year anyway, because my own experience tells me that now is a good time to notice what you love to do, whatever it is. Listen for God's call in your life. What is your *vocation*? What is your true work?"

■ ■ ■ ■ ■ ■ ■ ■ ■
Some people live in order to work. Other people work in order to live. Think of examples of each type among people you know. What is the difference between these approaches? Which appeals more to you?

Sister Mary Margaret swept the class with her eyes, then looked down to her desk and picked up a paper. "Time to turn to your home*work*," she declared.

The teacher's brief statement left Cathy with more questions than answers. She wondered why some of the courses in her high school were known as "vocational" courses. Those courses offered skills to prepare students for full-time work right after high school. But the teacher had suggested that you could also be "vocational" if you were heading to college. Cathy also wondered about the many kinds of work her father had done, including being a salesman, a computer installer, a store manager, and a stay-at-home dad. Could God call one person in all these different directions? Then there was that sly remark about "home*work.*" How was that related to the other work Cathy would do in her life? The biggest questions, though, were two that would linger with her for many years: What is *my* work? Is God calling me in a special way?

What do you want to be when you grow up?

Ask a five-year-old this question, and you are likely to get a pretty interesting answer: "A cowboy." "A princess." "A movie star."

Ask a teenager, and the stakes are higher, the answers less immediate, even though adulthood is much closer. "I'm not sure yet," she may mumble politely, while inside she is thinking, *Look, I'm only 15. My friends and I are not into that. We are thinking about our classes, going to the mall, and deciding what movie we will see this weekend.*

Right now, questions of future work can seem far away; you'll have time to think about them later. But high school is a great time to begin imagining different possibilities, a great time to begin thinking about what is important to you in your future work. During this time you are actually getting some experience at work. Studying is work. Raking leaves and washing dishes are work, even when you do these things as unpaid chores in your own family. And many teenagers work for pay as well.

Work is a practice that begins now. Work is about more than money, more than a job, and more than a career. Work is about all the different ways in which we take our God-given gifts and talents and our different life experiences and use them to make a contribution in the world.

The problem is, not every *job* feels like *work*.

You have had a lot of opportunities to observe how adults—your parents, your teachers, and others—relate to their work. You probably know some adults who find their work satisfying. Overall they feel a sense of accomplishment and the pleasure of making a difference in the lives of others. They are tired at the end of the day, but they also feel energized.

Other adults come home tired but not at all energized. These people hate going to work; their energy is drained by the tasks they have to do and the conditions in which they work. You do not get the sense that they are excited about what they do. Their job provides an income, but it does not feed their souls.

Some people would say it would be nice not to have to work—just to lie around and let someone else fetch us whatever our heart desires. This scenario isn't going to happen, of course. For almost everyone, work provides a *way to live* at the most basic level: Working earns food and shelter and other necessities. Most people *have* to work, for pay or in the home or on the land, if they and their family are to survive.

We do not work only to survive, however. Many people who have good work *don't* wish they could lie around all day. (Some days, yes, but not every day!) Work can offer great satisfaction as we use our energy toward worthwhile contributions.

Work is good—but not all day every day. God intends for people to have rest each day and a Sabbath each week. Check out the "Time" chapter. ■ ■ ■ ■ ■ ■ ■ ■ ■ ■ ■ ■

WORK

My father said, "Try many things. When you find what you love, do that. *Then* figure out how to make a living with it." What wisdom! . . . When people ask me, "Where do you work?" I answer, "Everywhere." They say, "I mean, what is your job?" I say, "I have no job—my work is my life—teaching, healing, loving, decorating, playing, struggling, helping.". . . The Native way is more freeing, more celebratory. You get all the "work" done—meeting the needs of housing, feeding, clothing, transporting, etc. But you do it in harmony, in union with all Creation and the life cycles. —JOSÉ HOBDAY, OSF, SENECA-IROQUOIS

The very first story in the Bible describes the creation of the universe as "the work that God did." And throughout the story of God's care for our world, we hear God's activity described as "work" again and again. God feeds the animals (Psalm 104) and gathers people together like a flock of chickens (2 Esdras 1:30; Luke 13:34). God is a potter who makes human beings, a physician who heals, a judge who pronounces sentences, a mother who nurses a child. We human beings do jobs like these: raising livestock, manufacturing useful objects, and providing assistance through health care, legal advice, or child care. When we do that work, we are taking part in a process of creativity and care that started with God and that is still in God's keeping.

Work is an important part of a way to live in relation to the loving, challenging life of God. Good work feeds us spiritually as well as physically, while at the same time making the world a little more just, a little more peaceful, and a little more hospitable for others. But sometimes you look for work and you only get a job.

Finding a passion for work

The writer and minister Frederick Buechner once said that a person's vocation can be found in the place where his or her deep gladness meets the world's deep hunger. This is the place where we may find the work God is calling us to do—the work that will both satisfy us and benefit others. Finding this place is not always easy, however. You need to pay attention to yourself. Where is *your* deep gladness? You also need to pay attention to what is outside of yourself by coming face-to-face with the world's deep

WORK

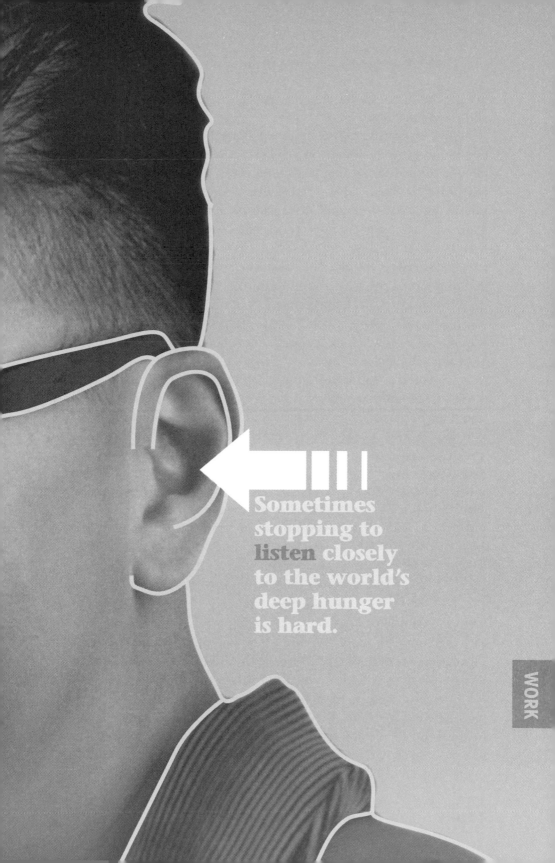

Sometimes stopping to listen closely to the world's deep hunger is hard.

hunger—for food, for healing, for beauty, for understanding, for shelter, and for so much else.

Achieving this kind of attention is difficult when you are surrounded by voices telling you what you *should* want to do. Too often these voices tell you to focus on money and status, even if it means neglecting the wisdom of Buechner's advice. One of these voices might even be your own. I nearly lost sight of my own deep gladness during a search for new work a few years ago. I was trying to decide among several possibilities when a friend gave me some important advice. "As you make your decision about which job to take," she said, "it's natural to think about what you'd be good at. But it is even more important to think about what you really long to do." That advice made a huge difference in my thinking. Because I got in touch with my "deep gladness," I was able to risk taking the work I really wanted, not simply the job I already knew how to do. That work proved to be the right choice for me.

Not long ago I asked Raynie, a sophomore at a San Francisco high school, if she knew anyone who had a clear and intense sense of having found the right work. She told me about her dad. Ten years ago he had a job as a lawyer in a big downtown firm. The firm offered to make him a partner, which got him thinking about what he really wanted to do with his life. He decided to leave the firm, and now he directs an organization that develops the leadership skills of middle- and lower-income folks so they can fight for what they need.

■ ■ ■ ■ ■ ■ ■ ■ ■ ■
Trying to figure out what your work should be? The "Choices" chapter offers suggestions about how to make important decisions like this.

Raynie says she has learned a lot from her father about the meaning of work. "My dad works hard; he comes home tired most nights. But it's pretty amazing when I go to meetings with him. The people talk about how to create more affordable housing, how to provide health care for low-income folks, how to improve schools. They have made a big difference in terms of the quality of life in the city. And besides, my dad loves his work."

Sometimes stopping to listen closely to the world's deep hunger is hard. Raynie's dad was moved by the cries of community groups in his city for better neighborhood services. When he stopped to think about what he wanted to do with his life, he realized that these groups had been speaking to him about one piece of the world's deep hunger for justice. What need crics out to you? The cry may not come from "the world" as a whole but from one person who asks you to use your gifts in a way you may not have thought about yet. Do your friends often ask you to explain math problems? Are you someone to whom they turn for advice about relationships? Do little kids especially like being with you? These questions express *hungers* these people are asking you to fill; do you find *deep gladness* when you respond to one of them? If you are one who especially notices pollution and wants to do something about that, the earth itself may be crying out to you as if hungry for your care.

Often others help us get in touch with the place where our deep gladness and the world's deep hunger meet. They can help us see more in ourselves than we are able to see on our own. Other people can help us see the depth of our passions and also how we are called to respond to the world's urgent needs.

The Gospel of Mark tells about a foreigner, a Syrophoenician woman, who helped Jesus to understand his mission more fully. In the midst of his ministry in Galilee, Jesus decided to rest for a while—a difficult thing to do because many people wanted to hear his teaching and experience his healing. One woman, a Greek born in Syrophoenicia, sought him out and begged him to heal her daughter, who was very ill. Jesus answered, "Let the children be fed first, for it is not fair to take the children's food and throw it to the dogs." He declined to help her because his ministry, as he then understood it, was to the Jews alone. But this tenacious woman would not take no for an answer. "Sir, even the dogs under the table eat the children's crumbs." Because this foreigner had a need to see her daughter cured, she challenged Jesus' understanding of his ministry. He listened to her, recognized the truth in her claim, and changed his answer. "For saying that, you may go," he told her. "The demon has left your daughter." The Syrophoenician woman returned to find her daughter healed. And Jesus

■ ■ ■ ■ ■ ■ ■ ■ ■ ■ ■

Too many times teenagers are focused on money. They think, *I want to be rich when I grow up.* They base their choice of a career on how much money they will make and not what it is they desire to do. After reading Raynie's story, I realized that we need to really search for what it is we long to do. It may take some time until we find the right thing for ourselves.

—ANGELA FERNÁNDEZ, 15

WORK

left this encounter seeing his own life's work stretched beyond the boundaries of the Jewish people (Mark 7:24-30).

As we seek to hear where the world's deep hunger is crying out to us and how it might affect the work we do, we need to be open, as Jesus was, to the voices of people in need.

The difference between "work" and "job"

Unfortunately not every job is one that engages the deep gladness of the person who holds it. Many jobs are menial and tedious, and these become oppressive when good pay and safe conditions are absent. The need to make a living forces some people into these jobs all over the world, both close to home and in the distant places where many popular brands of shoes and clothes are made. A vivid example of this kind of job is provided by Omar Gil, a young Mexican:

I come from Mexico City. My father had a business there, a small bookstore, until I was 11 years old. Then, because of the devaluation of the peso, his store went broke. My parents looked for work in Mexico City, but they couldn't find any, so they decided to come here to the border, to Nuevo Laredo. We came here looking for a way to subsist.

So I went to school on the border. When I finished preparatory school, my plan was to go back to Mexico City to the university to study physics and mathematics or law. But I couldn't continue my studies because we didn't have the money. I had to go to work.

But working in the maquiladoras [factories built in Mexico by U.S. corporations], it's not really possible to go to school, mainly because of time. Also, the pay is low, and my job is very insecure. Despite all this, I haven't lost hope yet that I'll be able to go back. It's just that I'm not 100 percent sure anymore. Now there are other factors as well. I don't have any time to rest, and I'm getting physically exhausted. It's very hard.

I've been in these factories since I was 19 years old, and now I'm 26. I've gotten more and more worried, because I don't have time for any kind of personal life. I leave work so tired that on weekends I don't even want to leave the house to go anywhere. I just want to rest. All my personal development has been put on hold so that I can just rest, so I'll be able to work. I feel like my youth has passed me by.

PUBLIC SERVICE ELECTRIC AND G

Omar has a job, but this job is not good work. It does not engage his gifts or his gladness. Even worse, this workplace violates many standards of justice. (See the "Justice" chapter to learn about some teens in the U.S. who are organizing protests to help Omar and others employed in the *maquiladoras*.)

An example from north of the border shows the distinction between work and a job in a different way. Although many people around the world take jobs because they have to, some U.S. teens get jobs for other reasons. My friend Patricia recently had a conversation with a bagger in our local grocery story that made me wonder about the role of jobs in American teenage life. Josh, a 16-year-old from our neighborhood, was helping Patricia load groceries into her car when he noticed her bumper sticker: *My child is an honor student*. He sighed. "I wish I could be an honor student," he told

A Prayer

Gracious and Loving God, I give you thanks this day for the gift of my present work.

I hold in prayer those who are jobless and those who have yet to discover their work.

I hold in prayer the young people throughout the world and in my own community who must have a job to help their families and who, therefore, cannot continue their studies.

Have mercy on me for the times I have failed to love.
I praise you for giving me the opportunity to share in the work of re-creating this world.

My prayer is that my work makes the world
a little more just,
a little more peaceful, and
a little more hospitable for everyone. Amen.

WORK

her. "How many hours a week do you have to be at the store?" asked Patricia. He told her that he was putting in about 20 hours a week so he could buy a car. "Riding a school bus and borrowing a car from Mom or Dad are getting old real fast. But it's hard to keep up with school and have time for friends and keep this job going. I get tired. Besides, this isn't the most exciting work, even though I do like lots of the people I see on the job." As Patricia drove away, Josh stood in the parking lot for a while, wondering whether he was spending too many hours away from the things he really cared about and whether he really *needed* a car after all.

A lot of the jobs available to American teenagers do not provide much personal fulfillment. These service-sector jobs pay very little, offer few benefits, lack prestige, and build toward no future. Large corporations thrive on a steady supply of teens to fill hundreds of thousands of positions like Josh's. They are happy to have this cheap supply of relatively undemanding employees.

Do teens benefit from these jobs as much as their employers do? Often the answer is yes: Some teens have the satisfaction of contributing to the real needs of their families, and some learn self-discipline and grow in responsibility in ways they never quite managed with schoolwork. Others, however, have bad experiences and develop negative attitudes about jobs in general. The money is nice, of course, but it is not always spent wisely enough to justify what earning it costs.

Whether in the case of Omar, whose job is terribly unjust, or in the case of Josh, whose job is merely tiresome, differentiating between the *jobs* these young men hold and the *work* God is calling them to do is important. Perhaps Omar's vocation is to tell the story of oppression in the factories along the U.S. border. Josh may still be seeking his vocation, but he is fortunate that the work he does at school gives him opportunities to continue his vocational search. In both cases, their truest *work* might not be what they get paid for. Instead, their true work will begin when they engage the process of creativity and care that started with God and that is still in God's keeping.

"Work is the way you occupy your mind and hand and eye and whole body when they're informed by your imagination and wit, by your keenest perceptions, by your most profound reflections on everything you've read and seen and heard and been part of," writes the philosopher Alice Koller in her book *The Stations of Solitude*.

WORK

My work is being a student

Writing this book was work for all of us authors, including the teenagers. All of us also have other work. "School is what I do," one of the teens told our writing team. "That is my work at this point in life."

You can learn quite a bit about work from what you do at school. You learn that success requires effort on your part. If you pay attention, you can discover the world's deep hungers in the stories you read in English, the problems you encounter in biology, or the issues you discuss in social studies. Maybe you will have a teacher like Sister Mary Margaret who shares her deep gladness with you and encourages you to discover your own. You also can learn what a difference your attitude makes in everything you do.

Nick, a freshman at a California high school, learned this last lesson early. When he saw the math grade on his first report card, he was furious. At home after dinner, Dad wanted to talk about it, but Nick had nothing to say. Inside he was fuming: *How can this be? Murphy must have messed up on his math when he figured the grades. I turned in all my homework on time; almost all my grades were As or Bs. How could he give me a C–?*

The next morning at school, Nick told Mr. Murphy that he didn't understand his grade. It seemed like forever before the teacher found his grade sheet. "You're right about your homework," he told Nick. "But your quarter grade was a C– because your test scores were very low. I assign final grades based on what you know, not on how much work you do."

"But that's not fair," Nick protested. "I put a lot of time into this class."

"Yes, you did. But I am not going to change the grade." The bell rang. "If you'd like, we can talk more about this later. I need to get ready for my next class."

Nick raced out of the room and immediately bumped into Phil. "Hey, would you believe that Murphy gave me a C– for my final grade? I just don't get it. Last year homework counted for something."

"Welcome to high school. Same thing happened to me. I finally figured out that for him and a lot of other teachers around here, what is important is that you really understand the stuff. It's like—are you just doing it for the grade or do you want to learn something? After I figured out what was important to me, my grades started going up."

Like Nick, you may have noticed that in high school, teachers' expectations change. Good grades don't come just because you put in the time;

you also have to take responsibility for really learning the material. To succeed in high school you need to develop the ability to judge how much you know and what you need to study. Instead of studying primarily to make respectable grades, you begin to notice and study more seriously the ideas within each subject area that you are genuinely curious about. School work is tremendously important in shaping what your future work will be. But—surprise!—that distant outcome depends on your ability to focus on what you are doing *now*.

Your own curiosity can become a powerful energy source for this work. All subjects won't interest you equally, but certain ones will capture your attention. Get into it! The more responsibility you take for your own learning, the more you will enjoy schoolwork. Jumping through someone else's hoops gets old and boring pretty fast.

This is not just about work!

Work that touches our deep gladness and feeds the deep hungers of the world can be a blessing for us and for others. Each of us has unique gifts and a unique perspective on the world's hungers, and everyone in a community benefits when one person

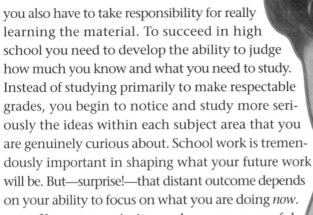

finds his or her true work. Having a good job is infinitely better than having a job that is unrewarding, financially or in other ways. Identifying your true work is even better, whether or not you can get a job doing that work. But figuring how your work fits within a way to live is even more important.

You are coming to the age of paid employment at a time when the world of jobs is in turmoil. Most American adults are working long hours, many at more than one job. Job stress prevents many from ever noticing what their true work is. To make the work situation even more confusing, experts predict that almost everyone will be employed in several kinds of jobs during the course of their lives. If it were ever possible to define oneself by a job—as in, "I'm an accountant; what are you?"—that time is passing. Today's circumstances are driving us back to our true identity. When

■ ■ ■ ■ ■ ■ ■
You may or may not be paid to do your work.

—ALICE KOLLER
in *The Stations of Solitude*

asked who I am, I now realize that even more than identifying myself as a teacher, I identify myself as a child of God. Even more than being a student, you are a child of God.

The deepest truth about each of us is ultimately a God-truth. God took delight in our unique creation at birth, and God longs to take delight in the ongoing creation of our lives. This is about more than our jobs, and even about more than our work. We are made by and for God. We discover the blessing of our work, the blessing of the place where our "deep gladness" and the "world's deep hunger" meet, when we stay in touch with this God-truth.

Work is one aspect of a full human life, but it is not a whole life. We need to think about work, not in isolation but as part of a whole way to live. Within this larger frame of reference, our work needs to meet our basic needs and contribute to our own well-being and that of other people. Yet work is not everything. For most of us, our work will not be written on our tombstone or remembered by friends after we are gone. But work is important. Work is a way of offering our gifts to others and to God. ■

WORK

DON RICHTER
WITH JACK DEPAOLO

‖Play

Sports can be playful. But free, unstructured play is even more important than sports. Playing frees our minds and bodies and helps us deal with the demands and restrictions of everyday living. Playing helps us see and do things in new ways. Besides that, it's fun to play!

■■■■■■■■■■■■■■■ —Jack DePaolo, 16

See Jack play

"Hey Jack, think fast!" I turned around just in time to see a tennis ball fly past my head, barely brushing a tuft of hair. "Missed, Mike," I sarcastically proclaimed. "You just got lucky," Mike replied.

I ran across the backyard to get the tennis ball. As I was running, I began having flashbacks about all the ways I've used tennis balls in my life. You see, in my family tennis is BIG: My mom played in college, and both my parents enjoy playing now. So tennis balls have been as much a constant in my life as TV and Cheerios. Some of my earliest childhood memories are of rolling fuzzy yellow balls back and forth with Mom and Dad. And over the years I've discovered just how versatile this small round object can be.

■■■■■ **In the beginning, God created the tennis ball. . . .** That's how I figured it anyway.

When I was five or six and learning how to swing a bat, Dad pitched tennis balls instead of hard balls. Good thing too, because I thought it was great fun to blast balls right back at him! Tennis balls are a lot less painful than baseballs when you get hit by one.

Now at the ripe old age of 16, I still play games with tennis balls. Thousands of forehands and backhands; hundreds of serves, overheads,

PLAY

and volleys—tennis is the game that feeds my soul! I gotta admit that there are times when playing a competitive sport feels more like *work* than *play*. But on balance, I love being outdoors on a cool sunny day, bouncing around on a well-groomed clay court, smacking a fuzzy yellow ball with plenty of topspin—*Pow*—watching it sail over the net in a split second and land a foot from the baseline—*Pow*—anticipating where the ball will land as it rebounds back toward me—*Pow*. The back-and-forth rhythm is like rolling the ball back and forth with my parents as a toddler. It's like having a conversation with a close friend—lots of back-and-forth banter with plenty of good-natured ribbing.

"Hey, Jack, he's rounding third and heading for home!" Speaking of friends, Mike was now crouched in catcher's position, waiting for the throw from center field. In a single motion, I grabbed the tennis ball off the ground and sidearmed it to him. Mike made the tag at home and yelped, "He's outta there!" Replaying our Little League days, we tossed the ball back and forth until Mike missed a catch. Abe—my chocolate-brown Lab, not my little brother—retrieved the ball in his slobbery mouth. Now we played a game of keep-away with the dog. Mike and I kept dropping the slimy ball, though, because we didn't want to touch it.

The ball got more slobbery each time Abe intercepted it. Finally we gave up on throwing and began kicking the gooey glob like a soccer ball. Apparently my dog is not a soccer fan. After a few kicks, Abe decided the game was over. He grabbed the ball in his foamy mouth, galloped around the corner of the house, and stashed his new toy in his favorite hole. Oh well, playing with that old tennis ball was a fun way to pass 10 minutes of a long summer afternoon.

Lots of ways to play

Don: How many different ways did Jack seriously mention playing with the tennis ball? I count at least seven. Amazing how many games you

■■■■■
Try this: Invent
a simple game for two
to four players that uses
only a tennis ball. Play your
game and ask spectators to
guess the rules by observing.
Reflect: Was your game competitive (winners and losers)
or cooperative (playing
together to reach a
common goal)? Was
it fun?

PLAY

can play with a simple tennis ball. There must be a little voice inside each of us urging "Play ball!" Something deep down that wants us to play and have fun instead of going through life all gloomy and glum.

Each time the authors of this book met to work on our chapters, we also found ways to play together. After a full day of intense conversations, for instance, we'd divide into teams to play Capture the Flag.

Jack: Now without naming names, I feel compelled to point out that one team always "won" because *a certain team captain* would drag opponents out of the neutral zone so they could be tagged and sent to jail.

Mark Yaconelli: That wasn't cheating. It was creative rule bending.

Jack: Hey, this is *our* chapter. Stay in your own!

Don: As I was about to say, playing is a great way to build relationships while having fun. Fun making is vital to a life well-lived. But play is about more than any game with a beginning and an ending. *Playfulness is a way of being in the world. Playing provides enjoyment, promises freedom, and promotes truth.* Even work can be approached with a playful spirit. On the other hand, a sport can lose its playfulness and feel like a job. We want to encourage a playful attitude toward whatever you happen to be doing at the moment.

Turning things upside down

Don: Consider the attitude of the *court jester*. In days of yore, a jester would not only entertain an audience but also get them laughing at—and thinking about—their own stuck-upness. A skillful jester could make folks see the world with fresh eyes by puncturing their prejudices and pomposity, showing them how foolish their own behavior could be. Jesters had to be quick on their feet, though, because this playful truth telling could be risky!

I sometimes imagine Jesus as a jester—a quick-witted, playful guy with a big smile on his face and a twinkle in his eye. You can see his jester skills when he tells parables that prod people to reframe their lives. Having a little problem figuring out who your neighbor is? "Well now," Jesus muses, "suppose you're lying facedown in a ditch after being beaten and robbed, and the very person who stops by to help you is the kind of person you most fear and despise. Could you possibly bring yourself to consider *this* person your neighbor? Or would you rather just lie there in the dirt and die?" (You can almost see self-righteousness squirming in its seat.)

■ ■ ■ ■ The word *liturgy* means both worship and work. Yet worship can be playful too, as our writing team experienced by celebrating our time together with a piñata. The piñata dates back to the early 16th century when Pedro de Gante, a Flemish Franciscan monk, established a village school for Indian children in "New Spain" (Mexico). Gante discovered that the best way to convey the gospel message to children was through their own language, customs, and local games, such as the piñata. The piñata, according to Gante, is gargoyle-shaped to symbolize the forces of evil in the world. When we try to defeat evil by ourselves, we often feel like we're swinging blindly at a moving target—hence the blindfolded player swinging at the piñata dangling from a rope. But by working/playing together, we eventually strike enough blows to break evil open, scattering blessings (candy) upon the whole community. Gante trusted that this simple children's game could become holy play and teach important lessons about the life of Christian faith. ■ ■ ■ ■ ■ ■ ■ ■ ■ ■ ■

Or what if a Roman soldier marches by and officiously orders you to carry his backpack for a mile? (This happened all the time in countries the Roman Empire occupied.) You could always boil with anger or seethe with resentment, but instead Jesus suggests a playful third way. Carry the pack without complaint for one mile, as requested. But when the soldier reaches out for his pack at the next mile marker, continue walking and say, with a friendly smile, "Hey, I'm just getting warmed up. I'll be glad to carry this thing another mile for you. This is fun!"

Now the soldier is off-balance, because by law he can force you to carry his pack for only *one mile*. If he lets you carry the pack an extra mile, he'll get in trouble with his superiors. And if he tries to explain that you *offered* to carry it, they'll laugh in his face and throw him in the brig. So this mighty soldier is reduced to pleading with you to give him back his pack. *Puh-leeez.*

Do you see what Jesus is up to here? This is radical play. The kind of play that upsets the powerful and self-important and delights those who

PLAY

are weighed down and oppressed. The authorities—who have lost all sense of playfulness in their own lives—do not like this unconventional activity one bit. They huddle together and vow to put an end to Jesus and his jester ways.

Even Jesus' own friends lose their sense of play from time to time. One day Jesus hears his disciples arguing among themselves about who will be first in line, sit at the head of the table, and get the biggest reward in heaven. So what does Jesus do? He puts a child on his lap and tells these "grown-ups" that unless they change their ways and become like children, they will never enter the kingdom of heaven (see Matthew 18:1-5; Mark 9:34; Luke 9:46). Then Jesus probably plays a few rounds of scissors, paper, rock—the first-century version anyway—with the proud youngster.

Jack: Those disciples sure sound like slow learners. Because a short while later, when people are bringing children for Jesus to touch and bless, what do you think the disciples do? They try to keep the children away from Jesus. "Time to stop fooling around and get serious!" they scold the parents. Well, once again, Jesus has to remind his followers about whose hearts are in the right place. Jesus says this to them:

> Let the little children come to me; do not stop them; for it is to such as these that the kingdom of God belongs. Truly I tell you, whoever does not receive the kingdom of God as a little child will never enter it (Mark 10:14-15).

Don: Theologians have spent centuries wondering what it was about children that Jesus wanted his disciples to imitate. I think children's ability to play must be near the top of the list. When little kids play, they open themselves to learning important new things about the world—sometimes literally seeing it upside down as they hang by their knees. We all need to keep playing—stretching our bodies, laughing when we feel clumsy, learning new games, finding new playmates. When we play, we open ourselves to new ways of seeing ourselves and who we are becoming.

■■■■■■■■■■■■■■■■■■■■■■■■■■■■■■■■■■

Play is the reset button God gives us to get a fresh take on a situation and to renew our lives.

Pushing your reset button

Jack: My little brother used to throw temper tantrums when he didn't get his way. At home he'd flop around on the floor like a fish out of water. And the tantrums in the car were worse. He hated being strapped in his car seat. He'd start shaking and screaming like a wounded animal. You couldn't reason with him; he was so beside himself he couldn't even tell you *why* he was angry. But after a while he'd start talking to his stuffed Scooby-Doo dog. He'd just forget his frustrations and act as if nothing had happened. Playing with Scooby-Doo was like pushing his reset button.

Don: I'm sure glad computers come with reset buttons. Ever have a computer lock up on you? Perhaps you're running one program too many and suddenly—**WONK**—the screen freezes, the keyboard stalls, and you can't even run the standard shut-down operation with your mouse. What do you do—besides panic that you might lose that important paper you're writing? You push the reset button and hold your breath until your system reboots and gives you options for retrieving your documents.

Jack: I wish I could simply push a reset button when my life gets overloaded and everything gets chaotic.

Don: Well here's the good news: *Play is the reset button God gives us to get a fresh take on a situation and to renew our lives.* Sure, life is more than a game. Yet even when times are difficult and tense, people who know how to play can envision new possibilities. A playful spirit knows how to improvise, how to juggle, how to think outside the box. A playful mind knows how to combine things that don't ordinarily "belong" together, how to wonder about different ways to do something, including ways that might seem silly or improbable at first. Some business consultants actually make their clients play with children's toys so they'll also start playing with ideas for new products.

> ■ ■ ■ ■ ■ ■ ■ ■
> **Learn to juggle. What you learn to do with your hands, you can learn to do with ideas and new concepts too.** ■ ■

No one is born knowing how to play a sport, but most of us have a natural capacity for the kind of *free play* we're advocating. Remember how Jack tossed the ball around with Mike and Abe? No set rules or defined goals. They just made it up as they went along. We need to nurture this kind of child*like* (not child*ish*) play as we grow older.

PLAY

Jack: Ever tried to play a game of Clue with a three-year-old? It's pointless. A three-year-old loves to throw the dice, bend the cards, and scatter the playing pieces all over the board. A three-year-old has no interest in guessing who did it in what room with which weapon. It's fun to play with little kids in their own world, like when you're baby-sitting. When I'm with my little brother, he doesn't have to "learn how to play the game" and he doesn't need lots of expensive toys to have fun because

- we can play drums in the kitchen with the pans and Tupperware,
- we can build a fort out of old bedsheets,
- we can play hide-and-seek with no toys at all.

I can't play board games with my little brother yet, but we have fun making up games as we go along.

Don: Can you recall horsing around with a few friends recently? Making it up as you went along? Perhaps you were just kicking a paper wad to one another or tossing a Frisbee or sliding down a grassy slope in the rain. Maybe you were making up silly lyrics to a song or composing nonsense poetry with those little refrigerator-magnet words. By the way, those magnets remind me of these "text boxes" I'm learning to use in writing this chapter. I'm sure you're already proficient in the art of desktop publishing, but for me this is a new venture. It's been fun playing with different ways to arrange words on the page, but if you're not careful, you discover that all of a sudden, without any warning, you . . . get trapped in a text box without even realizing it. Then you try to figure a way out, and the more you struggle, the worse it gets—until you remember to push the magic button and *voilà!* You're back in business again.

Playing under pressure

Jack: When you're a ninth-grader, sometimes you feel trapped in a box that you didn't design and that you have little control over. You're boxed in by all sorts of expectations. The consequences of not meeting all the expectations different people have for you seem enormous. "Time to stop fooling around and get serious!" Sound familiar? You worry whether you're accomplishing enough every day and living up to your potential.

Don: Well, no matter how old you are, it's still important to spend *some* time just fooling around. Seriously. Little kids learn how to interact

> **Notice the playfulness of nature: gurgling streams, dancing light, humming birds, fluttering leaves, twinkling stars. All creation wants to play with you.**
> ■■■■■■■■■■■■■■■ —MICHAEL JOSEPH in *Play Therapy*

with others and relate to their environment through play. That's why elementary schools have recess—or ought to (though some schools unwisely have replaced recess with more class-time instruction). Big kids need time for play and recreation too.

Look again at this common word *recreation*. Do you see another way to say this word? What happens when you view your play and physical activity as *re-creation*?

- Your body is re-created, renewed, and restored.
- You are re-connected with God's playful creation.

Recreation frees you to see the big picture, whether you're feeling on top of the world or at the bottom of the barrel. As you are re-created by play, you come to know that

- you and all others are endowed with special *gifts* to celebrate;
- you, along with everyone, have certain *limits* you must accept;
- you can *expect the unexpected* and learn to react playfully and non-defensively;
- you can *maintain humor and dignity,* even when others try to grind you down.

Lively play can help you accept yourself as you have been created, with both gifts and limits. It can help you keep your balance when life is unpredictable and even when others are cruel.

Jack: Not all play is this good. Sometimes play can have a vicious side to it. When I was in the eighth grade, a classmate thought it would be funny to make a "What do you think of Jack?" tape. First he tape-recorded questions about me. Then he would ask one of my friends what she thought about the *principal* and tape her response right after the prerecorded question about me. He did this over and over, and then he went around school playing his "interviews" to get some laughs at my expense. Needless to say, when I found out what was happening, I was pretty mad. I told him he'd better stop, but all he said was, "Hey, DePaolo, I was just kiddin'." His "kidding" wasn't the free and fun kind of play we've been discussing in our chapter. That kind of mean-spirited practical joke puts people down.

Don: It takes courage to say "I don't want to play that game," especially when you're saying it to classmates and friends. But we don't need to get our kicks from harmful play that degrades other people or jeopardizes someone's safety—including our own. Pranks that get a laugh at someone else's expense are harmful play. Hazing that subjects teens to humiliating treatment in order to "join the club" is harmful play. These activities may seem funny, but they're certainly not fun for everyone involved. When in doubt, remember that healthy play provides enjoyment, promises freedom, *and* promotes truth—all three.

Can we still "play" sports?

Don: By the time you enter high school, a lot of your playtime is organized into games, contests, and competitive sports. Sports can help us play, but sports can also compromise play if we're not careful.

Jack: As you know by now, I enjoy playing tennis. Sometimes the competition and pressure can be intense though. When I'm not playing well, I get down on myself, and it's hard to keep the game in perspective and have fun. This is a challenge for all athletes—even the great ones.

Don: Keeping the fun in sports can be a real challenge, especially if your coaches don't have a playful spirit like Dean Smith. Not only the coaches but also teammates, fans, and the local media are invested in winning. Pressure from all these people is a lot to manage. So if you play a sport, here are a few points to bear in mind.

1. The need for coaching

Don: To play a sport, you *may* need to have some athletic talent, but you must develop some specific skills. Have you heard people say, "he's a natural-born swimmer" or "she's a natural-born soccer player"? Don't believe it! A person may have natural physical abilities like size and agility, but without learning the skills and rules of a sport, even a six-foot-six guy would be a lousy high school basketball player. Jack is a top-notch tennis player because he puts in a lot of time staying in condition, getting coached, and improving his skills. Even bred-to-be-tennis-professionals like Venus

PLAY

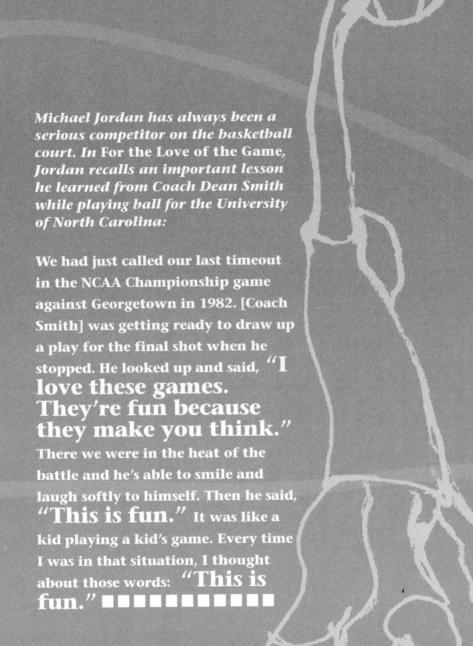

Michael Jordan has always been a serious competitor on the basketball court. In For the Love of the Game, *Jordan recalls an important lesson he learned from Coach Dean Smith while playing ball for the University of North Carolina:*

We had just called our last timeout in the NCAA Championship game against Georgetown in 1982. [Coach Smith] was getting ready to draw up a play for the final shot when he stopped. He looked up and said, "I love these games. They're fun because they make you think." There we were in the heat of the battle and he's able to smile and laugh softly to himself. Then he said, "This is fun." It was like a kid playing a kid's game. Every time I was in that situation, I thought about those words: "This is fun." ■■■■■■■■■■

PLAY

and Serena Williams, who have lots of natural ability, need constant practice to stay on top of their game. This is an important lesson to remember for other aspects of our lives, like the life of faith: the need for care and practice on a daily basis.

2. Leveling the playing field

Playing sports involves competition, and competition is generally healthy when the rules are explicit, the playing field is safe, and the play is fair. Sadly the arenas in which we often experience competition are not always fair. Have you ever played a game when the play was unfair? when the playing field was not "level," as they say? How did that make you feel?

Jack: One Sunday afternoon my friend's youth group went to the local park for a game of Ultimate Frisbee. They formed two teams, and the game began. After a few minutes, it became clear who the designated "players" and "spectators" were. The boys on both teams passed only to other boys, as if the girls were invisible. The girls clustered together on the sidelines and began yelling: "Hey, this isn't fair!" "Yeah, we came here to play too." "You guys need to pass to us and not just to each other."

One boy started mocking the girls in a whining voice, "Well, if you *girls* wanna play, you gotta stop standing around and get back on the field!" But another boy piped up, "Wait a minute. They've got a good point. We need to hear 'em out."

■■■**Playing games is a great way to stay connected to my dad when his physical condition makes other ways of relating a real challenge.** —TIM, 14

After discussing the conflict, the players decided to change the rules to make the game fair. The new rule was that boys could only pass to girls and girls to boys. Adding this new twist made the game fun for everyone.

PLAY

Play is derived from the German word *pflegen*: "to care for."

Following the game, these teens shared a picnic meal and talked about broader issues of fairness. They observed how their simple rule change had created a more level playing field for all players. They wondered together about rules that might be changed to make life more fair for folks who have been "standing on the sidelines" for many years. Respect for the level playing field in sports can teach us about fair play in other areas of life.

3. Keeping your eye on the shadow (as well as the ball)

Don: When it comes to sports, the game plays you as much you play the game. This dimension of sport can become an all-consuming passion for an athlete—even an addiction. A friend who teaches at a state university told me what he observed: "All the runners on the women's cross-country team had some kind of eating disorder. I thought it was a team requirement." These distance runners were so obsessed with their body weight and physique that they literally starved themselves in order to compete.

This is *the shadow side of sports*, when athletic competition moves beyond the boundaries of the game and begins to define your total reality. If you're feeling like an inmate, imprisoned by the constant demands of a sport, athletic competition is no longer healthy for you. When any sport produces a sense of self-loathing within you, the game has taken over, and you're no longer "playing" the game. Competing in this frame of mind will only drive you deeper into despair.

Jack: It's taken me a while, but I can now gauge when the pressure's starting to be too much for me. That means it's time to put down the tennis racquet and chill—maybe play a game of air hockey with my little brother or a card game with my friends. And there's always that slobbery old tennis ball my dog loves to chase! After an N.A.P. (see the "Time" chapter!), I feel refreshed and eager to get back on the court again.

PLAY

How do you throw paper wads into the wastebasket? Some folks shoot impossible hook shots from the far corner of the room. Some folks stand directly over the basket so there's no possible way to miss. And some folks stand back just far enough to make it interesting but just close enough so that they always make it. Ten out of ten. They "play it safe" and stick close to what they know will succeed. How about you?

■■■■■■■■■■■■■■■■■■■■■■■■■■■■■■■

Playing for life

Don: Play can teach us important lessons about who we are and who we're becoming. How we play reveals how we relate to the world, to other people, and even to God. Ask yourself these questions. In each case, consider what your *play* teaches you about your *faith*.

- Who brings out the playful side of me? How do they do it?
- Am I more comfortable with *scripted* play with predictable outcomes? Or am I willing to go with the flow of *spontaneous* play?
- Do I juggle only the number of balls I can keep under control? Or do I risk adding an extra ball to see how the pattern changes?
- Am I a good sport, a gracious loser as well as winner? Or am I a sore loser because I feel *entitled* to win every game?
- Do I designate a specific block as "downtime" in my planning calendar, after all the schoolwork and chores have been completed? Do I watch for opportunities to play with family and friends and animals?

There are lots of ways to play, and Jack and I have explored only a few of them. Keep a playful attitude toward whatever you happen to be doing at the moment. Find life-giving ways to play throughout your high-school years—and beyond. Surround yourself with playful friends, including Jesus the jester, that quick-witted, playful guy with a big smile on his face and a twinkle in his eye. But remember this: When you play with him, he likes to play for keeps! ■

DOROTHY C. BASS
WITH MARTHA SCHWEHN
AND JOHN SCHWEHN

‖Time

Teenagers often have strict schedules. In a society that is constantly telling us to do so many things, it is often hard to find time for God and time for the rest we need. This chapter is about taking regular moments to be instead of to do. If we learn this Christian practice, we can recognize the true value of time and notice the blessings God puts in our lives every day.

■ ■ ■ ■ ■ ■ ■ ■ ■ ■ ■ ■ ■ ■—**Martha Schwehn, 15**

It is the first day of high school, and the assistant principal is delivering some stiff instructions to John and Martha's freshman class:

- All students must be in their first-period classroom by 7:35 A.M.
- You have five minutes to change classes between periods. You will get a warning the first time you are not in your seat when the bell rings. The second time, you get a detention.
- Always carry your school schedule book. Use it to keep track of homework assignments, after-school practices, exam dates, and application deadlines.
- You cannot have a pass to the bathroom unless you have your schedule book with you.

John, who is definitely not a morning person, is worried. He doubts whether he can race from one wing of the huge school to another in only five minutes, especially if he needs to get something from his locker between classes. He wonders whether he'll be able to keep track of all his books and papers and get everything done on time.

When he got home that day, John sat down with me (I'm his mom) and reflected, "It's a pretty dramatic change from waking up in the calm environment of my bedroom to finding myself among hundreds of people chattering and running, just barely making it to class; from an environment where time doesn't matter to a place where time controls you, and missing the schedule could get you a detention. One thing school does, I have come to realize, is train me to live a basic lifestyle that will exist throughout my life. That lifestyle must be centered around time."

Rules about time shape the life of every high-school student. And rules about time will shape your whole life. These rules determine how fast things move, how much people try to get done each day, as well as how much unstructured time they have, how often they stop working to eat, chat with friends, sleep, or just plain think. Choices in all these arenas affect the quality of a person's life. So it's important to live in time in a way that results in a high-quality life.

John talked about a lifestyle that must be centered around time. What he really needs—what all of us need—is to move from that mind-set to a different perspective. We need a way to live well in time; we need a design for our time that allows us to know and enjoy God, ourselves, and other people. Christian practices can help us to learn this kind of design.

No matter how many rules other people set for your life, God wants you to take a Non Active Period—an N.A.P.—a time to rest, a time to be with God, a time to let down your guard and just *be*. This chapter starts with the time pressures teens face today, but by the end we'll all be sharing an N.A.P.

What are you doing?!

Here's what John's schedule book looked like about four weeks into high school: one week in the life of a ninth-grade, tennis-playing, horn-tooting guy.

Martha's schedule below shows one day—a Thursday in April—in more detail:

6:15	wake up
6:30	eat breakfast
7:00	catch bus
7:35	school starts
11:15	lunch
11:40	back to classes

September **18**

2:35 PM–National Honor Society
Meeting (A109)
6:00 PM–Freshman Volleyball vs. Lake
Central (Valparaiso)

September **19**

Powder Puff Football Game
ISTEP + Test 10, 11, 12
2:30 PM–German Club Meeting (C145)
2:30 PM–Key Club Meeting (A109)
4:15 PM–V & JV B Tennis vs.
Chesterton (Chesterton)
4:30 PM–V & VJ B Cross Country vs.
LaPorte/Merrillville (LaPorte)
4:30 PM–Freshman Volleyball vs.
Boone Grove (Boone Grove)
5:30 PM–V & VJ G Soccer vs. Hobart
(Fairgrounds)

September **20**

ISTEP + Test 10, 11, 12
2:35 PM–Hope Club Meeting/Officer
Nomina. (Room B224)
4:15 PM–V & JV B Tennis vs. Lake
Central (Lake Central)
5:30 PM–V & VJ B Soccer vs. Hobart
(Hobart)
6:00 PM–V & VJ Volletball vs.
Hammond Morton (Morton)

September **21**

Homecoming Parade & Bonfire
ISTEP + Test 10, 11, 12
2:30 PM–4:30 PM–Scholastic Games
(B223)
2:30 PM–Student Council Meeting
2:35 PM–Earth Awareness Club
Meeting (Room B224)
6:00 PM–Freshman Football vs.
Chesterton (Valparaiso)
6:00 PM–V & VJ Volleyball vs. Hobsrt
(Hobart)

Sp-find 20 place names
(spanish) and say What
they mean
Tennis Practice

NONE
Tennis Meet

None
Tennis Meet
5:30 Horn Lesson

Prewriting wkst find
copy of story due
tomorrow
Questions for Bio
Math
Tennis Practice

2:25	school ends
2:30	tennis practice
4:00	tennis meet, VHS vs. Merrillville
6:00	finish tennis meet
6:20	eat dinner
7:00	rehearse Sunday music at church
9:30	get home
9:45	watch TV, do homework
11:00	go to bed

What would your schedule look like? No single week or day could give the full picture, of course. You'd need a schedule for winter, another for summer (thank goodness for summer!), one for Tuesday, one for Saturday (thank goodness for Saturday!), and more. But how about right now—this week, this season? How do you feel about time in your life?

Look around and you'll see that lots of folks worry about time these days. Many feel time is their enemy: "I don't use time," someone said. "Time uses me!" Adults seem to think it is "in" to moan about how busy they are—though sometimes you have to wonder if they are moaning or actually bragging about all the stuff they have to do (and therefore how important they must be). Lots of teens also fill their schedules to overflowing. Machines that are supposed to save time—such as computers—should make things easier, but instead they seem to add to the stress. Do you ever get really aggravated because your computer is taking a few seconds too long to boot up? It's incredible how impatient we can become. Maybe we need to ask ourselves, *What is the Big Hurry?*

Choose a day or a week and write out your own schedule. Then think about your own life in time as you reflect on the issues raised in this chapter. ■ ■ ■ ■ ■ ■

Some teens just give up on this high-pressure scene. Watching lots of TV, playing endless video games, cutting class—these are ways of rejecting the Big Hurry. Unfortunately, reacting in this way also means missing out on lots of the good things that happen in time, including those that can prepare you for a not-boring future. Other kids let the high-pressure scene get deep under their skin and find themselves trapped in a different way. Kim, a senior, says, "My friends and I feel really stressed out about getting into college. We never have time to relax. The practice of living well in time calls out to me, but I just don't have time for it. I know that my friends and I just would not be able to change our schedules, no matter what."

Both groups are stuck. They are making the mistake of thinking that either they organize their time the way they do or they get a break by dropping out of the whole scheduling thing altogether.

It is easy to get so caught up in keeping up that we forget that our schedules are the result of many human decisions. Adults—like the ones in charge of your school—set rules. You make choices—to join a team, to take a study hall, to watch TV on school nights (or not). You cope with financial pressures by getting a part-time job. (If you do this, you know that employers' rules—such as "You have to work every weekend"—are also major time shapers.) Some families gather for supper most nights; many others go for weeks without sitting down together.

Time isn't made of stone. Schedules don't have to be the way they are. They are the result of many choices—some of them yours, some of them not.

If time isn't made of stone, what IS it made of?

When it comes to thinking about time, the pages of a schedule tell only a small part of the story. It would be impossible to squeeze our mysterious human experience of time into those flat little squares of a calendar. All hours do not feel the same size when you are in the middle of them. When it seems like there is nothing to do, time can start to drag; you turn on the TV, watch a boring show, and wish Friday night would get here faster. But time can also fly. You get with your friends, and you fall into a conversation or put on some music and—*poof!*—it's time to go home and you felt like you were just getting started. Even taking a shower can put you in the zone where you lose all track of time. Your body gets totally

Getting clean is only half of what I do in the shower. The rest of the time I spend thinking about whatever is on my mind and sorting things out as ■ ■ ■ ■ I let the water pour over me. ■ ■ ■ ■ ■

—JOHN, 15

relaxed, your daydreams take over—and before you know it, your sister is banging on the door, shrieking, "Get out! You've been in there for an hour already!"

Time is the *place* of all our experiences. Can you really be friends with someone you never spend time with? Can you play a sport or a musical instrument without giving it some of your time? Aren't you grateful for a teacher or a relative who always has time for you? Look at the other practices in this book, and you'll realize that every one of them takes time. When you are practicing your faith in these ways, you are alive and alert—to your own deepest needs, to other people, to the beauty of creation, and to the presence of God. That's what makes the practices of faith renewing instead of just one more activity you have to do. Remember Frank's story about searching for the whale (see the "Creation" chapter)? This story shows how even "wasted" time can be precious when you spend it with someone you love, doing something important. Frank and his dad bobbed up and down on San Francisco Bay all night long, and though they did not find a whale, they did experience the sacredness of time spent with each other and God in the midst of creation.

When have you lost track of time because you were so absorbed in something fine? When do you feel that you are *wasting time*?

Time has great value. But often we are too busy or too distracted to notice anything except that time is going too fast and we feel stressed *or* that time is going too slowly and we feel bored. It doesn't have to be this way.

Kaitlyn, who worked on the "Welcome" chapter, shared this story: "I ride the bus to school each morning. Most of the year, I have to leave while it's still dark. Getting out of bed and onto a bus this early is not too pleasant. But one morning I noticed the sun coming up. It made me think of this beautiful planet turning gently toward the sun and how wonderful it is that God made all this and shares it with me again every day. I thought of how God said, "Let there be light." And suddenly I was praying, "Thank you, God, for this amazing world."

A year later, Kaitlyn admits that she often forgets or is too tired to notice this morning gift. But on many days she does see it; and whenever she does, she smiles and thinks again about the connection between her day, earth's rhythm, and God. It is a quiet moment of thanks. What might

Time is built into creation itself. In the very beginning, before there is such a thing as time, God says, "Let there be light!" And there is light. It is different from darkness, and God separates them, naming the light "day" and the darkness "night." This is the birth of time itself. ■ ■ ■ ■

have been a dead time—awake too early, stuck on a bus with nothing to do, just waiting to get to school—becomes time that is alive with God's Spirit.

Sunrise, sunset

Given the choice, nearly all teenagers would rather enjoy their spiritual experiences at sunset than at sunrise. Most American teens have to get to school long before their bodies are ready to be there. High school starts early—too early, according to doctors who study sleep. The natural teenage body clock is set so that it is physically difficult to settle down to an early bedtime and even more difficult to get up early. In fact, scientific research shows that most American high schools are beginning classes hours before the student brain is operating at full capacity. Two Minnesota cities that learned these facts moved starting time one hour later, and within three years average SAT scores had climbed a hundred points! Researchers attribute those results to the fact that students were actually remembering material covered in first and second periods.

Teenagers have plenty of energy, and many like having lots to do. Still, there are times when a crowded schedule can be overwhelming. You get big assignments in all your classes at once, or you need to hold a part-time job, or you're on a team or in a play that requires substantial time. It's wise to plan ahead when you face weeks with extra demands, though sometimes keeping everything steady and in balance is impossible. Getting involved in more activities than you can handle is a sure path to stress, so avoid adding commitments that would stretch you beyond your limits. However, there is one commitment you can afford to add: a commitment to taking regular Non Active Periods. John likes this advice. He says, "I'm not ashamed to admit it: I love to take naps. Coming home from the busy traffic of the outside world and getting comfortable on the sofa feels great, and it refreshes me for the rest of the day."

Follow John's example and get some rest. Follow Kaitlyn's example and seek out those moments in time when you can offer your attention to God and to what God is doing all around you. Taking time to notice blessings is part of living an abundant life. We need to take time to enter the quiet, still space of God's love. God's love is always there. The question is whether we can let go of our distractions—the noise, the worries, the things we need to do, the stuff we want to buy—long enough to see, enjoy, and receive that love.

Slow food and quiet moments

Our family—my husband, Mark, John, Martha, and I—enjoys a time of focusing on God's love twice each day. (Well, maybe not every day; sometimes one or more of us aren't home, but this is our basic pattern.) At supper, we bow our heads and say grace before eating. *Grace* is a wonderful word; it means "free gift," something you receive because of the giver's generosity, not because you have worked for it or deserved it. Saying "grace" when what you've been hearing all day is "hurry up" and "try harder" is like taking a nice deep breath and slowly letting it out.

Often the eating that people do these days is more like taking in fuel. Just like a car—a machine—people pull into a station and pump in the stuff to keep their wheels turning for a while longer. Notice how many gas stations double as fast-food joints? Think about it: "Fast" food is food that takes as little time as possible.

When you add time to a meal, the meal changes. When you are about to eat—wherever, whenever—try sitting for a couple of minutes in silence. Breathe. Think about where your meal came from. The food came from nature and from human work. Thank the Creator! Experience your connection with those who worked to bring this food to the table and with the people who are hungry today. Add time to the meal, and you can add companions too—a friend or two perhaps. Take time, in other words, to remember that you are not a machine taking in fuel but a human being, made in God's image. You can add time to a meal and consciousness about its source even when you are eating a meal from a fast-food restaurant—as long as you treat it like "slow food." If your family, like

During the school year, 39% of 15- to 17-year-olds hold jobs, working an average of 18 hours a week. **High-school students average 51 minutes of homework a day, 21 hours of television a week, and 15 shopping trips a month.** Nine out of 10 pray each week; 56% attend religious services; 35% read the Bible outside of church; and 32% belong to a religious youth group.

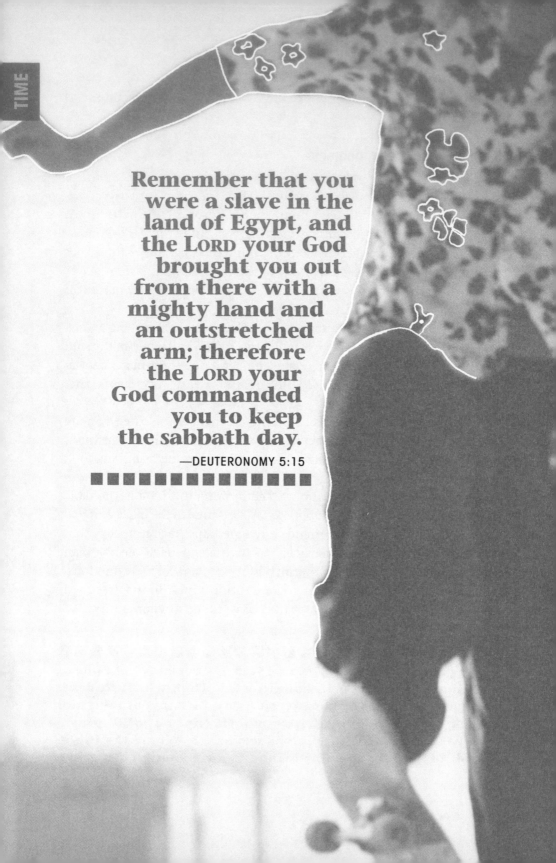

Remember that you were a slave in the land of Egypt, and the LORD your God brought you out from there with a mighty hand and an outstretched arm; therefore the LORD your God commanded you to keep the sabbath day.

—DEUTERONOMY 5:15

many today, doesn't take time at meals, maybe you can be the one to invite other family members to do so, even if it can happen only once in a while.

The other time our family regularly takes for God comes at bedtime (right before our daily BIG N.A.P.). "Now I lay me down to sleep," we pray together, one parent and one teen, "I pray thee, Lord, thy child to keep. When in the morning I awake, help me the path of love to take. This I ask for Jesus' sake. God bless . . . (here comes a long list of loved ones, plus several other people we are especially concerned about just now) . . . Amen."

Whether we are adults or teens, praying this way transforms us into little children again for a moment, relieved of duties and trusting Someone much bigger than we are to watch over us, to keep us, while we rest. We enter the quiet, still space of God's love. This end of one day becomes the beginning of the next, for we are more likely to take "the path of love" in the morning when we remember that God loves us and also loves the people we'll be seeing.

Prayers before supper and at bedtime are not usually intense spiritual experiences. Often our attention strays, and we don't feel the presence of God. On the other hand, if we did not save this time in our cluttered days, we might not remember the grace and blessing of God at all. And occasionally these small amounts of time set aside for prayer grow bigger. When we need to share a heartfelt sorrow or to express healing words for a hurt we have caused or a deep sense of gratitude, we do have the time.

You can choose from numerous other ways to take time for God every day. To do any of these, you'll need to be silent for at least a little while. That will mean turning off the television, the radio, the computer, and the CD player in order to be present not only to God but also to yourself. Here are some of the practices you could choose:

■ ■ **Most teenagers need 9 hours and 15 minutes of sleep each night, says Dr. Mary Carskadon, a professor of psychiatry and human behavior. But conflicts between the body clocks of teens and the schedules of most high schools make this nearly impossible; they average seven hours on school nights. Laboratory tests show that rhythms of hormone release in teenagers make it natural for them to stay up later at night and to sleep later in the morning. School systems could honor teens by starting classes an hour later. What are some reasons most schools do not make this change?** ■ ■ ■ ■

- Write in a journal, not just about events but about your hopes, fears, dreams.
- Try a prayer exercise from the "Prayer" chapter.
- Read a short passage from the Bible each day, slowly. Ponder what it means for you.
- Take a walk. Breathe deeply. Notice what is around you.
- Pray over the phone with a friend, maybe even an adult friend, in the evening.
- Read a poem more than once. Let the rhythms and images sink in. Write a poem.

Breaking the patterns

At times steady rhythms are helpful. But aren't there also times when life can seem a little too steady and predictable? One day you need a bathroom pass, so you get out that old school scheduler to get one. When you look at the schedule, you realize you've been in school for months and *will still* be in school for months to come. Then it snows. At least if you live in the Midwest like we do, it snows.

Martha remembers a wonderful snow day: "I woke up early Monday morning and tuned in to the local radio station. Our town is notorious for toughing out the snow, but on this particular day, the school board must have seen that the buses would never get through. When I heard the announcement of a snow day, I immediately picked up the phone and called my best friend to see if she had heard the news. What a wonderful surprise! That day was filled with sledding, snowball fights, hot chocolate, and many laughs. I love snow days—I think because they are unexpected, something offbeat that lets you out of your daily schedule."

The day is offbeat! The rhythm is broken, and you are free! On a snow day, what the clock says and the bells' ringing in the empty school corridors don't matter. You play as long as feels right to you—that is, until you are too cold, your friends have to go home, or the image of cocoa suddenly floats into your mind. You are not living by the clock; you are living inside an event that has its own pace. You don't have to justify your use of time at all. How great to have a day like that!

The Jewish people have had a day that is something like a snow day for thousands of years. In fact, they have had such a day once each week—a day that is off the beat, a day when clocks and bells don't matter. This day is the Sabbath. One of the Ten Commandments is to observe this day: "Six days you shall labor and do all your work. But the seventh day is a sabbath to the LORD your God; you shall not do any work" (Exodus 20:9-10). STOP! Cease! Enough is enough! The Lord has declared this a Non Active Period!

Observing the Sabbath is a commandment. But in Jewish tradition the Sabbath is regarded even more as a gift, because each Sabbath is a reminder of how much God cherishes earth and the human beings made in God's own image. After creating the heavens and the earth, plants and animals, and finally, people, God sees that it is all very good. So God rests for a whole day, spending time with these creatures—being rather than doing, enjoying rather than working. God blesses this day (see Genesis 2:1-3). It's a wonderful day of grace.

Later, however, humanity turns away from God, and God's chosen people end up in slavery. Slavery is the opposite of Sabbath. In the book of Exodus, we read about how the Hebrew people were trapped in Egypt—making bricks for Pharaoh all day every day, unable to have any time off work at all. They cried out, and God heard their cry and led them out of bondage. Once they were free, God commanded them to keep the Sabbath. You are not slaves anymore, God told them. One way to remember that you are free is to take a whole day off, every single week, even when you think you don't have time to rest. And make sure that your animals and the people who work for you get to have a day off too!

In the very busy world of the 21st century, many adults work as if they were slaves—some because of severe financial need, some because their employers do not treat them fairly, and some because they are obsessed with work itself. Teens need to be aware of how a slave-labor mentality might develop in them during and after high school as well. And then—whether Jewish or Christian or practicing another faith—teens need to listen to this ancient word about freedom and accept the gift of Sabbath time—time to be rather than do; time to enjoy other people and creation; time for genuine, deep freedom.

Sabbath is not just empty time. Sabbath time is restful and renewing because it reorients us to God. It is time full of God, and for that reason, a time of true freedom. Therefore, the Sabbath has been and continues to be a day of worship as well as a day of rest for the Jewish people.

Saying "grace" when what you've been hearing all day is "hurry up" and "try harder" is like taking a nice deep breath and slowly letting it out. ■ ■ ■ ■ ■ ■ ■ ■ ■ ■ ■ ■

Rest and worship go together for Christians too. Jesus was a Jew, and he went to the synagogue to pray on the seventh day of each week. After Jesus' death, his followers continued to rest on this day, but they also met on Sunday, the first day of the week, to remember his resurrection. Over the centuries, the two celebrations gradually merged. Sunday became the traditional day of Christian rest and worship, the day on which we celebrate Sabbath.

When we gather to worship on Sunday, we remember Christ's resurrection and celebrate that God is mightier than death itself. God is mightier than anything that threatens to separate us from the true freedom God intends for us and for all people.

Like many other teens, Martha and John started going to youth group at church on Sunday evenings when they entered high school. They hadn't been sure they would enjoy youth group, but now they refuse to miss those gatherings. They have become a great way to begin each week. John comments, "We're all there trying to figure out together what it means to be who God has made us and called us to be, instead of what advertisements or peer pressures tell us to be. We eat together, worship God together, study the Bible, and talk about really important issues in our lives. We also have fun."

Martha agrees and adds, "I don't care if I have homework to do; this feels important enough to set that aside until later. I like it that Jeremy (our youth director) says we can come as we are. I usually wear my pj's and slippers. I feel accepted—like I can come as I am, on the inside as well as on the outside." For John and Martha, going to youth group has become one of the rhythms of their life with God.

Time for God, time for life

There are many ways to stop and notice God, even in the middle of 24/7 craziness. These ways might come to you all of a sudden, like Kaitlyn's insight on a dark school bus. You might have grown up with ways to pay attention to God, as Martha and John grew up saying prayers at bedtime.

Or reading this chapter might be the first you've heard about the idea of taking time for God. Maybe you are a visitor to a church youth group, wondering whether you have time for this sort of thing!

Do you have time? You may think you don't. But either *(a)* you're kidding yourself, because you aren't really that busy, or *(b)* you really are too busy but shouldn't be. Think about it—and then admit that you can't afford not to stop for a slow, deep breath of God's love. You do have time. Enough time to say, "Ah, this light is beautiful; thank you, God!" Enough time to say "grace." Enough time to turn in trust to the One who watches over you as you sleep, asking this One also to watch over whoever is in need. Enough time to sing a song of praise that Life is stronger than Death. Enough time to gather with a group of friends each week who can help you to be truly free, because you are seeking God's will for your life.

As you grow into the person you will be for the rest of your life, don't forget that God intends for you to enjoy a Non Active Period on a regular basis. Get some rest, and notice God's presence, each and every day. ■

‖‖Truth

Truth telling is a choice teenagers face every day. People—teenagers especially —are sometimes dishonest because of pressure to succeed, fear of losing relationships, and overwhelming situations. Thankfully, through making confessions, surrounding yourself with people you can be your truthful self around (like at church), and taking careful risks, you can put your words, actions, and heart in sync with one another and begin to live truthfully, which in turn will bring you closer to everyone—including God. ■ ■ ■ ■

—**Betsy Crowe, 15**

I was just getting settled at my desk one fine spring morning when my colleague Rachel poked her head through the doorway.

"Just got off the phone with Grand Lake. We've got a tough one," she said. I grabbed my coffee, a pad of paper, and a pen and followed Rachel into her office. We were lawyers specializing in the rights of students with disabilities. School districts hired us for advice about their legal duty to provide an appropriate education for students with special needs. Almost all our cases were tough ones.

Rachel reminded me about Laura, an eighth-grader in the Grand Lake school system who had a progressive neurological disease that had begun to damage her hearing. Laura's hearing loss created a new set of educational needs.

Rachel explained the situation: "Laura starts high school next year, and she has her heart set on going to Silver Lake High School. It's where she's always wanted to go—right down the street from her house. But the school district thinks she would be better off at the other high school, Northfield."

I knew Northfield was a high school with a number of hearing-impaired students. The instruction and activities were set up to accommodate students with hearing loss without setting them apart. At Northfield, an American Sign Language (ASL) interpreter was a regular part of the classroom. At Silver Lake, where Laura wanted to go, the interpreter would be on hand just for her. I already knew Laura was self-conscious about her hearing loss. I wondered how she would feel having an adult following her around all day, calling even more attention to her. Would she be able to focus on learning at all?

"What do the parents say? I mean, have they looked at Northfield?" I asked.

"Not yet." Rachel looked concerned. "We're hoping they will go today. You know, her parents are really prominent in the community. The special ed director says they want Laura at Silver Lake because it is more prestigious—the rich kids' school. Plus, according to the school counselor, Laura's mother can't accept the hearing loss."

Our secretary opened the door and handed me a fax. "From Grand Lake," she said.

I scanned the page. "The school people were right about the parents. They don't want Northfield. They've sued the school district. They are asking the judge to order that Laura go to Silver Lake High School."

As the lawsuit developed, we learned that one of Laura's concerns was that her friends from eighth grade would all go to Silver Lake. Her parents had other concerns, but for Laura, the issue of friends was big. She didn't want to be separated from them. I could understand that. But Rachel and I firmly believed Laura would make friends at the other school where many students, hearing and deaf, could **Being truthful is** communicate in Laura's new language, ASL. If she went to Silver Lake, as the parents' suit demanded, Laura would be the only deaf person. We worried that Laura would be isolated, lonely, and left out. That kind of isolation could keep her from learning.

On the first day of the trial, Laura's attorney called Brittany Simpson as a witness to convince the judge that separating from friends bound for Silver Lake would traumatize Laura. Brittany raised her right hand and swore that the testimony she was about to give was the truth, the whole truth, and nothing but the truth. In response to questions from Laura's attorney, Brittany said she was one of Laura's good friends, that they hung out together at school and did stuff together on weekends.

TRUTH

more than not telling a lie. ■■■■

. . . the truth, the whole truth, and nothing but the truth

On cross-examination, I asked Brittany some questions to find out more. Here is a sample of what I asked (not from the real trial transcript):

Ms. Wiginton: How did you and Laura get to be friends?

Ms. Simpson: We were in the same art class. I kind of felt like sorry for her because no one really talked to her. So I like started sitting by her and stuff, and I found out about her condition and that she is like really cool and stuff. I'm like her only friend.

Ms. Wiginton: Did you have classes together other than art?

Ms. Simpson: Not really. I mean, Laura is like really smart and so she takes the more advanced stuff. But part of the year we had the same lunch.

Ms. Wiginton: Do you sign?

Ms. Simpson: Kind of. I mean, I know most of the letters and some words. I'm learning. It's cool.

Ms. Wiginton: How many times have you been to Laura's house?

Ms. Simpson: Um, I'm not sure. I mean, well, . . . I remember going over one time with my boyfriend to like pick her up.

Ms. Wiginton: How many times has Laura been over to your house?

Ms. Simpson: Well, she hasn't really like *been* to my house. I mean, like her parents won't let her come over and all because they don't know my mom. They're like really protective since she can't hear.

What do you think Brittany's testimony proved?

Getting the whole story

In the legal system, lawyers have certain ways—practices—of trying to get a view of the *whole* truth. We examine what people *say* is true in light of what they *do* with time and money, whom they hang out with, where they go, how they treat other people, and more. If how people *live* matches what they *say*, we think they are telling the truth. If how they live *doesn't* match what they say, then we tend to believe they are not truthful. Brittany said she and Laura were good friends, but their actions showed that the two girls spent very little time together. Brittany could not even speak Laura's language, ASL.

Truth encompasses the *whole* story—what we say *and* how we live our lives. The truth comes out in who we are and what we do every day. Living truthfully calls for bringing our words, our actions, and our deepest values as close together as possible. There are many obstacles to living a truthful life—to getting our words, actions, and values in sync. Let's look at three.

1. Pressure to succeed

Every school has rules against cheating. Yet in a 1998 survey of students listed in *Who's Who Among American High School Students*, 80 percent of high-school students admitted they had cheated at least once, and half of them said they considered cheating "no big deal." What's going on?

Teenagers are taught that they must get good grades in order to get into a good college so they can get a good job. In our culture, we act like this progression is carved in stone. In a way, it's not surprising that people do whatever it takes to make good grades, even lie and cheat. Allie, a teenager from Boston, sums it up: "Think how hard it is to get into college. If I have to copy some homework to keep my grades up because I had to play a sport or work, then that's what I'll do."

To resist being dishonest at school, teenagers have to withstand the incredible power of the pressure to succeed. Even teachers sometimes contribute to and support the pressure to succeed at the cost of living truthfully. They may look the other way, let students grade one another's papers with no monitoring, or refuse to believe or act on reports from peers. One way to resist the pressure to succeed is to find other ways of thinking about success. Maybe success is not about good grades, prestigious colleges and high-powered jobs. Maybe success is about finding what you love to do and doing it well. Living truthfully may mean being true to your own gifts and finding people who support that.

Betsy says, "I have cheated before, but I would rather make an A on my own."

2. Fear of losing relationships

In preparation for writing this chapter, Betsy conducted an informal survey of her friends. She asked them to describe situations when they had trouble telling the truth. Every answer included a concern about not wanting to hurt another person's feelings. Why? They were afraid they might lose a friend.

Allie—the teenager who talked about cheating—also talks about the value teenagers place on relationships. She says that unlike cheating in school, "Cheating in a relationship is huge, because it's like totally emotional. Cheating on a test is dishonest, but it's a totally, totally different thing." Relationships are different for an important reason. We figure out who we are by experiencing how we are like or not like other people our age. We find our place of belonging in the world through our friends.

But here's the tricky part: Teenagers want their friends to know them, yet they're also afraid that if friends do get to know them and discover they are not alike, those friends will abandon them. This two-sided situation can make it difficult to be truthful. You may tend to say what your friends want to hear or go along with what they do just to stay in relationship—even if it means betraying yourself. Living truthfully requires finding relationships with people you can trust with your real self.

Teenagers also think about relationship with their parents. Allie provided an insight into the dynamics of that relationship. She said she copies homework when she can't get it done in order to get good grades, go to college, and so forth—accomplishments that will please her parents. What would happen if she got caught cheating? "My parents would kill me."

Like Allie, many teenagers don't want their parents to know they have "done wrong," because they will get in trouble. And, in truth, lots of parents don't want to see their teenagers as they really are. But there may be another fear too. Down deep, Allie may be afraid she'll lose her relationship with her parents if they know "bad" things about her. Allie protects herself from that possible loss by hiding whatever might threaten their connection. And down deep, Allie's mom and dad may be afraid themselves, fearful that they have failed to raise Allie well. Living truthfully means getting real with parents about your own giftedness, desires, hopes, and fears. Living truthfully brings freedom for real, authentic connection with friends and family.

3. Overwhelming situations

When I was in junior high school, Carol and I were best friends. We spent the night together every Friday. We had a Craft Clubhouse for kids in our

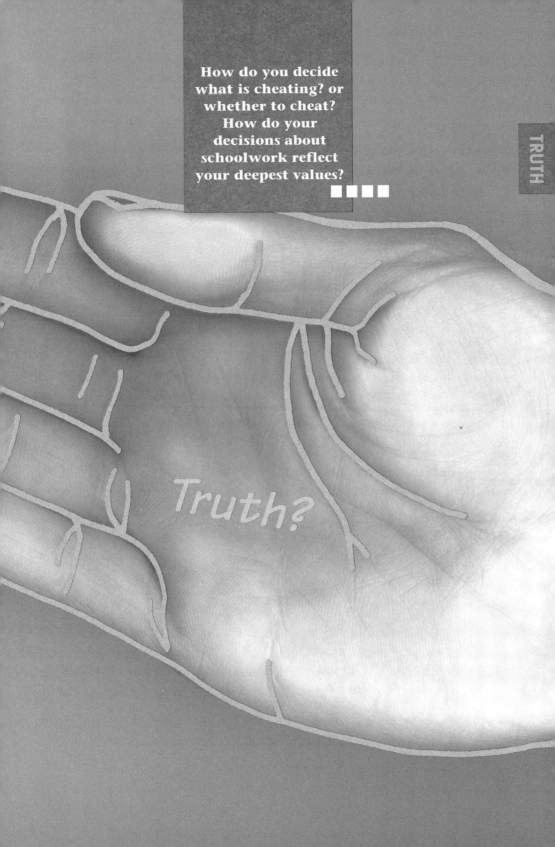

How do you decide
what is cheating? or
whether to cheat?
How do your
decisions about
schoolwork reflect
your deepest values?

Truth?

neighborhood during the summers. We told each other everything and trusted each other completely. She was like part of my family. But at the end of seventh grade, Carol abruptly and without explanation stopped being my friend. She wouldn't talk to me in person or on the phone. She wouldn't reply to the notes I stuffed in her locker. She would barely look at me when we passed in the hall. This broke my heart.

I couldn't figure out what was going on. I was sure I had done something wrong, but I didn't know what. I felt ashamed. I didn't talk to anyone about the situation. I went over and over it in my head. Finally I concluded that Carol was embarrassed to be my friend because I had tried out for cheerleading and had not been selected. Whether a girl was a cheerleader determined her social status. I wasn't popular. I noticed Carol was hanging out with the new cheerleaders and their clique. I was convinced: She dumped me because I was a loser. And if my very best friend—the person who knew me better than anyone—thought I was a loser, I probably was. This shameful conclusion about my lack of worth colored how I saw myself and how I related to my peers for years.

■ ■ ■ ■ ■ ■ ■ ■
How do you know when someone you trust doesn't tell you the truth? How does it feel? How does it affect your relationship with that friend?

When I went to my 10-year high-school class reunion, I saw Carol. She looked beautiful, happy, and successful. I was glad to see her, and she seemed pleased to see me. We talked for a while and discovered that we now lived in the same city. She said she would call when we got back home.

Carol came to see me and my new baby daughter, Betsy. Here's my memory of what she said that sunny August afternoon:

> Do you remember when we stopped being friends? There is something I should have told you about a long time ago. When I saw you at the reunion, I knew the time had come. At the end of seventh grade, my mother had a lot of problems. She did really strange things—like getting drunk in the middle of the day or coming home drunk. I didn't know what to do except get out of the house and ride my bike until I thought she was sobered up. I was scared and confused and ashamed. I couldn't let anyone come to the house because I never knew what Mom would do. I couldn't tell anyone.

Now my heart broke for scared, confused, lonely 12-year-old Carol and for the pain she had experienced. I had never thought something might be wrong in *her* life. All those years ago, we didn't know how to—we couldn't—get the truth out. I think lots of teenagers carry around secrets that can't yet be told. Living truthfully may involve finding someone to trust with your truth—someone who can help you hold the secret until it is safe to tell it, someone to help you cope and avoid drawing wrong or hurtful conclusions as I did. Carol gave me a great gift when she told me her story. Sometimes we never know the truth of another person's life or why things happen. When we don't, living truthfully may require a generosity to forgive our friends and ourselves for hiding truths that can't be spoken because they feel so overwhelming.

The story of my lost-and-found friendship with Carol shows how hidden truths hurt people. I'm sure Carol's mom and dad hurt. Carol hurt. I hurt because of the broken friendship. I was also hurt because I believed I was a loser. Carol's confession shone a different light on that years-old conclusion. I had believed something that was not true.

Where are we in this consideration of living truthfully? We have identified some things that make it hard: the pressure to succeed, the fear of losing relationships, and dealing with truths we can't yet tell. We know that hidden truths hurt us and can keep us out of the relationships we long for. What do we do then to live truthfully? Here are three ideas:

Making your confession

Many people practice confession to help them live truthfully. The word *confession* brings three images to my mind: a courtroom, Roman Catholics, and Saint Augustine.

In movies and on television (rarely in "real life"), the most exciting moments of courtroom drama often come when a witness blurts out a startling confession. The audience usually has suspected the truth, but the good guys have had trouble proving it. This confession clears everything up. Why does the witness confess? Maybe a brilliant lawyer breaks down the person during cross-examination. Maybe the witness decides he or she can't let someone else take the blame. Whatever the plot device, I think this is going on: The witness can no longer face living an untruthful life—one where what she or he *knows* and what she or he *says* are totally separated.

For centuries, Roman Catholics and other Christian communities practiced the sacrament of confession in a certain way. The person confessing (the penitent) would kneel on one side of a screen and recite a list of his or her sins to a priest on the other side. Sensing the penitent's sincere sorrow and honest desire to avoid sin in the future, the priest would then pronounce *absolution* ("I absolve you from your sins, in the name of the Father, and of the Son, and of the Holy Spirit. Amen") while the penitent prayed an *act of contrition* ("Oh my God, I am heartily sorry for having offended You. I firmly resolve with the help of Your grace to do penance and amend my life"). Today this sacrament—usually known as the sacrament (or rite) of reconciliation—may take place through a screen, face-to-face, or in a special service of reconciliation.

Almost all Christians—Protestant and Catholic—practice confession as a regular and important part of worship. We recite prayers aloud telling God and the gathered community that we have not loved God with our whole hearts or loved our neighbors as ourselves. Most services also include a time for silent, individual confession when we can reflect on the specific ways we have fallen short. These practices of confession may reveal uncomfortable truths we need to know about ourselves. It takes courage to face these truths honestly, to admit before God and others, "I'm not the person I really want to be. I want to change the way I'm living so that my life has integrity."

> ■ ■ ■ ■
> **Jesus said, "I am the way, and the truth, and the life."**
> —JOHN 14:6

Saint Augustine is one of the most influential Christians of all time. Although written in the fourth century, *The Confessions* of Saint Augustine is still read in college classes today. Augustine's *Confessions* is a spiritual autobiography. He writes about what he did during his life and asks himself, *What was I expressing when I did this? What was I looking for?* For example, he remembers that late one night when he was 16, he and his buddies stole the ripe pears from a neighbor's tree:

> We took great loads of fruit from it, not for our own eating, but rather to throw it to the pigs; even if we did eat a little of it, we did this to do what pleased us for the reason that it was forbidden. . . . I loved the theft itself and nothing else.

In reflecting on his crime in *Confessions*, Augustine realized that if he pursued only his love of stealing, he would never find the truth, goodness, and beauty he wanted for his life. This kind of reflection over a long period of time led Augustine to God, whom he believed to be the source of liveliness he had sought in the garden prank. He came to see God as the center for bringing his actions and values closer together.

The courtroom, the Christian act of confession, and Augustine—all of these suggest that one way toward living a truthful life is to make your own confession. I don't mean a catalog of your bad deeds or a public admission of a lie. Your confession is your personal reflection about how your words, deeds, and truth line up—about who you are. You might write in a journal, draw, write poetry. Augustine wrote his confession to God. Other people have put together a confession addressed to the child they hope to have someday, to a grandparent, to a friend, or even to themselves. You may decide to have one person with whom you share your confession. He or she may help you reflect on the truth you are living. It takes some effort to live a truthful life.

Being part of a community that promotes truthful living

Simon Peter, Jesus' disciple, gives us a great example of living a truthful life, even though he did not always tell the truth. From the day Peter met Jesus, he had been Jesus' most vocal and passionate defender. Peter always claimed, before anyone else, that he would do whatever was necessary for the cause. Jesus even called Peter "the rock" on which he would build the church (Matthew 16:18). But during their last meal together, Jesus predicted that Peter would deny that he knew Jesus at all.

Confessing means Be honest about what you have said and done. Name uncomfortable truths as well as your deepest longings. Examine how the way you live and what you believe fit together or fall apart.

Peter was aghast. "Not me," he said. "I will never do such a thing." When Jesus was arrested later that evening, Peter secretly followed the soldiers and Jesus. Jesus was taken inside the high priest's office; Peter tried to blend into the group outside by the fire. The situation was tense; the outlook bad. These people were out to get Jesus, and Peter was afraid.

> Now the chief priests and the whole council were looking for testimony against Jesus to put him to death; but they found none. . . . While Peter was below in the courtyard, one of the servant-girls of the high priest came by. When she saw Peter warming himself, she stared at him and said, "You also were with Jesus, the man from Nazareth." But he denied it, saying, "I do not know or understand what you are talking about." And he went out into the forecourt. Then the cock crowed. And the servant-girl, on seeing him, began again to say to the bystanders, "This man is one of them!" But again he denied it. Then after a little while the bystanders again said to Peter, "Certainly you are one of them; for you are a Galilean." But he began to curse, and he swore an oath, "I do not know this man you are talking about." At that moment the cock crowed for the second time. Then Peter remembered that Jesus had said to him, "Before the cock crows twice, you will deny me three times." And he broke down and wept (Mark 14:55, 66-72).

I believe in the

Some rock. This was Peter's moment of truth. With the second crow, Peter knew the uncomfortable truth about himself: He was afraid, and out of that fear, he had lied about his best friend. His heart broke.

But that's not the end of the story. In John's Gospel, Jesus and Peter are reconciled when Jesus returns after his resurrection. Jesus asks Peter three times, "Do you love me?" Each time, Peter answers yes. Jesus gives him three instructions in response: "Feed my lambs. Tend my sheep. Feed my sheep." He is telling Peter that even though he lied about their friendship,

■ ■ ■ ■ ■ ■
What are the hard truths to tell in your life? What are you not willing to lie about? With whom do you always want to be truthful? What are you willing to endure for the sake of truthfulness? ■

Peter is still the one to care for Jesus' followers. Peter's painful moment of truth in the high priest's courtyard initiated his doing what Jesus hoped for—starting the church. The church became the community where Peter would be reminded of his friendship with Jesus, receive encouragement when he was fearful, and be with people helping one another live truthfully.

Someday you may have a moment of truth like Peter's—an experience when you will feel caught by fear and feel trapped by a dilemma. But the good news is that you don't have to face it alone. You can be part of a community of people who are committed to living truthfully.

The church is a community of people who seek to live truthfully. For Christians, how we live is closely related to what we believe. Therefore, when Christians gather for worship, we speak our beliefs about what is true right out loud: God is real. God loves humanity. We are more than the sum of our fears and doubts and mistakes. We can mess up (like Peter) and still be loved. We have hope for goodness. In many churches, central Christian beliefs are summarized in the strong words of creeds and confessions of faith that have been handed down through the centuries. Congregations often recite these ancient creeds as part of their service of worship.

Holy Ghost . . . the forgiveness of sins . . . the life everlasting.

—FROM THE APOSTLES' CREED,
an ancient statement of Christian faith

People in church may not always feel full of conviction when they say the words of the creeds or prayers. But participating in the rituals of the church is valuable. Here the community *testifies* about its deepest beliefs and affirms its desire to live in harmony with these beliefs. By joining in, you practice bringing your mind, body, heart, and soul together. And you may find in this community people with whom you can talk honestly about the details of your own effort to live truthfully.

Taking well-chosen risks in truth telling

The servant girl who recognized Peter took a risk to tell the truth. Jesus was accused of being a rebel, gathering forces against those in power. Peter was one of his followers. How was this servant girl to be sure Peter would not retaliate if she exposed him? And why would she think anyone would listen to her—a lowly servant and a powerless girl—anyway? She was gutsy. She confronted Peter directly. When he denied who he was, the girl spread word to the others that Peter was one of Jesus' friends. Her courage to speak out had an unintended consequence. She brought about Peter's moment of truth—and his starting point for establishing the church.

This servant girl's bravado shows us that speaking the truth can lead to changes. Bringing truth out from hiding opens the way for new possibilities. Living a truthful life—bringing words, actions, and deepest values together—may mean trying something new, doing something different. It's OK to start small.

You might start with a friend. I know one teenager, Evan, who always blames his parents for anything that doesn't go right. Nothing is ever his fault. Instead of sympathizing with Evan for the thousandth time, his best friend, Brad, finally took a chance and said something difficult: "Evan, I don't know what to say to you anymore. I think you need to talk to a counselor who is trained to know what to say." Evan got mad. But now there is the chance for honesty in the friendship—and the chance that Evan may look for more and better ways to take care of himself. Most of all, Brad is living truthfully.

■ ■ ■ **Living truthfully also means** ■ ■ ■
**revising what you believe as more
truth comes to be known.**

Little Black Crow, a Native American teenager, recently took a more public kind of risk in her hometown of Alvarado, Texas. For a long time, she had been embarrassed by the use of an Indian as the high-school mascot. But she had been afraid to say anything. She finally posted her feelings in an Internet conversation among Native Americans. They encouraged her to speak up, to stand up for who she is. Little Black Crow began speaking up first in e-mails, then to reporters and the school board. She expressed her belief that the use of the mascot was discriminatory and degrading. While some people said Indians should regard the mascot as an honor, Little Black Crow disagreed, saying it did not feel like an honor, especially since no Indians she knew were bright yellow and purple.

Little Black Crow's outspokenness resulted in a number of remarkable outcomes. The local newspaper wrote about her campaign, which had generated national support. Storm Reyes, a Native American woman from Tacoma, Washington, traveled to Alvarado to speak to the school board. She had promised Little Black Crow she would do what she could to effect a change. Although the school district did not completely change the mascot, modifications were made to the mascot costume, and the purple and yellow Indians painted on picnic tables were repainted in a solid, more dignified color. And perhaps most importantly, people were thinking more about an image they had taken for granted before Little Black Crow spoke out.

To risk speaking out against wrong requires support, passion, and perseverance, but it can start a movement toward justice (check out the "Justice" chapter).

In Laura's case against Grand Lake Schools, the judge took a risk and decided to send Laura to the school she did not want. For many reasons besides the issue of friends, the judge decided that Laura's potential educational gains outweighed what she might leave behind at Silver Lake—even though the transition would be painful. The judge believed Laura needed friends who could sign and communicate with her and with whom she shared the experience of hearing impairment. If Laura and Brittany wanted to get together, they certainly could; they would just be at different schools. In this case, the judge's courage to make a difficult decision about truth brought goodness. Before long, Laura loved Northfield. She made friends and did well. Her parents even thanked the school district. (The endings of cases don't always work out that well, but it sure is nice when one does.)

What does it mean to live a truthful life? It's not just saying what you wish were true—as Brittany did when she testified that she and Laura were friends. It's living what is true by always trying to bring your mind, body, heart, and soul into play and as close to one another as possible.

Why is living truthfully difficult? Pressure to succeed may cause you to put achievement ahead of other values. Your desire for friends may cause you to keep silent about what you feel, know, or believe. Fear of losing your parents' love may cause you to hide anything that might anger or disappoint them. Confusing and scary situations may overwhelm you, so that you become unsure whether or how to tell the truth.

■ ■ ■ ■ ■ ■ ■ ■
How do you feel when you don't tell the whole truth to a parent? How does the hidden truth change the relationship?

How can we help ourselves live truthfully? We can make an ongoing confession, being honest about what we have said and done, naming uncomfortable truths about ourselves, claiming our deepest longings, and examining the fit between what we know about ourselves and the way we live. We can be part of a community of people, like the church, who are also trying to live truthfully. We can take some well-chosen risks that bring mind, body, heart, and soul closer together.

May you be blessed in living a truthful life. ■

‖Choices

All people face making important choices—especially teenagers. We have to make many decisions that will affect the rest of our lives. I hope that this chapter will help young people learn how to make decisions that are wiser and more life-giving. ■ ■ ■ ■

—**Matthew Mistal, 15**

To be alive and to be human mean that we must make decisions. There's just no way around it. Whether we are deciding which socks to wear in the morning, which friends to hang out with, or which career to pursue, our lives are filled with opportunities to decide. Sometimes I look at my dog, Jackson, and wish I could be like him. He only has to decide how much to eat, when to get up from a nap, and whether to play with his ball or chase the spray from the sprinkler. Instincts he was born with drive him; he doesn't have to make complex decisions as we humans do. Nor does he quite have the intellect to make such choices.

In truth, some people do try to live like my dog. They listen only to their most basic instincts regarding food, sleep, or sex. They focus on getting what they want when they want it. Many people who live this way ultimately end up letting other people make decisions for them—in prisons, mental hospitals, or dysfunctional relationships. In a way, they end up like my dog, because someone else determines what they can eat, where they can live, and what they can do. Their lives lack the richness they were meant to have.

Discernment is the Christian practice that teaches us to give careful attention to our own deepest selves and to God. This practice can help us to make wise decisions as complicated beings in a complicated world.

Making choices as humans

What does it mean to be human—and to be fully, truly alive in all our humanness? In the Bible, the psalmist sings about how the sea roars, the field exults, and the trees of the forest sing for joy, all declaring the glory

■ ■ ■ ■ ■ ■ ■
Some common choices youth are allowed to make are:
- **friends**
- **music**
- **clothes**
- **hobbies**
- **activities**
- **their level of participation in school.**

What choices do you make? ■ ■ ■

of God (Psalm 96). Trees giving glory to God? What can that possibly mean? Thomas Merton, a monk who lived not so long ago, said that a tree gives glory to God by fully being a tree—by living for the purpose for which it was created! Merton also said that as humans we give glory to God by being what we were fully meant to be—using all the capacities and gifts given to us by God. For a tree, this means putting its roots down deep in the soil to drink the rich nutrients into its trunk and branches, raising its leaves to the sky to receive the rays of the sun, growing good bark to protect its inner core, enriching the earth by giving off oxygen, and providing shade and comfort to the animals of the forest. These are the ways a tree gives glory to God, and the ways it lives into its gift for the world—by being what it was created for. If trees were removed from large portions of the planet (like the rain forests of South America), the whole earth would lose something very important and would be thrust into cataclysmic climate changes.

How do we as humans give glory to God and figure out what gifts we can offer the world? Instead of simply accomplishing a few functions, like a tree's, we have to choose among hundreds and thousands of possibilities. And unlike the tree, we have more than our genes to guide us. We have heart, soul, mind, and strength, and we are called to love God with all of these. Being truly human means answering the call to love God with all that we are. It also means loving our neighbors by offering our gifts to the world.

Discovering how to love God and our neighbors is not usually an easy process, however. God gave us a *heart* to know what makes us happy or sad. God gave us a *soul* to make us yearn for a more satisfying way of living. God gave us a *mind* to think and to create solutions to difficult problems. God gave us physical *strength* to build the world we dream of. We are

172

We are complicated beings—much more complicated than dogs or trees.

■■■■■■■■■■■■■■■■■■■■■■■■■■■■■■

**The commandment to love God with all that we are is
known as the Shema, from its first word in Hebrew
in Deuteronomy 6:4-9. Jesus repeats this commandment
in Mark 12:29-30:**

Hear, O Israel: the Lord our God, the Lord is one; you shall love the Lord your God with all your heart, and with all your soul, and with all your mind, and with all your strength.

complicated beings—much more complicated than dogs or trees. And so living into our full humanness requires careful attention to who we are and to the presence and call of God in our lives.

To paint or not to paint? Brad was a young man facing a choice. He stood in knee-high wet grass just beyond the amber glow of a street lamp, which was shining dimly on a supermarket wall, as he and his friends prepared to decorate the wall with their aerosol weapons. It was 2:00 A.M., and their parents thought they were camping in Mark's backyard. Even though they had not discussed it, Brad knew that Mark would draw his signature space rocket, and James undoubtedly would draw a large black widow spider, an allusion to his skateboarding nickname. It was exciting to imagine how their artwork would shock adults the next morning as they rushed into the store for coffee, or how it would amaze the bleary-eyed insomniacs who would arrive even sooner. But Brad could also envision the rage of the store owner who would have to clean the paint from the side of the store, not to mention the ire of his own parents should they discover his involvement. He pressed the plastic tip of the can to check the contents. *Psssst* . . . the paint flowed red and free into the air. But he hesitated to apply it to the wall. "Come on, Brad!" His hands froze in midstroke as he realized that he did have a choice.

To dance or not to dance? Carmen also faced an important decision. She sat on the edge of her bed and bit her tongue as her father stood in the doorway with the business college application in his hands. Through her tears she looked up at the walls of her room, which were covered in a collage of posters featuring her favorite prima ballerinas and photos of herself, in leotards or tutus, on her toes or at the barre, posing with proud instructors or bowing after the dozens of dance recitals she had given since the age of four. She had absolutely no interest in going to a business college, but the intensity of her father's voice made it clear that he wanted her to pursue a degree so that she could have a "real" career. She had always hoped to study with a regional ballet troupe and to pursue a career in dance. Her mother told Carmen that she could choose, but her mother also kept talking about how a business degree would broaden Carmen's future options, not narrow them. Carmen sat with the pen in her hand, wondering how to decide what to do. .

Think for a moment about Brad and Carmen. Brad got caught up in his friends' desire to spray paint a wall. Carmen felt the weight of her father's desire that she study business. Like many teens, both felt the pressure of other people's desires. They didn't know how to decide what to do.

There always seem to be more than a few people willing to tell young people what to do and how to do it! While taking instructions works fine for my dog, who seems pleased when I tell him what to do, it just doesn't fit the human spirit. Simply following orders or giving in to pressure will not help us become the people we want to and could become. As human beings, we yearn for more. We yearn to live into the greater possibilities we sense will open up if we glorify God with all that we are. How can Brad and Carmen—and how can you—consider choices in ways that involve heart, soul, mind, and strength?

Feeling trapped

Both Brad and Carmen felt like they were caught in a cage. They felt overpowered by people who were trying to choose *for* them rather than encouraging them to reflect well and carefully on the choices they faced.

Many youth today feel trapped in similar ways. Pressure comes from more than parents and friends. Numerous industries in today's world specialize in telling young people what to do. The *clothing industry* wants you to buy certain clothes, so their *advertisers* proclaim you can't be lovable

■■■■ The glory of God is ■■■■ a human being fully alive.

—IRENAEUS, a second-century Christian leader

or beautiful unless you look like supermodels wearing the right brand of clothes. It's not good for business if you believe you already are lovable and beautiful without buying their clothes and without looking like their models. The *entertainment industry* wants you to buy its movies, music, videos, electronics, and magazines, so they hire big advertising firms and spend billions of dollars each year to persuade you to do so. Their message implies that happiness can be found at the cash register, which seems harmless enough until you realize that you can't buy happiness.

Perhaps the most confining cages of all, however, are those we create with our own superficial desires. Sometimes we desire what's not best for us, and then we become our own worst jailers. Like adults, youth can also become captive to shallow desires. If you think you can't do without candy, junk food, and television, those desires can become more important in your life than they should. Those shallow desires can prevent you from living the abundant life Jesus offers. Other desires, such as being popular or extremely muscular, can also keep you focused on shallow illusions, so that you don't think clearly about how to glorify God with your life and offer your own gifts to the world.

Candy, junk food, and television are OK when used in moderation. When you become addicted to them, however, your health can suffer, and you can lose the ability and desire for good food and wholesome activity. Superficial desires tempt you in ways that obscure your deepest desires—for life, love, justice, peace, and God. Sometimes you can become so addicted to shallow imitations of real life that you lose the ability to recognize and live real life—vital, enthusiastic, juicy, glorious, full, real life.

Knowing your deeper desires is often tricky, especially when shallow imitations are so seductive. For example, your deepest self may yearn for a true friend, but you may constantly bypass opportunities to form deep, lasting friendships because you are so crazy to be included in the "popular" crowd. Or you might know deep down that you want to dance, but you don't, because your parents oppose it or because some teens think people into ballet are stuck up. Another person may "want" to dance only because it is a form of rebellion against her parents. Where are the cages? Where is the promise of richness of life?

You need sources of wisdom when you do this kind of choosing. Distinguishing between what is illusion and what is real and true is difficult without someone to share your thinking with. You need a relationship

A simple but good decision. Once I was trying to decide whether to help my mother with yard ■■■■■■■■■■■■■■■■ ■■■ work, or to go with my friends and play. I sat down and thought about how much it would help my mother, who works full time. I also thought of how it would improve my relationship with her. I also decided that Jesus was always helping people in need and would approve of this work. These insights helped me make a good decision.

—MATTHEW, 15

with God, formed through reading the Bible, through prayer, through worship, through meditation. You need the wisdom of older folks who have walked these paths before. And you need the wisdom of a community you can trust.

A Christian community is a good place to discuss your choices with other people—people who also want to live in a way that glorifies God and offer their own gifts for the healing of the world. You don't build this kind of community by stifling your own voice and merely listening, however! In a faithful community, you risk offering your own voice in conversation with others. Even here, however, the path to a wise choice may not be easy and straightforward. Most often choosing is a long and arduous journey of sorting through your own thoughts and desires as you also listen carefully to others on the journey.

Where to start: ASK QUESTIONS!

When youth are trying to figure out how to live, they often hear the adult rationale "That's the way we've always done it." This explanation rarely convinces youth to follow a particular path in their search for truth! What's more, young people usually notice when adults have not thought through their answers. (That's when a lame reply like the "always-done-it" reason appears, isn't it?) The natural questions raised by youth—"But why?" and "Why not?"—are important steps in *anyone's* process of making good decisions. In fact, adults need to hear these questions as they too seek to be fully human and to give glory to God with their lives.

A new eighth-grade Sunday school teacher faced a class of 20 bored, uninterested youth. As the fearful teacher stood in front of the group, one unimpressed boy asked, "Why do we have to attend Sunday school anyway?" The teacher thought he should honor the questions of the class, and he had an idea of where to turn for answers. At his request, the eighth-graders got up and followed him (with increasing nervousness) to the room next door, where the adult Sunday school class was meeting. With their teacher's encouragement, the young people began to question the adults about the history and meaning of Sunday school: Why do we go to Sunday school? Why should we get up early after a late Saturday night, dress up in

Asking questions is a gift that youth can

**What makes *you* angry? sad? frustrated? concerned?
What do you choose to do about it?** ■ ■ ■ ■ ■ ■ ■ ■

uncomfortable clothes that we don't like, sit in a hot stuffy room, and listen to adults tell ancient stories that seem irrelevant to our lives?

At first the adults stuttered, hesitated, and fumbled for answers drawn from their own understanding and experience. But after a while, the adults—some of whom had thought the same questions for years but hadn't said anything—decided not merely to defend Sunday school; they made it clear that they were ready to wrestle with the questions the youth were asking. As it turned out, these questions prompted some adults to examine their own questions about Christian education in their church. This process helped to change the way the people in this congregation practiced their faith. The people decided that the Sunday school wasn't working, so they shifted their education time to Wednesday nights. Every week, people would have dinner and then divide into intergenerational groups for learning. These adults even encouraged youth to ask lots of questions in these groups, because they had learned that asking questions is a gift that youth can offer to adults—indeed, to the world! In turn the youth began to trust the adults in their congregation with their big questions about how to live.

Young people have influenced larger societal changes by asking hard questions about practices and attitudes they believed were wrong. Think of the civil rights movement in this country. Think of the women's movement. Think of the end of apartheid in South Africa. In the face of injustice, young people's questions—"But why?" and "Why not?"—can open the path to change. These movements are discussed more fully in the chapter "Justice." For the purpose of *this* chapter, notice that the young people involved in these social-justice movements had to start by allowing themselves to ask difficult, even scary, questions about their society. They had to make the choice to be troublemakers. They protested. They yelled. They cried. They asked questions that made other people think new thoughts. Slowly changes came about, and justice and freedom increased. Just as young people have raised crucial questions about the world in the past, many continue to do so today—in congregations, at school, where they work, and in public life.

offer to adults—to the world! ■ ■ ■ ■ ■ ■ ■ ■ ■

Finding guidance in traditions

A young man named Ignatius, born into a wealthy Spanish family in 1491, longed only to be a knight and courtier, and he seemed on the way to fulfilling this ambition. But he was badly wounded in battle and then wounded again by the doctors who botched his leg operation. The long period of inactivity during his recuperation forced him to slow down and rethink his life choices. He started reading—his first step into the Christian practice at the heart of this chapter, the practice of *discernment*. As he read about the spiritual strength of young men in the past—like Saint Francis, who renounced his father's wealth for a life of poverty and service—he glimpsed a way to live that he found incredibly inspiring. *The Imitation of Christ* by Thomas à Kempis, a book still read and loved by millions of people today, gave Ignatius an even stronger image of what life with God could be. Taking his faith seriously and seeking to live it fully, he realized, would take more strength, even more heroism, than being a knight. Living his faith fully became his deepest longing.

For seven years, Ignatius sought out experiences and mentors that would propel and encourage him along his chosen path. He gave up what the historians call his "youthful pleasures" and learned to live simply. He spent a lot of time with the Bible. (You can learn about his imaginative method of Bible study in "The Story" chapter.) He traveled to different cities, lived among the poor people, visited the holy sites around Jerusalem, and developed a life of prayer. Finally he decided to go back to school. There he found what he needed most: a community. In 1540 this community became an order within the Catholic Church, the Society of Jesus, known as the Jesuits.

Christian tradition has long honored the importance of *discernment* or deliberate decision making, and the members of various Christian communities have tried to assist one another in making wise choices for centuries. As with Ignatius, the sifting process usually begins with letting go of bad habits that lead to poor choices. Indeed, the earliest records of candidates' preparation for Christian baptism document lengthy periods of *renunciation*—attending to and rooting out negative patterns of behavior in order to make space in their lives to listen to and respond to God. These early Christians also knew that they would need the support of a community as they grew into the new habits and disciplines that would replace the old ones.

Drawing on the experience gained during his own quest for a way to live, Ignatius taught the members of his community to examine their lives each day by asking two simple questions: "Where did you feel most alive?" and "Where did you feel life draining from you?" Even today, thousands of Christians all over the world are in the habit of reflecting prayerfully on these questions each evening. The specific wording of the two questions may vary, but the intention has remained the same through the years— to take time, usually with a companion, to have a close look at where God is at work in your life.

Regularly asking these two questions in a spirit of prayer is known as the *examen*. This process assumes that making good decisions begins with being thankful for the goodness in our lives. *Where do you feel most alive today?* In what seem insignificant moments, observations, objects—the simplest of food, the touch of a friend, the shimmering of the sky, the fragrance of a burning candle—we may see God breaking through to us with abundant life. Such simple pleasures can offer great delight if we make it a habit to notice them. The second question prompts those who do the *examen* to take note of more painful experiences by reflecting on whatever may be weighing them down and blocking their communion with God and others. Ignatius taught people, through steady, faithful use of these questions, to listen to their own deep desires, not merely to what others might tell them to want.

Other Christian communities have adopted specific ways of practicing Christian discernment. Ever since the 17th century, members of the Society of Friends (Quakers) have taken time to sit together in silence as a way of listening to their hearts in light of God's calling. When Quakers face a choice, they meet together to discern the spirit of the gathered community. They believe that wise choices are not the result of heated debates followed by voting "yea" or "nay" on an issue, with one side's winning and the other side's losing. Rather, a Quaker meeting begins in silence and builds toward *consensus*—a sense of common purpose—by persuasive speaking and attentive listening, interwoven with periods of silent reflection. Friends who are not in complete agreement may always "stand aside" from an emerging consensus. Yet if anyone at the meeting "stands against," the decision is postponed until another day.

In our own time, groups of Latin American Christians known as "base communities" have contributed to our understanding of how to make good choices. These communities gather regularly to pray, study the Bible, and discuss how they are called to be involved in the loving, challenging life of God. They pay close attention to the poverty, injustice, and suffering all around them, and they ask what the good news of Jesus means for them, right in their own barrios and villages. Often their practice of discernment leads them to the practice of seeking justice. Many people have learned to read in these communities, because they wanted to read the Bible for themselves and also to participate in movements for political and economic justice. Their example encourages North American Christians also to listen to our own hearts and to God's Word as we examine the poverty, injustice, and suffering of the world. Do you ever think about the people who make the clothes you buy at the Gap or Wal-Mart? Do you ever wonder if they have enough to eat? Or if they get paid well enough to feed their families? Or if they have toilet breaks? The Latin American base communities have taught us to ask such questions and to understand how our everyday choices impact other people all over the world.

All these discerners, from the early Christians to the present day, teach us that *traveling companions make a difference* on our journey into Life with a capital *L*. Others who are on the same journey can help us stay on the right path. Each of us needs to have friends who become our community of faith, people whose daily lives are guided by their openness to God. Some members of this community may be sitting next to us in church, while others lived centuries ago.

Choosing a way to live may take years. Without other people to support you, the journey can feel terribly lonely. With every looming decision, you feel like you're standing by yourself at the proverbial fork in the road. Within the community that has Jesus at its heart, you're not standing on

■■■■■■■■■■■
For what moment today am I most grateful? For what moment today am I least grateful? . . . When did I feel most alive today? When did I most feel life draining out of me?

—The Ignatian Examen
from *Sleeping with Bread*

Quaker Clearness Committee ■ ■ ■ ■ ■ ■ ■ ■ ■ ■ ■ ■

Quaker tradition invites anyone seeking to make good decisions to call together a small support group of church members and friends. This support group is called a *clearness committee*. The committee meeting begins and ends with silence, maintaining a spirit of openness and prayerful waiting. The members of the committee simply ask questions of the person seeking clarity to help surface issues, concerns, and understandings. The clearness committee does not give advice or try to solve the person's problems but focuses instead on the person seeking clearness. The intent is to lead seekers, through their own answers and considerations, to a conclusion affirmed by all committee members. Quakers say that through this discernment process, "way will open." □ □ □ □ □ □ □ □ □ □ □ □ □

the road alone but are held up on the shoulders of other people who are on the same journey, who know your story and the stories of God, and who desire, for you and for themselves, a life that is fully, truly alive.

Learning to choose well

If we want to live well, we need to learn the slow, deliberate practice of discerning between helpful and harmful choices. Here are a few ideas about how to make good choices—some of them developed long ago and some of them the contributions of youth who are making good decisions today. This list may not be complete, but it offers worthwhile guidance when you must make one of the complicated choices confronting young people today.

1. **Slow down.** Never make important decisions in a rush.
2. **Determine what's really happening.** Attempt to describe the situation fully and clearly in writing or in conversation with a friend.
3. **Find someone to talk to.** Seek out a friend, parent, teacher, or expert who can give alternative perspectives on the problem you face and help you identify several possible solutions. Seek support from your faith community—your pastor or youth minister, a small group of faith friends, or one or two older members of a warm congregation that wishes for your best.

4. **List the options that are open to you.** What are the benefits of each option? What are the risks? Whom will it hurt? Whom will it help?
5. **Think about each option.** Pray about it. Which feels the best in your soul, in your body, in your mind? Which engages your strength? Which makes you feel like the life is draining from you?
6. **Imagine what Jesus** would do, think, say, or feel if he were facing your decision.
7. **Decide** what *you* will do. But . . .
8. **Take some time before you act on your decision.** Before you act, reflect on the decision again—and again and again if you or your discernment community thinks you should.

The value of these steps is pretty clear when it comes to a major decision, like Carmen's decision about what to do after high school. At first glance, however, the steps probably seem less relevant to the smaller decisions Carmen and Brad make every day—which shoes to wear, which parking place to take, what to say to the homeless man on the corner, whether to go to the mall with friends—or even whether to spray paint a wall. It's true that everyday decisions like these may not require going through every single step. But that does not mean that the Christian practice of discernment matters only in BIG things. When we have thought and prayed and discussed big decisions this carefully, discernment becomes a part of the way we live. Ultimately these steps for paying attention to God and to our lives can become habits that influence even the small decisions we make every day, because we have come to know ourselves at a deep level and to realize that all our thoughts and actions take place in the presence of God. At that point, we are *really* out of the cage of other people's desires for us and fully, truly alive, so that our lives can glorify God and enable us to contribute our own unique gifts to the healing of the world.

Getting into the habit of choosing well

As any musician or athlete will tell you, bad habits are the worst enemy of good play. These must be rooted out, while good habits are being instilled. For example, Tiger Woods, the youngest master golfer ever, has spent thousands of hours refining his technique, removing the flaws in his swing.

In golf, every little twist, twitch, or wiggle affects the direction of the ball. Tiger could undoubtedly hit the ball without this kind of refinement, but for the control he desires, he must be on guard against any slight arm or leg movement that might pull the ball in the wrong direction. Some golfers spend a lifetime trying to figure out how to overcome these movements. In America, where we are so used to getting what we desire immediately—fast food, 100-plus cable channels, supersonic air travel, and more—we tend to ignore this kind of long, steady attention to detail. Slow, deliberate process—the kind that Tiger employs in his practice sessions—generates the best results. This deliberate, careful approach offers still more: It clears a space within which we can experience life more fully. For Tiger Woods, this careful practice leads to the sheer delight of playing golf simply for its own sake.

Similarly, there is something delightful about inviting God into our decisions and exploring our lives in God's presence. There is something delightful about using our hearts, minds, souls, and strength in the midst of a problem. In the midst of a dilemma we may discover or reaffirm our gifts, hopes, commitments, and relationships.

The Christian practice of discernment would be helpful to Brad as he stands paralyzed by doubt in front of a clean supermarket wall and to Carmen as she makes vocational decisions within the complexities of her family situation. This practice would encourage them to slow down, to seek support, and to look beyond their impulses. This practice would encourage them to pray for God's guidance and also to have some truthful conversations with friends who share their faith. By discerning deliberately, they probably would not only make a wise decision but also find themselves reflecting on how their lives might glorify God and become gifts of healing for the world. ■

▌▌▌Friends

You know those people who are nice to everyone, even to the unpopular kids? Maybe they are a model for how Jesus wants us to treat people. In this chapter we talk about people who purposely show Christ's love in the way they treat others and include different kinds of friends within their group. One of the ways God shows his love for us is by giving us the ability to be a good Christian friend. So enjoy!

■■■■■■■■■■■■■■■■ —**Katie Lytch, 15**

In a memorable scene from the movie *Remember the Titans*, the high-school football team basks in the golden glow of an upset victory over its rival. Gerry, the team captain, is surrounded by the popular crowd at the high school. They invite him to a party—a party for white students only. Suddenly he has a tough choice to make. Should he get into a flashy car with this group, which includes his girlfriend? Or should he celebrate with a smaller group of his teammates, including his new best friend, who is African-American?

This movie is based on the true story of racial tensions surrounding the integration of a suburban Washington, D.C., high school in 1971. But Gerry could face the same choice in thousands of other high schools today: Should he go with the popular crowd or be true to his friends?

Being popular vs. being a good friend

Everyone wants to be popular, right? Or do they? Gerry was popular. At his moment of decision, however, he realized that being popular was not necessarily the same thing as being a good friend.

Being popular implies that a large number of people view you as someone they want to hang out with. Being a good friend means being loyal, not betraying confidences, and listening when someone is struggling with a problem. Some people are both, but usually, being a really good friend suggests you put more of your time into fewer relationships. We all want to *have* good friends. But are we always ready to *be* good friends? What if being a good friend to one person gets in the way of being popular with many others?

Some people are so eager to be popular that they don't stop to think about what friendship actually means. They may insincerely flatter in order to win the approval of the "in group." They may try to stir up rivalries between friends, hoping to divide them and take one of the friends for themselves. They may even resort to cruel pranks they think will enhance their popularity. For example, one boy announced to his entire Spanish class that another boy had a crush on the teacher. The first boy wouldn't stop teasing, even when it became obvious that the other was *not* taking it as a joke. The boy doing the teasing tried to elevate himself in the eyes of a certain group at someone else's expense. But his behavior did not make *anybody* eager to hang out with him.

Chris transferred into a new school in his senior year. He didn't try to force his way into any particular group. He just began to make friends with the other students in his classes and joined some after-school activities. Soon his new friends started including him in larger gatherings. By the end of the year, he had quietly built up a network of friends that crossed many of the social groups in the school. His primary group of friends was composed of student council members and people from a Bible study that met at a friend's church. But his circle also included Muslims, friends of various races, and people who lived in much less affluent neighborhoods than his suburban subdivision. His friends' parents liked Chris too. Once a mom even asked him to talk to her younger son about self-respect, because she suspected the boy was smoking pot; she trusted Chris to advise him.

What attracted people to Chris as a friend was his sincere caring for others. Chris conveyed a sense of well-wishing in the way he talked to people. Because he felt loved by God and was at peace with himself, others felt peace and acceptance when they were with him. Chris cared about people; he didn't just use them and then drop them when he became popular. It was more important to him to *be* a friend than to *have* friends. Good friends, he knew, cannot be collected like baseball cards.

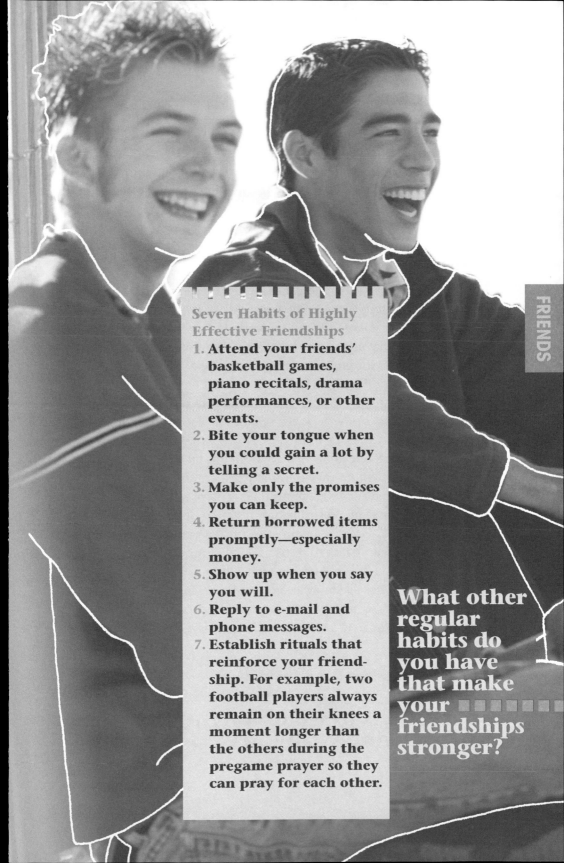

Seven Habits of Highly Effective Friendships

1. Attend your friends' basketball games, piano recitals, drama performances, or other events.
2. Bite your tongue when you could gain a lot by telling a secret.
3. Make only the promises you can keep.
4. Return borrowed items promptly—especially money.
5. Show up when you say you will.
6. Reply to e-mail and phone messages.
7. Establish rituals that reinforce your friendship. For example, two football players always remain on their knees a moment longer than the others during the pregame prayer so they can pray for each other.

What other regular habits do you have that make your ■ ■ ■ ■ ■ ■ friendships stronger?

Moving to a new school and making new friends are not easy. Chris's attitude made a difference. He realized that being "most popular" in the senior class yearbook is not what matters. What matters is relationships. God created Chris to be in relationships with others, and Chris knew that he wanted to be in relationships that were mutual, enjoyable, and supportive. He figured that his classmates probably wanted the same kind of relationships. God gave Chris—and everyone else—the capacity for friendship.

Learning friendship skills

Being a friend, unlike being popular, is a skill you can work at with a reasonable expectation of success. The first mark of good friendship is *having sincere respect for someone*. When you approach being a friend as doing the person a favor, that person feels humiliated. Consider Paola, an exchange student from Brazil. She grew resentful when people in this country took her places and bought her lots of American stuff but never showed any interest in her personally. At first she enjoyed the trips to the mall. But an empty feeling grew inside her when no one asked to see the photographs of her home country that she wanted to show them. Paola felt like a charity case, not a friend. She knew that good friends take the trouble to find qualities in each other that they genuinely respect and admire.

The second mark of good friendship is *developing a balance of give and take*. Have you ever seen a relationship in which one person seemed to do all the giving? This might be fine for limited periods, but over time the giving should flow in both directions. A relationship can be out of balance when one friend does not give enough. On the other hand, one friend may give and give while feeling awkward about receiving anything in return. An incident before a recent party demonstrates good giving *and* good receiving. One girl was planning a surprise birthday party. A friend who would

■■■■■■■■■■■■■■■■■■■■■■■■■■■■

I believe having a strong relationship with God is based on having a strong relationship with Christian friends.

—BRYAN, 14

Love is patient; love is kind; love is not envious or boastful or arrogant or rude. It does not insist on its own way; it is not irritable or resentful; it does not rejoice in wrongdoing, but rejoices in the truth. It bears all things, believes all things, hopes all things, endures all things. Love never ends.

■ ■ ■ ■ ■ ■ —1 CORINTHIANS 13:4-8*a* ■ ■ ■ ■ ■ ■

not be able to attend offered some paper plates and napkins for the party. Although the girl throwing the party thought these plates were too plain, she received them graciously, thus allowing her friend the pleasure of giving. Small gestures like this one add up over time to habits that sustain excellent friendships.

A third mark of good friendship is *being honest.* Friends who are honest with each other know they are in a relationship they can trust. Friends can relax together because each one is confident that the other person isn't pretending to be a friend just to have someone to hang out with. Knowing that the person you are with is sharing his or her true thoughts and emotions feels good and encourages you to be honestly yourself in return.

Loving one another

When Christians talk about relationships, we often use the word *love,* as in "love your neighbor as yourself." We don't typically use this word to describe our friendships, however. If we had a better sense of what *love* means, maybe we would. In the Christian tradition, *love* is part of every relationship, but it does not always manifest itself in the same form. Over the centuries, Christian thinkers have drawn on the ancient writings of both the New Testament and non-Christian philosophers to identify four main forms of love. Today they are still known by the Greek names they acquired in the ancient world. Thinking about how these types of love shape our different friendships can increase our understanding of ourselves and our relationships.

Storge is family love, the natural affection that exists (or ought to exist) between parents and children, between grandparents and grandchildren.

Philia is the primary, basic form of friendship love. It is characterized by the qualities of good friendship we've been discussing—mutual respect, balanced give-and-take, and honesty. All true friendships are based on *philia*.

Eros is romantic love, a strong body-and-soul attraction to another person. This kind of love generally focuses on one person in particular, at least for a while. The passions produced by *eros* can be overwhelming. "Keeping the fire in the fireplace," as my camp counselor used to say, can be a real challenge! When *eros* develops between friends, it is important to keep *philia* strong as well, so that mutual respect, balanced give-and-take, and honesty can help to manage *erotic* feelings. (The word *erotic* comes from *eros*.) The introduction of *eros* love in a friendship can change the friendship dramatically. The shift to *eros* love is a boundary that some friends make a conscious choice not to cross. Reading the "Bodies" chapter in this book may help you consider what physical boundaries could define a worthy way to live when *eros* enters a friendship.

QUESTION: I've never had a date. Am I weird?

ANSWER: No. A lot of people don't date until they get through high school. In fact, being older when you start to date may help you to handle it better.

At times, being a friend involves a fourth kind of love, a love that goes beyond *storge*, *philia*, and *eros*, a love that leads to extraordinary effort and even self-sacrifice. *Agape* is the Greek word for this special kind of love, the kind of love God shows. *Agape* enables you to love and care for another without regard for being loved and cared for in return. This kind of love might lead you to let go of a grudge against a friend for hurting you—even if the friend never apologizes. Or *agape* might enable you to stand with a friend when the friend is humiliated—even when taking that stand is no benefit to you. Or *agape* might give you the strength to lovingly confront a friend using alcohol or drugs destructively. Sometimes showing *agape* love forces you to risk losing a friend.

Friendship can be risky. When friends need our *agape* love, we need to ask God for the strength to respond. The support of a community that has Jesus at its heart is also important at such times. Jesus, the ultimate role

Friendship is one of the most important things in my life, second only to my faith. I am blessed with incredible friends, but my best friend means more to me than any other. We are sisters in Christ.

—MIRANDA, 17

model of *agape* love, gave himself completely, even to the point of dying on the cross.

A Fellowship of Christian Athletes group demonstrated *agape* love when a member got pregnant. Instead of shunning Whitney and Kevin, the FCA decided to embrace this couple and show their support for them. "We just opened our arms wide to them," one member told me. "Some kids ridiculed us, but we said, 'We all make mistakes. God forgives us. We are practicing forgiveness for our friends.'" (See the "Forgiveness" chapter.)

When friendships change

Jennifer felt hurt when her longtime friend, Sonia, dropped her shortly after they started high school. When Jennifer, who is white, asked Sonia, who is African-American, why she never returned her calls anymore, Sonia said it was because Jennifer's ancestors were probably slave owners. Jennifer thought Sonia was unfair to blame her for her ancestors' wrongdoing. But she reasoned that being a friend to Sonia in this situation required her to respect Sonia's need for space.

Did Sonia do the right thing? Sonia still liked Jennifer, but she needed to be with others who shared her desire to explore African-American identity. How does the decision Sonia faced compare with the decision Gerry faced in *Remember the Titans*? It is a rare privilege when you can have an honest conversation about race among friends of different races. Maybe an honest discussion between Sonia and Jennifer would have helped them to understand each other's point of view.

The image of God as "Father, Son, and Holy Spirit" (the Trinity) shows us that God's own life is a life of relationship.

There are times and reasons for giving space in friendships. Sometimes we even need to let friendships end. Brenda realized it was time to let go of certain friendships during her sophomore year in high school. She was doing very well in her classes, and some of her friends started to make fun of her and accuse her of acting uppity. After taking an honest look at herself and them, she felt that the problem was not her behavior but their jealousy of her grades. Since she was unwilling to let up on her schoolwork just to please them, she began calling some of the other students in her class on weekends.

FRIENDS

I don't think we need to worry when young people choose to sit with people like themselves, with whom they may share common experiences and interests. When those groups are racially similar, we get nervous because it reminds us of the imposed segregation of the past, but in fact connecting with people like yourself can be an important part of identity development. **We should also work to provide opportunities for young people to connect across lines of difference, however.**

—BEVERLY DANIEL TATUM,
Why Are All the Black Kids Sitting Together in the Cafeteria?

An ebb and flow in your friendships over time is normal. Few high-school seniors remain tight with the same group of friends they had during their freshman year. One typical change in high-school friendships occurs when all-girl and all-boy groups shift into mixed groups. As you or some of your friends start to date, your group may undergo major changes. Such changes can be hard on you, especially if you feel that some friends are losing interest in being with you.

Sometimes you may feel so bruised by friendships that aren't going the way you'd hoped that you wonder whether to go it alone. You may feel like retreating to the couch in front of the television, or you may try to avoid the rejection of face-to-face encounters by having most of your chats online. Having some downtime, away from social pressures, might be a welcome relief for a while. But shutting yourself off from social interaction for days or weeks at a time will only make you more lonely and sad. An important part of your life will be missing.

God and friendship

God built a need for relationships right into human beings. Shortly after creating the first person, the Genesis story says, God realized that it was not going to work for this one person to be all alone. So God set about creating companions. First God made animals and birds, bringing them to the person to name. But not one of them was a suitable "helper and partner"— until God made another human being (see Genesis 2). Companions cheer us in our loneliness by sharing life with us. Think about walking down the hall between classes. What a difference in your day a wave from a passing friend can make.

Through friendships, God teaches us to love our neighbors, ourselves, and God. We learn to love our neighbors as we put ourselves in other people's shoes and care deeply about how they experience life. We learn to love ourselves as a friend listens to our hopes and dreams and doesn't laugh at us. And we also learn to love God through our friendships.

Two boys learned how friendship teaches us love of God when they got lost on a wilderness trip in Oregon. One boy thought his life might be over, but the other—a good friend—assured him that they were safe with God in whatever happened because God would walk with them even in the valley of the shadow of death (see Psalm 23). Because the first boy trusted his friend, he was able to remain calm and to trust God as well. His confidence in God has stayed with him long after the two survived their ordeal.

Having friends is so basic to the way God created human beings that even Jesus sought out friends. Instead of going around Palestine on his own to perform miracles, heal the sick, and teach about the kingdom of God, Jesus called twelve friends to join him in his ministry. He relied on three friends in particular—Peter, James, and John. He asked these friends to come with him at crucial times in his life, such as when he met Moses and Elijah on a mountain (see Mark 9:2-10) and when he prayed in the garden of Gethsemane on the night before he died (see Mark 14:32-42). Jesus' choice to include a circle of friends in his ministry demonstrates how God wants us to conduct our lives.

A clique vs. a circle of friends

In the opening scene of the movie *10 Things I Hate About You*, a new boy is taken around the high school and oriented to the different social groups. His guide points out the the Beautiful People ("unless they talk first, don't bother"), the Coffee Kids ("they're very edgy—don't make any sudden movements"), the Cowboys ("the closest they've come to a cow is McDonald's"), the Future M.B.A.s ("all Ivy League–accepted—yuppie greed is back"), and finally the Don't-Even-Think-About-It group (which includes the most desirable girl to date).

While this portrayal of high-school cliques may be exaggerated for the sake of humor, most teenagers can readily identify different groups

. . . the Coffee Kids ("they're very edgy—
don't make any sudden movements")

in their high school. Seven high-school freshmen who go to six different schools in our city recently came up with a list of 41 cliques! Some cliques they named were common to more than one school (like "the smart people" and "the jocks"), while others were unique (like "the anorexics" and "the grunge skaters"). Each group claimed its own special place in the cafeteria. I bet you can name the cliques in your high school too.

Clique is a negative term implying snobbery and exclusiveness. But it is normal and healthy to establish friendships with particular people in regular and stable ways so that a circle of friends develops. You may enjoy the same activities as certain other people or simply like spending time with them. As part of your loyalty to one another, you establish informal understandings about who is in your circle. A dependable circle of friends can give you a secure feeling. Yet by creating an "inside" of the circle, you automatically create an "outside." This divide between "in" and "out" is the tricky part.

Jesus had twelve friends who formed a definite circle. Yet he also had good friends besides these twelve disciples, including Mary, Martha, and their brother, Lazarus. He cared so much for them that he wept when Lazarus died (see John 11:17-44). And Jesus' friendships also extended beyond the people who were like him. In fact, he associated with those who were shunned—tax collectors, sinners, and groups that were hated, such as the Samaritans. Jesus' circle of friends was an ever-growing, welcoming circle.

What is your circle of friends like? Is it open and welcoming, or is it enclosed by high walls with a border guard to check the credentials of anyone who wants in? Does your circle include friends from another culture? race? age-group? economic level? Think about how you could influence your friendship circle to welcome different kinds of newcomers.

Spiritual friends

Another kind of friendship is the *spiritual friendship*. A spiritual friendship includes not two persons but three. These friendships help two people grow closer not only to each other but also to God.

Some spiritual friends are *companions*. (Remember learning in the "Food" chapter that *companions* means "those who share bread"?) These folks who share your faith in a regular, familiar way—perhaps family members and people who go to the same church you attend. Companions practice their faith together, in worship and in daily life.

Which of your friends match these descriptions?
1. **Companions**
2. **Mentors**
3. **Soul friends**
4. **Famous friends**
5. **Kindred spirits**

Other spiritual friends are *mentors,* older, wiser friends who guide you in exploring your relationship with God. One boy I know has found a good mentor in his wrestling coach, who also happens to belong to his church. They meet for breakfast every Sunday morning to talk about their faith.

Soul friends are people around your own age with whom you can share lots of personal stuff. You confide in them about your deepest joys, struggles, and longings.

Famous friends are those you don't know personally but who show you a way to live through their teaching, music, or example. Martin Luther King Jr., Saint Francis of Assisi, and Dorothy Day are famous people who have inspired many teens in this way.

Finally there are *kindred spirits*. These friends have religious beliefs different from yours, or perhaps they don't consider themselves religious. Even so, you find talking with these friends about important issues gives you new insights about God and your life.

When I was a teen, I had many spiritual companions in my church and school, but I looked for soul friends and mentors among the friends I had at summer camp in another state. During the school year, my camp friends and I kept in touch through letters and through prayers for each other. I admired my camp counselors and wanted to grow up to be just like them in their commitment to God. As an adult, I have never attended any of my high-school reunions in New Jersey, but I do return to the camp in New Hampshire where I grew close to God and to many spiritual friends.

Spiritual friendships are wonderful, but even these friendships can face difficulties. On a church choir tour, Cheri discovered that three of the boys were breaking the covenant they had written for their trip by drinking alcohol. She knew these guys well; they were her friends. Yet she also knew their behavior could jeopardize the safety of the group, and she felt hurt by their disregard for the group's covenant. With a heavy heart, Cheri realized what it would take to be a good friend to these boys and to her group. She told the adult leaders what she had seen. The leaders then called a meeting, and the adults and teens together decided that the boys would be sent home.

But that wasn't the end of the story. During the remainder of the trip, Cheri and the other choir members called the boys often, just to keep in touch. The boys sensed that those they had hurt still cared for them. And so when the church bus pulled into the parking lot at the end of the trip, the three boys were waiting to meet it. Cheri was overjoyed. Tears flowed as they sang their final concert together back in their home church.

On the night before he died, Jesus shared a meal with his disciples. "This is my commandment, that you love one another as I have loved you," he said. "No longer do I call you servants," he told them, "but I have called you friends" (John 15:12, 15, paraphrase). He invited them to share his relationship with God and the Holy Spirit, and he showed them that being his friend included being good friends to one another. The circle of people with Jesus at its heart—the people called Christians—has been making friends ever since, within the circle and beyond the circle, reaching into a wide world of human beings, each one unique but each created by God to be in relationships. ■

⦀Welcome

We usually think of welcoming as greeting someone we know with hospitality. In these significant years of our lives, it means a lot more; it means opening our hearts to all people and accepting them as equal children of God. I welcome you into our chapter, and I hope you find the strength to pursue this promising practice. ▪ ▪ ▪ ▪ ▪ ▪ ▪

—**Kaitlyn Filar, 16**

WELCOME

Your name is Garrett. You're president of your school's Young Republicans. Your hero is Ronald Reagan, and you're addicted to C-SPAN.

Your name is Chrissi. You're the head cheerleader. You'd like to be Sarah Michelle Gellar, and you can't get enough of *Dawson's Creek*.

Your name is Dale. You're a World Wrestling Federation fan. The Rock is the best, and you never miss *Thursday Night Smackdown*.

You're Summer, an environmental activist who loves whales. You're Joel, and you love Jesus. You're Crystal, a New Age devotee whose hero is the goddess within.

You're a jock, a bookworm, a computer geek. A Trekkie, a preppy, a rapper, a Goth. Real people? No. Stereotypes? Of course.

The lunch-table game

Kaitlyn, my niece and writing partner, and I were looking for a creative way to explore the Christian practice of "welcoming" with the other authors of this book. Kaitlyn suggested playing "the lunch-table game." Sitting in her family's boat in the middle of North Carolina's Lake Norman, Kaitlyn and I spent a wonderful spring afternoon together inventing the names and identities above for the game. The stereotypes came easily. We were surprised at how readily we judged and laughed at people who were only figments of our imaginations.

A few weeks later, when all the authors gathered in Montreat, North Carolina, we were even more surprised by what the game revealed. To begin, we gave everyone a slip of paper with a name, an identity, a hero, and a favorite TV show written on it. "Picture yourself in a new high school, on the first day of school, at lunchtime. Roam around the lunchroom and form yourselves into lunch tables of six people each," we instructed. Folks with similar interests eventually found one another, and some unexpected alliances were formed. But some people never found a place to sit.

When the game was over, the participants talked animatedly: "Boy, that took me right back to high school, to that queasy feeling in the pit of my stomach," one adult said. "And lunch period was the worst. I was afraid I would never have any friends to sit with." Other adults nodded in agreement.

"I really felt the pressure to sit with someone—anyone!—but I didn't want to sit at the losers' table and be branded a loser myself," one of the teens admitted. "So I spent the whole time trying to get cool folks to like me, even when it meant concealing my true identity."

The surprise to us was *everyone's* fear of being a loser, right down to the popular football quarterback and the perky head cheerleader. Everyone worried about fitting in and being accepted. And no one in our pretend lunchroom ever felt "at home."

Feeling "at home"

The word *home* means different things to different people. For some of us, *home* signifies a place of security and comfort, a place where we are accepted just as we are. For others, *home* is not a comforting image and may even represent a place filled with threat and judgment. Some people are homeless because they have no physical shelter. Others may dwell in a house, yet they do not feel that it is a "home." Whatever our associations with the word, we all long to feel "at home"—to find shelter in friendships

Think about a time when you were not welcomed at school, on a sports team, at a party, in the cafeteria, or elsewhere. ■■■■■■■■■■■■■■■■■■■ How did you feel?

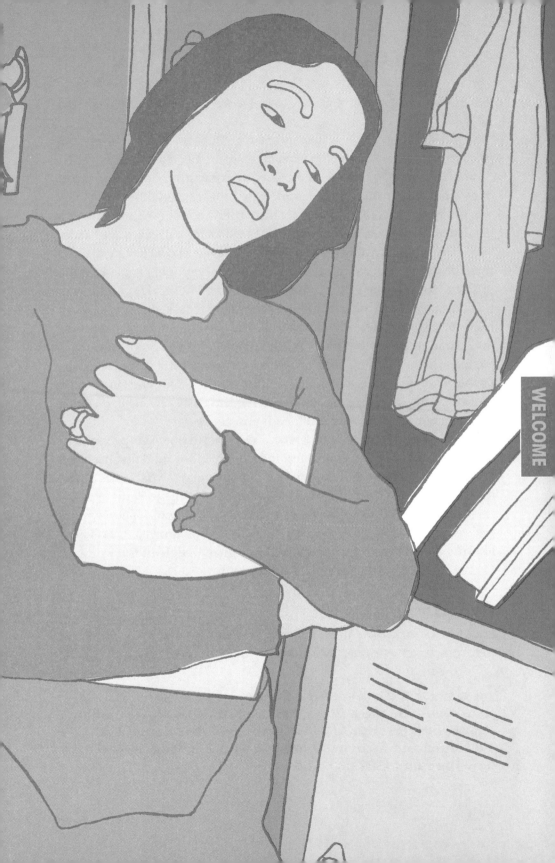

WELCOME

that allow us truly to be ourselves, to feel *welcomed*, to have a place at the table.

Most of us find this security by seeking out people like ourselves, people who seem "safe." High-school lunch tables usually reflect this tendency, divided by gender, race, athletic prowess, or extracurricular interests. Most of us repeat that pattern in our work, worship, and social lives as adults. The entire world looks like one gigantic high-school lunchroom—rich divided from poor, black from white, able-bodied from disabled, and so on.

This is not the world Jesus envisioned. The Son of God never embraced these divisions, never accepted the idea that only special people earn the privilege to sit at the table. Quite the contrary. The stories of Jesus present an extensive record of the kind of company Jesus kept. Sure, he spent time with scholars and religious leaders—the powerful and popular people of his time. But when he chose his first disciples and friends, he called simple fishermen. He hung out with foreigners, prostitutes, beggars, lepers, people who were lame and blind—all sorts of sick people and sinners and outcasts. Jesus also broke the cultural rules of his day by eating and talking with women, considering them friends and equals.

Jesus could relate to outsiders because he was a homeless person himself. He started life in an animal feeding trough and wound up on a cross. He was born a refugee and executed a criminal—hardly what you'd expect for the Son of God. But that was the point. God came to earth as a vulnerable, poor child to let us know that God understands all our sorrows and pains, all our loneliness and insecurities. Jesus showed us how profoundly God loves all the wounded, frightened people of the world. In God's home, everyone has a place at the table.

Welcome home

Jesus has a special place in his heart for homeless people. One of his most well-known stories features two brothers who both become homeless (Luke

What if we invented a TV show called *Anti-Survivor?* Jesus would be the host. And instead of people being voted out of the tribe, they'd be voted in. Everybody would be welcomed and included. Everyone would belong. Isn't that how life should be?

In the Middle Eastern culture of Jesus' day, it was disgraceful for an elderly man to run, not to mention running to embrace a disobedient son who by law deserved severe punishment. ■ ■ ■ ■ ■ ■ ■ ■ ■ ■

15:11-32). The younger brother leaves home willingly; the older brother feels displaced—he no longer feels "at home." The younger son takes his inheritance in cash, travels to a distant country, and soon squanders all his money in reckless living. With no place left to call home, this young man experiences a wake-up call one day: While feeding pigs, he wishes he could fill his belly with some of their slop. *Time to go back to Dad, apologize for my behavior, and beg him to let me work on the farm as a hired hand,* he reasons to himself.

As the younger son approaches what used to be his home, the neighbors are probably wagging their heads. "What a disgrace!" they mutter, wondering what the father will do with this no-account fellow. But then an unbelievable thing happens. While the young man stumbles down the road rehearsing his apology speech, the father sees him coming and *runs* with arms wide open to embrace his returning son. The giddy father even announces he will host a special feast to celebrate the younger son's homecoming. Party time!

You can imagine who is not too thrilled about all the festivities! The older son has always respected his father and has worked hard on the farm for many years. Even though he is now due to inherit his father's estate, the older son resents his younger brother's enthusiastic welcome back home. He stands outside the house and fumes. He will not go in and celebrate this worthless scoundrel's return. Any place that welcomes his brother no longer feels like home to him.

That's where the story ends: The younger son feels welcomed back home; the older son feels homeless; the patient father encourages the older son to forgive and embrace his repentant brother. Opening our hearts to strangers is a challenge. Perhaps a bigger challenge is opening our hearts to friends and relatives who have become strangers to us because of their actions or beliefs. What will the older son do? Will he join his father in receiving the younger son back home? Or will he stand outside the house to his last day, still angry and resentful?

Finding a place to belong

I grew up in Hershey, Pennsylvania—"Chocolatetown, U.S.A."—raised in the First United Methodist Church on Chocolate Avenue, where the street-lights have domes in the shape of Hershey's Kisses. Hershey was a great place to be a kid. The air often smelled like candy. The chocolate factory, a few blocks from my home, gave out free samples, and my sisters and I had a strategy for taking several tours in a day and coming home with a fistful. We'd spend summer days riding the carousel and roller coaster in our town's amusement park, then stop on the way home at the drugstore on the corner of Chocolate and Cocoa Avenues for chocolate Cokes.

An upper-middle-class white kid in a wealthy town, I attended the best schools in the area. The "script" for me (we all have one, based on such factors as our skin color, economic class, gender, and education) directed me to grow up to live the same way. But an event happened when I was 13 that changed the script. Dr. Martin Luther King Jr., the great civil rights leader, was assassinated. I sat in my comfortable Hershey living room and watched on TV as people in Harrisburg, 13 miles away, burned parts of the city in response to the tragedy.

That's when I learned that not every child in America grows up in a town with a chocolate factory, an amusement park, four swimming pools, and nine golf courses. That lifestyle of privilege was not the way for me to live. That's when I began to step outside my "comfort zone," going into inner-city Harrisburg as a 14-year-old to volunteer in a church. I didn't understand it then, but I

Go through one day paying close attention to how you act toward others. Are you welcoming to everyone? If not, think about why you act as you do and how you might act differently. ■ ■ ■ ■

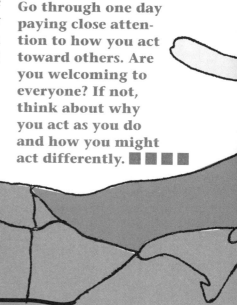

Jesus has a special place in his heart for homeless people.

WELCOME

think I was going where I didn't "belong" in an effort to say that we all belong—in the world and to one another.

That volunteer effort was a small step but the first on a long journey that has taken me to many unexpected places. My life has been richer and far more exciting than if I'd simply followed the predictable script. Looking back 32 years later, I can say I'm grateful for every scary, exhilarating, poignant moment along the way. And though I've been lonely at times, I've never been alone on this journey. A community has always supported me.

As a young adult, I lived for 15 years with Sojourners Community in inner-city Washington, D.C. Sojourners was an intentional Christian community, comprised of people who worshiped together twice a week and lived with one another in several large households, sharing all our money (as parts of the early church did, according to Acts 2:43-47 and Acts 4:32-37). We published a magazine, still in existence, also called *Sojourners*, which focuses on social justice, human rights, simple living, peace, and care for the environment, from a Christian viewpoint.

sojourner:
a temporary
resident

We started several outreach ministries in our low-income neighborhood, including a day-care center, a tutoring program for children, a housing ministry, and a food program.

Community members also volunteered at an overnight shelter for homeless women. One Christmas Eve when I was there, in the middle of the night, two women started arguing. Sheila accused Mary of stealing her coat while she slept. Mary called Sheila a liar, prompting Sheila to call Mary a "no-good-good-for-nothing." Mary responded without hesitation, "Oh yeah? I'm better than you'll ever be. I'm an aristocrat of the highest order—with the Rothschilds on my mother's side and the Three Wise Men on my father's!"

I was moved by Mary's effort to connect herself with one of the wealthiest families in the world—and with the wise gift-bearers at Jesus' birth. Out of her brokenness and powerlessness, Mary was claiming that she was somebody; that she too was a friend of Jesus, a beloved child of God. *That she belonged.*

A place at the table

That night at the shelter, the words of another Mary came to my mind, the song of praise that Jesus' mother sang when she was pregnant and visiting her cousin Elizabeth:

> [God] has scattered the proud in the thoughts of their hearts.
> He has brought down the powerful from their thrones,
>   and lifted up the lowly;
> he has filled the hungry with good things,
>   and sent the rich away empty (Luke 1:51-53).

Mary's son echoed the same refrain in his most famous sermon:

> Blessed are you who are poor,
>   for yours is the kingdom of God.
> Blessed are you who are hungry now,
>   for you will be filled.
> Blessed are you who weep now,
>   for you will laugh (Luke 6:20-21).

Mary's song and Jesus' sermon proclaim an upside-down world indeed—a world in which those who think they've got it made and those who enjoy a lifestyle of privilege suddenly realize, *This is no way to live!* And those with empty hands and hearts full of sadness are embraced by God and given new life. Not a life of *no* needs but a life of needs met. Not a life of *no* tears but a life of tears wiped away. Not a life of *no* hunger but a life of hunger satisfied. That's the way life will be around God's great banquet table, Jesus explained.

The invited guests will be no-shows because they think they've got it made. The banquet interferes with their comfortable lifestyle. Instead, those who know they *need to be filled*—people who are poor, blind, or lame—will take the seats of honor around this table. A popular African-American spiritual calls God's great banquet table "the welcome table." So it is! The table extends God's welcome to everyone who desires to join the feast. And those who are seated already feel blessed and grateful to be there.

Jesus took his teaching about hospitality a step further. Hospitality encompasses more than taking our own place at the welcome table, Jesus said. Hospitality calls us to bring others there too. Indeed, Jesus told us that *he himself* might be one of the very people who need our welcome and our care. And we won't even recognize him because he'll come to us disguised as a stranger!

I learned this lesson about hospitality at the Sojourners Neighborhood Center, where we gave out food every Saturday morning. Each week up to 300 families came for a bag of groceries. Always before opening the line, we volunteers joined hands while Mrs. Mary Glover offered a prayer. Mrs. Glover, a longtime resident of the neighborhood, had first come through the line herself for food. She offered the same prayer every week, starting by thanking God for waking her up that day and for giving her another opportunity to serve. And she always ended it the same way: "We thank you for the feet that are coming through this line for food today and the hands that are giving it out. We know, Lord, that you're coming through this line today, so help us to treat you right. Yes, Lord, help us to treat you right."

"For I was hungry and you gave me food, I was thirsty and you gave me something to drink, I was a stranger and you welcomed me, I was naked and you gave me clothing, I was sick and you took care of me, I was in prison and you visited me." . . . And the king will answer them, "Truly I tell you, just as you did it to one of the least of these who are members of my family, you did it to me." ■■■■■

—Matthew 25:35-36, 40

WELCOME

The people in the line looked like strangers to me, but Mrs. Glover was able to see the face of Jesus in everyone she met. She *lived* Matthew 25:35-36, 40, where Jesus surprises folks by saying that wherever they have met someone in need, they have met him.

But just who are the people who are in need? In high school, they are the new student, the loner, the person with a disability who is teased, the person who suffers under a stereotype based on race or dress or speech. That's the obvious answer. But each one of us is also a person in need. Jesus broke down the walls that separate people into "them" and "us." Each one of us has known what it feels like to be lonely or afraid, to be a stranger in need of welcome. We welcome Jesus when we welcome one another. We honor Jesus when we honor every person we meet.

Guests who become hosts

Hospitality—especially to strangers—has been at the heart of the Jewish and Christian traditions for thousands of years. The early Israelites were reminded often to care for "the sojourner, the widow, and the orphan." The earliest Christians met in one another's homes, sharing generously with one another and people who came to them in need. During the time of slavery in this country, Quakers and other Christians opened their homes as way stations on the Underground Railroad for slaves escaping north to freedom.

In the 1930s—when the Nazis launched a campaign that led to the murder of six million Jewish people in Europe—the small village of Le Chambon, France, harbored and saved the lives of thousands of Jews. Anne Frank, whose diary has become a classic, was harbored for a time by Christian friends. When war was raging in Central America, Christians across this country launched the Sanctuary Movement, opening their homes and churches to shelter refugees fleeing the violence.

Often the people whom we see as recipients of our hospitality in fact become our hosts. I was in the Central American country of Nicaragua in 1983, helping to set up a peace witness in the war zones there. Armed forces known as *contras*, who were supported by our government, were carrying out raids against people in the countryside, injuring and killing many. I went to Nicaragua, along with other Christians, to offer some peaceful and prayerful protection to the people there.

While traveling to the tiny, isolated village of Jalapa, our group received word that *contras* had taken over the road ahead. We stopped and spent the night on the floor of a Baptist church, which we shared with refugee women and children who had fled their mountain homes. Throughout the night, we heard the sounds of gunfire in the distance and crying children up close. We awoke before dawn, ready to move on toward Jalapa. The refugee women had risen even earlier. Already they had stacked firewood in a dome-shaped clay oven outside. They were slapping out tortillas as a glint of sunlight appeared behind the mountains on the eastern horizon.

Those women had fled with their children and little more than the clothes they wore. They didn't know where they would spend the following night or where their next meal would come from. But they invited us—prosperous strangers from a country that was sponsoring a war against them—to partake in their meager breakfast. They shared everything they had with us.

While eating the women's tortillas at dawn, I was reminded how puny my own welcome to people often is, how rarely I share the best of what is mine with others. As I've traveled in many parts of the world, I've been amazed to find that the people who have the least are the most generous, the most gracious and welcoming. All those people have been my teachers. They have taught me a way to live.

With arms wide open

Every person has to decide where to stand in this world. If you claim to follow Jesus, then you need to go where he said you can find him—among the people in need (see Matthew 25:34-40). How you respond today to the lonely or outcast student in your midst helps to shape the patterns and practices that will serve you when you get out into the world beyond high school. When you make welcoming others a part of daily life, you join a long faith tradition marked by bold risks and enormous joy.

The band Creed sings a song called "With Arms Wide Open." The lead singer, Scott Stapp, wrote this song the day he learned he was going to be a father. In the song, he anticipates welcoming his new son "with arms wide open"—naming him, holding him, nurturing him. Stapp sings his hope that his son, having been welcomed in this way, will grow up to

As a teenager in a highly diverse environment, you must learn to tolerate all kinds of people. Welcoming someone is the key to accepting them. Many teenagers end up sacrificing their own beliefs just to belong anywhere where they are accepted. Then these teenagers begin to judge one another harshly. They close their minds to please the group or clique they belong to. As a Christian, I feel it's my duty and privilege to welcome all people as Jesus did. Although at times I catch myself neglecting strangers, I try to recognize this and correct it. This is what all of us need to do as Christians, as teenagers, as humans.

—KAITLYN, 16

greet the world "with arms wide open"—more open, in fact, than Stapp himself has been. It's a wonderful wish: to go through life with a posture of welcome and openness to whatever—and whomever—comes along.

Welcoming isn't always easy. You take a risk when you welcome someone considered unpopular or "different." Your motivation may be misunderstood by the very person you're trying to include. Or people might take advantage of you, demanding too much and "wearing out their welcome." But if a spirit of welcome pervades your life, you can make a difference in the world.

In 1988, I was welcomed to South Africa, at a time when that nation suffered under the stranglehold of racial separation and hatred known as apartheid. Whites controlled the country, while blacks lived in utter poverty. Those who joined the anti-apartheid struggle for freedom were arrested and imprisoned, some killed. I had gone to South Africa as a journalist with *Sojourners* magazine, in an effort to help tell the rest of the world the truth about what was going on there.

Jam-Jam, a young man active in the freedom struggle, welcomed me—a total stranger—at great risk to himself. He had just been released after 10 months in prison, where he had been kept in a cold cell, fed only cornmeal infested with worms, and tortured. He showed me around the black township where he and other blacks were forced to live.

Before long, a *casspir*—an armored personnel carrier—appeared, and eight members of the South African army jumped out and surrounded us, pointing rifles. We were interrogated by an officer of the security police. The officer angrily threatened to put Jam-Jam back into prison because Jam-Jam knew that it was illegal for a white person to be in a black area, yet he was showing me around.

I will never forget what happened next. In response to the threats, Jam-Jam reached calmly into his back pocket and took out his small New Testament. Putting it right up to the face of the angry officer, he said simply, "Sir, I am a Christian." The officer, confronted with the power of the gospel of Jesus Christ, had nothing to say. He let us go.

Today apartheid no longer exists in South Africa. In 1994, Nelson Mandela became that country's first black president—after spending 29 years in prison for his anti-apartheid activities. South Africa has been transformed, in large part because of the courage of faithful Christians like Jam-Jam, who held on to a vision of a South Africa where blacks and whites

WELCOME

could live peacefully, welcoming one another as equals, as people created and loved by the same God. They drew their courage from Jesus Christ, who taught them to love their enemies, who welcomed everyone into his community of followers, who welcomes each of us now.

A welcome-table world

On the night before he died, Jesus gathered his friends around a table and shared his last meal. He broke the bread and shared the cup at a welcome feast, reminding his friends of his deep and sacrificial love for them and for the world. He washed their feet, declaring each of them to be worthy of God's enormous love.

We, like all of Jesus' friends, are truly wonders of God's creation. When we know this to be true of ourselves and of every human being we encounter, then a spirit of welcome guides our path. Then we can move beyond living in a divided "lunch-table world" to living in a "welcome-table world." We can approach life as one gigantic welcome feast and every day as an opportunity to show to the world our deep and abiding love for God and God's beloved children. This is the way I want to live. ■

▌▌▌Forgiveness

You know that feeling of hurt: a numbing ache that makes your heart sore or the pain that feels like boiling molten lava inside your chest, just waiting to erupt at any minute. Many instances and situations can cause hurt, even ones in which you least expect to experience heartache and pain. You may have felt betrayed by a close friend, a parent, or even God. The gospel says that forgiveness is the way to heal the hurt. This chapter explores how hard it is to forgive but also why forgiveness is important and how it can happen. ■ ■ ■ ■ ■

—Judy Kuo, 17

It is a serious thing when a relationship gets broken. Someone you count on to be there for you suddenly isn't there anymore. Someone you trust proves unworthy of your trust. Whenever it happens, however it happens, when a relationship gets broken, your world gets broken too. There is an empty place where someone precious once existed, and injustice where once there was harmony. And in the midst of the world's brokenness, you yourself feel broken too. Depending on the situation and personalities, people respond in many different ways. You may rage in anger, lashing out at others because someone lashed out at you. Or you may weep quietly in despair, going into a shell and avoiding the pain of future relationships. Or both. Sometimes people dwell in that anger or cling to those tears for the rest of their lives.

This chapter is about the Christian practice that makes it possible not to get stuck in the brokenness: forgiveness. It's a hopeful chapter. But like the practice of forgiveness itself, it has to start with a look at the jagged

FORGIVENESS

edges of our lives, the places where relationships do in fact get broken. Places like these:

- You find out your best friend has been saying bad stuff about you behind your back.
- You get dumped by a boyfriend or girlfriend.
- You find out your folks are getting a divorce.
- Your sister dies in a car accident.
- You are ridiculed by a teacher or coach you thought was cool.
- You are laughed at by a group of kids at school.
- Your stepdad molests you.
- Your boss yells at you again for something that wasn't your fault.

Some of these places are more terrifying and harmful than others, but everyone dwells in jagged places at different times in their life.

Real-life stories of broken relationships

Denise's story. I usually get along well with my folks. This past spring they went out of town for the weekend, leaving me behind on my own for the first time. Before they left, I asked them if I could have a few friends over on Saturday night. They said that would be fine. I invited four friends over. The problem is, somehow the word got out that my folks were out of town. Before the evening was over, there were more than 40 teenagers in my house and outside in my yard. There was beer everywhere. The neighbors called the police because of the noise. I was humiliated when the police insisted on calling my parents. They drove home in the middle of the night. When I tried to explain what had happened, they refused to listen and grounded me. Over and over, they said how disappointed in me they were. I was furious. Furious at whatever supposed "friend" passed the word that my parents were away. And furious that my parents put all the blame on me. It was so unfair. I didn't even know half the kids who showed up that night.

Eric's story. My dad left us when I was a little kid, and my mom and sister and I moved in with my grandparents. My grandfather has pretty much been my dad. He was cool even though he was old. I could always talk to him. He came to all my games at school and stuff. Then two years ago my grandfather was diagnosed with cancer. He had a really tough time

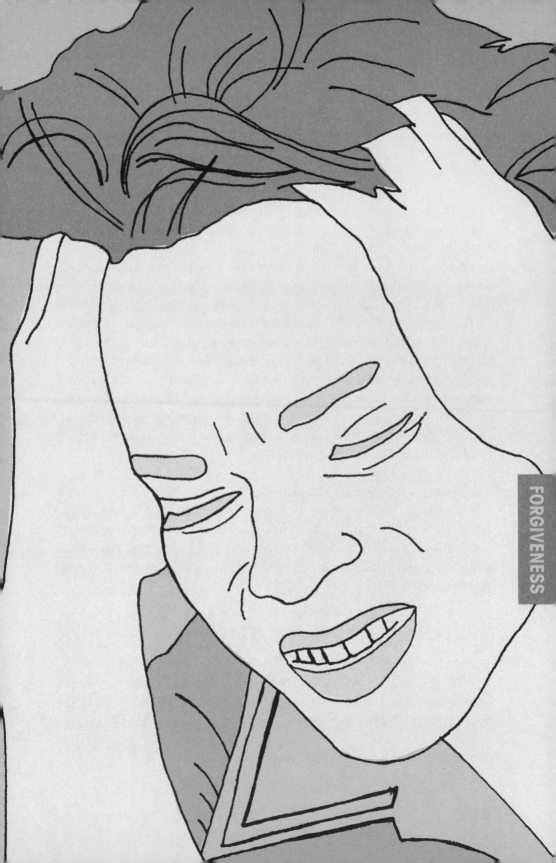

of it. He was in the hospital a lot and went through all this chemotherapy. I prayed and prayed to God to heal my grandfather. But my grandfather died three months ago. He was suffering a lot. Now I don't think there is any God. I mean, why would he let my grandfather die that way? Why wouldn't he listen to my prayers? It hurts my grandmother and mom, but I refuse to go to church now. I didn't even go to my grandfather's funeral.

Michele's story. Hunter and I had been going together for over a year. We were even voted "cutest couple" in our class. Everyone liked Hunter. All my friends kept telling me how lucky I was to have Hunter and what a great guy he was. In our second year of being together, Hunter and I pledged our love for each other, and then Hunter began asking to have sex. I really wanted to wait until I got married, but Hunter would get frustrated. When I told my friends, they all thought we were already "doing it." I mean, I knew I loved Hunter and he loved me. Anyway, one afternoon we did it at his house when no one else was home. It was really beautiful, and it was like we really were in love with each other. We continued to have sex together for a few more weeks, and then something changed. Last month, after almost 18 months of being together, Hunter broke up with me. He said he didn't feel like he was in love with me anymore. I couldn't believe it. I feel so used. I don't know what to do.

For very different reasons, Denise, Eric, and Michele are angry, sad, and confused. And they have a right to these feelings. Important relationships have been broken. Each has experienced the betrayal of a trust. For Denise, it was trust with her parents and friends. For Eric, it was trust with God. And for Michele, it was trust with her former boyfriend Hunter and her friends.

> ■■Then Peter came and said to [Jesus], "Lord, if my brother sins against me, how often should I forgive? As many as seven times?" Jesus said to him, ■■■■■"Not seven times, but I tell you, seventy-seven times."
>
> —MATTHEW 18:21-22

Our need for relationships

We are created for relationship. That means we can't exist on our own. God created us as beings who need to relate to others and to God. Try as we might, we cannot exist on our own.

Can you picture yourself as a hermit in a cave on a deserted island? It might be a nice fantasy when you've had a bad day at school, lost a big fight with your brother, or been grounded by your parents. In fact, though, even folks who aren't very sociable are part of many relationship webs. The family web still exists even when it gets torn. The webs of relationships in a school, a church, or a neighborhood are the same. When the web of relationships is strong and holds you safe, it's wonderful. But that is not always the case. Sometimes the web of relationships gets sticky and closes in around you in an uncomfortable way. At other times, the web unravels, and you feel like you've lost the support of those around you.

We need relationships with other people just as we need air and water, and they bring us much of what is good in our lives. Think of the trusting relationships Denise, Eric, and Michele enjoyed before their trust was broken. How sad if Eric, who had lost his father early in life, had never known the close relationship with his grandfather. How wonderful that Denise cares so deeply about her parents' opinion. Even Michele and Hunter's relationship was a good one for both of them for many months.

But relationships are never risk-free. In fact, they tear easily—though the tears don't always result in complete breaks. Even in strong relationships, people experience misunderstandings. Our very need for relationship is one reason jealousies arise and feelings get hurt. No relationship of any value can grow and deepen without some tensions, and no relationship can continue for long without some conflicts. No human interaction can happen without the possibility of pain, injury, suffering, betrayal, and alienation. The only way to avoid these risks is to head to that cave on the island. The problem with heading to the island is that you would have to break all relationships—not just the ones causing difficulty at the moment—and besides, that island is simply not for sale, even if it is nice to think about buying it occasionally.

Relationships can tear for many reasons. One kind of tear results from selfishness. Selfishness overlooks the valid concerns of someone else. Hunter acted out of selfishness when he pressured Michele to have sex. The kids who turned Denise's gathering of friends into a drunken bash also acted

FORGIVENESS

selfishly. They were not concerned about others, and they were not concerned about what God wants for people. They were concerned about what they wanted. They were stuck on themselves.

Another way of tearing the web turns selfishness inside out: Someone is inappropriately selfless. Michele's behavior provides an example. By failing to be true to her beliefs, she contributed to breaking the trust between Hunter and herself. Michele gave in to Hunter's plan, completely ignoring her own goals and plans for life. Losing one's "self" in a relationship can be a danger.

If Michele allows the bad choice she made in this relationship to become a significant part of her self-image, she could end up feeling unworthy of love in the future. She would then be doing wrong again—this time by discounting her value as a human being—to God, to herself, and to the other people she will love in her life.

Human beings have always had trouble with the intricate, difficult work of relating to one another. We are often selfish. And we often sell ourselves short. Christians have a word for the problem at the root of both forms of brokenness: sin.

Many people today dislike this hard, old-fashioned word and insist that everyone is really good way down deep. That's true in one important sense: God created humanity good (see Genesis 1:27-31). However, an honest look at human history shows how far we can fall from goodness and how often we have fallen and continue to fall away from it (see Romans 3:23). God created us not only good but also free, and people have chosen evil again and again. That choice results in our hurting others. It also means we get hurt by others.

Another look at the three real-life cases

Denise trusted her parents and thought her parents trusted her. In her own opinion, it wasn't her fault that her little gathering of friends got out of hand. However, it is possible that Denise contributed to the problem by being too selfless when lots of people showed up at her house that night. Did she try to stand up to them? Did she seek adult help in getting the situation back to where it should be? Or did she lack the courage to go against the crowd? As for the "friend" who betrayed Denise by spreading word that her parents were away, that sin was one of selfishness. This

The family web still exists even when it gets torn.

When the web of relationships is strong and holds you safe, it's wonderful.

Sometimes the web
of relationships gets sticky
and closes in around you in an
uncomfortable way. At other times
the web unravels, and you feel like you
have lost the support of those around you.

person's act not only tore her relationship with Denise but rippled outward to harm several other relationships as well.

Denise's parents contributed to breaking their relationship with their daughter by jumping to conclusions and not listening to her concerns. They felt she had betrayed their trust and were furious about driving home in the middle of the night from their weekend vacation. (Who can blame them?) Motivated by anger and probably some serious embarrassment—as in, "What will the neighbors think?"—they grounded Denise. The parents perhaps had behaved selfishly when they had decided to go away without making arrangements for Denise's supervision, because it turned out that Denise was not ready to handle a weekend at home on her own. Denise's relationship with her parents is precious to her and to them. How can it be healed?

Eric is angry at God. In Eric's mind, God let him down by allowing his grandfather, whom Eric loved so much, to die an early and miserable death. Getting angry is not a selfish act on Eric's part. It's OK to get angry at God. God can take it. In fact, the Book of Psalms (a book of poems in the Bible) includes vivid expressions of anger against God, and we are invited to join in weeping or shouting or singing these words in our own times of need. Jesus prayed one of these psalms on the cross, crying in agony to God. (Learn more about these psalms and expressing anger and grief to God in the "Grieving" chapter.) So anger, which makes many people uncomfortable, is not wrong, and Eric is not acting selfishly. But Eric may experience even more hurt if he does not seek to move beyond his rage. Right now he is stuck and allowing himself to become further cut off from the web of relationship with God and other people. He needs healing for these relationships.

Michele was betrayed. She loved Hunter as much as she was able, and perhaps Hunter loved her too. But after having sex, Hunter moved on, leaving Michele feeling devastated, betrayed, hurt, and alone. Having sex is an extremely intimate and vulnerable way for two people to be in relationship. Rejection of that intimacy and vulnerability betrays a person at a deeper level than many people can stand. Michele is angry at Hunter, angry at her friends for encouraging her to risk herself with Hunter, and angry at herself. Sometimes she contemplates revenge, but mostly she just feels like trash. These strong emotions will probably cause more tears in her web of relationships both now and in the future, as well as in her relationship with God. How can she find the healing that will allow her to create stronger relationships with God and others?

Ways of coping

When a broken relationship tears you and your world apart, you have two choices for dealing with your pain.

1. You can hold on to that pain and carry it with you until your emotions explode or you collapse from exhaustion.

2. You can seek healing by practicing forgiveness, which will take the weight off your shoulders and help you hand it over to God.

Many people choose the first option. They let the wrong someone inflicted on them or the wrong they inflicted on someone else harden in their clenched fists. They may clearly appear depressed, but other times they may not even realize how much they are hurting. Their pain continues to grow because those clenched fists can't reach out for good new relationships. Instead these people hurt more, and often they hurt other people too. This choice may seem easier than the second, but it can be very destructive. People who hold on to the hurt may cope through expressions such as the following:

The perpetual victim. Perpetual victims habitually blame others for everything that goes wrong, including their own wrongdoings.

The doormat. Instead of blaming others, doormats blame themselves for the bad things that happen to themselves and others. People who respond this way will take full responsibility for their pain and the pain of others, even when they didn't cause it. They have low self-regard and often put themselves down.

The angry abuser. People operating out of this mind set have decided to hurt others before they can be hurt. Having experienced broken relationships, they carry a perpetual chip on their shoulder and want to make sure they are never hurt again. Angry abusers often demand and threaten, frequently getting angrier than appropriate for a specific situation. They may seem to be in control, but their existence is truly lonely and miserable.

The caustic cynic. Rather than lashing out at others, these people sit along the sidelines of life and throw darts of sarcasm and negativity at anything that shows vitality and possibility. To an innocent listener, the advice may seem well-meaning, but in truth caustic cynics want all attempts at health and wholeness to fail so they can say, "I told you so."

The denier. Another way of dealing with pain is to deny that it exists. After being hurt, deniers think they can just decide to get over it. This attitude attributes too little importance to the pain and hurt that truly happened, to the right to be sad and angry, and to the need for healing. Following this approach prevents learning from past mistakes. People in denial often have difficulty expressing feelings, appear stronger than they are, avoid conflict at all costs, and refuse to accept help.

The projector. People who cope in this way project blame for their pain onto a person who may have nothing to do with the real source of the pain. They can get very upset over minor issues because they are taking their own hurt feelings out on someone else. They often refuse to talk about what is troubling them.

Certainly there are other ways of holding on to hurt beyond these six, but these six types are classic responses for many people, including teenagers. Often you'll encounter someone who exhibits bits and pieces of behaviors from all these types and others.

We could say of any one of these: This is *no way* to live!

An un-easy way to peace

Christians often pray a short prayer that eases our death-grip on the hurts we have suffered or caused. Jesus taught his disciples this prayer, the prayer known for centuries as the *Lord's Prayer* or the *Our Father*. One line in particular calls us into a way to live very different from the *no-way* options we've been considering: "Forgive us our sins, as we forgive those who sin against us." When we offer this prayer, we are asking God not to reply to the wrongs we have done with punishment or revenge or the cold silence of disapproval—and we are also declaring our willingness to move toward healing in relation to those who have hurt us.

This prayer is not for perfect people. (And who might they be anyway?) It's for every sinful one of us. We read it in the Bible, a book full of stories about those who chose evil rather than good—and also a book full of compassion for those who have suffered abuse and pain. We learn this prayer from Jesus, who brought the world forgiveness by suffering a painful death as the innocent victim of other people's selfishness.

IT'S NOT YOUR FAULT! ■■■■■■■■■■■■■■■■■■■■

If you know someone who has been or is currently being abused, you may want to read this page with that person. Also be sure to help him or her tell a VERY trusted adult.

Do you struggle with abuse? You may be getting physically beaten up or verbally put down or sexually molested or raped. **This is not your fault. You did not bring this on yourself.** Go back and read these last two sentences out loud. This is not happening to you because of *your* selfishness or *your* sinfulness. This is not happening to you because God wills it or wants it. This is happening because of the selfishness and sinfulness of the abuser. This is not your fault!

One of the reasons people remain in abusive situations is that abusers are so good at convincing their victims that the situation is their fault and that somehow they brought this on themselves. This is a lie. If you are in such a situation, get help. Find an adult you trust, tell him or her what is going on, and ask for guidance in finding further help. If you have tried telling an adult before and it didn't work, try again. Situations of abuse often involve an imbalance of power. That's why stopping abuse is so hard if you are the victim. It takes courage to stop the abuse. But with God's help you can do it (see Philippians 4:13 and 19).

You need help from people experienced in dealing with abuse. These people may be strangers to you now, but their expertise can help you in stopping the abuse and then in working through your thoughts and feelings about the abuse. Consider contacting your pastor, youth minister, counselor, guidance counselor, rape center, or crisis center.

In cases like yours and in many other painful situations, forgiveness will take time, perhaps even a whole lifetime. Take care of yourself first, then you can work on forgiveness. It will be more work than you can imagine, but you are well worth all the effort! ■ ■ ■ ■ ■

Jesus' life, death, and resurrection show us that sin, pain, and death are not the end of the story (see The Story according to Emily in "The Story"). After Jesus was executed, God raised him from death. The first words Jesus said to his shattered disciples as they huddled terrified behind locked doors were "Peace be with you" (John 20:19). And he has been going around saying "Peace" ever since, inviting people to let go of the wrongs they have suffered and the wrongs they have done so that they can live their way into a more peaceful future.

"Peace." This is God's gift to us in Jesus: "For the wages of sin is death, but the free gift of God is eternal life in Christ Jesus our Lord" (Romans 6:23). Even though we have sinned and fallen short, in other words, God is giving us a gift. No matter what we have done, our sins and wrongdoings will not be held against us. The web of relationships that was broken between us and God is now repaired by Jesus. Jesus can also help us repair the torn webs of our relationships with others and with ourselves.

Through this gift of forgiveness, God throws away the scorecard and declares that everyone wins. This gift comes from God to us. But it's not supposed to stop there. Those of us who have received this gift now have the chance to share it with others. We get to go around saying "Peace."

Forgiveness. The word is not unfamiliar. But it is often misunderstood.

Forgiveness is NOT . . .

- easy
- covering up your feelings
- approving or tolerating the wrong that was done to you
- getting even
- acting out of moral superiority
- a sign of weakness
- just mouthing the words
- excusing the person who hurt you
- dismissing the right to seek justice and compensation for harm
- inviting someone to hurt you again
- a solitary act
- forgetting
- a onetime event
- simple
- going to make it feel all better

Forgiveness is . . .

- hard work
- acknowledging your feelings of pain, hurt, and sadness
- naming the wrong that was done to you
- a sign of remarkable strength
- holding the other accountable for what they did to you
- overcoming fear, shame, and blame
- a decision to move beyond the suffering
- moving on and taking steps toward health and wholeness
- a process
- a declaration of hope in a better future
- a decision you may need to make many times for the same event
- figuring out how to deal with your relationships—with God, yourself, the person who hurt you, and others
- learning how to avoid being hurt in that same way again
- a process that takes a long time

Forgiving is difficult because . . .

- you might feel embarrassed
- you don't know how to go about it
- you have never seen someone do it
- you try to do it without God's help
- you still want to feel superior to the other person
- you've gotten used to feeling inferior to the other person
- other people view it as weakness
- it takes courage
- it doesn't come easily or quickly
- it requires confronting difficult feelings
- people say "I'm sorry" all the time and don't mean it
- getting to the point of peace could take a long time

Come to me, all you that are weary
and are carrying heavy burdens,
and I will give you rest.
—MATTHEW 11:28

Handing your burden to God

You may want to get a real brick and hold it as you read this next section. Picture this: Let's say you go through life with a backpack like one you use at school. Each wrong you've experienced in your life adds a brick to your backpack. You can choose to carry those bricks your whole life—like a grudge. But it takes a heck of a lot of work to carry those bricks with you wherever you go. Imagine how hard and how tired you would be after a while. By not forgiving, you end up using all your energy to lug those bricks around. It's exhausting! That's why people say that when they forgave someone, "it was like a weight was lifted from my shoulders." How heavy is your backpack?

There is another way. You can work through the process of forgiveness and give up those bricks one by one. It takes work, but there are ways you can unpack those bricks.

If you are yearning to lighten your load, look for other people to help with the lifting. People who are grateful to God for the forgiveness they have received themselves make excellent companions in the healing work of forgiveness. Join them to worship this forgiving God, and pray that explosive little line from the Lord's Prayer—in whatever version you know—right along with them (see below).

Eric was so angry at God that he didn't even go to church for his grandfather's funeral. If he tries to forgive God and goes back to church, however, he may start remembering that he has much to be thankful for, especially the loving relationship he shared with his grandfather. If this happens, anger will not be his last word with God.

> **Forgive us our sins as we forgive those who sin against us.**
> —Ecumenical, ICET

> **Forgive us our debts, as we forgive our debtors.**
> —Matthew 6:12, King James Version of the Bible

> **Forgive us our trespasses, as we forgive those who trespass against us.**
> —Catholic and several Protestant traditions

Both Denise and her parents also have some brick lifting to do; mutual forgiveness will take work and time, but good honest conversations may help them to move toward that point. Denise will certainly need to work at restoring her parents' trust.

As for Michele, self-respecting new relationships with friends, boyfriends, and eventually a husband will enable her to live beyond her brokenness. But she will be ready for these relationships only when she is on the road to forgiving Hunter, her old friends, and herself.

Moving into new relationships of trust may not come easily to Denise, Eric, and Michele, but they don't have to continue carrying those bricks around. They can unload them and walk freely into the future. Imagine that.

What about you? Imagine how you could be free to walk farther, to run with energy, to join with others, to move into the marvelous future that God has in store for you. Go ahead. Hand your burden to God. ∎

EVELYN L. PARKER **WITH**
RAYMOND RIVERA

▍▍▍Justice

Justice, for Christians, means acting in ways
that promote human flourishing—especially for
people who are poor, weak, and vulnerable. ■ ■ ■ ■
—**Raymond Rivera, 14**

AUGUST 30
Dear Evelyn, How's it going? I can't believe summer's almost over and school's about to start! Are you ready? I guess it feels different when you're the teacher. Do you still get nervous? I'll be in the ninth grade this year. I'm really excited about high school, but at the same time I'm a little uneasy. Since you and my mom are good friends, she suggested that I ask you a few questions I've been wondering about. Would that be OK?

AUGUST 31
Dear Raymond, Great to hear from you! Yes, the summer months have flown by. I'm still getting prepared for the courses I have to teach this fall—and yes, I still get nervous on that first day of classes. I worry about whether students will like me and whether they'll be interested in what I'm teaching. I'm delighted that your mother encouraged you to write to me and I'll be glad to respond to your questions—as long as they're not about geometry!

SEPTEMBER 2
Thanks, Evelyn. I think it will be easier for me to write about this than to talk about it. I'm a little worried about going to a new school. Especially with being Mexican-American. I know there are lots of us here in Dallas, but I also know what some people think and how they feel about us. I don't know—I just want to be respected and treated fairly. And I'm fed up with the racial slurs and insults. Mom told me that you had to deal with a lot of these same issues when you were a teenager. Any advice?

JUSTICE

Dear Raymond, I am honored that you feel comfortable sharing your concerns with me, especially about this topic. And I understand why you'd be worrying about these issues. Whether you're Mexican-American, Native American, Asian-American, or African-American, like me, you always have to wonder whether folks will treat you fairly or whether they'll "dis" you simply because of your skin color. Other kids have similar worries about being mistreated because of where they live, what their background is, or how much money their family has. Experiencing concerns is common when you're entering high school because everything about it is new to you. School ought to be a place where at least you could expect everyone to be treated fairly, and often it is. But injustice can and does happen in schools, just as in so many other places in society.

When I was young, schools were racially segregated, and I was excluded from some schools because of my black skin. After school integration, I was allowed into previously all-white schools, but I wasn't allowed into certain other places—including many of the churches in my hometown. Being *allowed* is not the same as being *accepted* and treated fairly. Sometimes things weren't fair because I was black, sometimes because I was female. I've been fortunate, though, to have a strong faith community in my life, and my Christian faith has taught me to claim my dignity and humanity even when others were denying it. And that's what I wish for you too, Raymond, because it's hard to stand up to situations of injustice when you're out there on your own.

There's much more I could say, but I'm interested in hearing your questions. I really want you to know you're not in this all alone.

JUSTICE

What are your concerns about fairness at school?

SEPTEMBER 9

Hi, Evelyn. It's really been bothering me that some of the churches in your hometown shut you out because of your skin color. Isn't the church supposed to be a place that accepts *everyone*? What gives?

SEPTEMBER 10

Raymond, you're right—the church is supposed to be a place where everyone is accepted. In fact, the whole way of life Jesus preached and taught about is based on *unconditional acceptance*. Jesus constantly upset the authorities because he accepted people others considered outsiders. He ate with sinners, prostitutes, and tax collectors. He touched lepers and women who had been labeled "unclean." Jesus' disciples decided that the church must welcome *all people*, not just Jesus' Jewish followers, and that in the church no divisions would exist between men and women or between slaves and free people. In the church, *everyone* would be truly free.

But following through on this ideal in the midst of a society that works the other way—Roman society back then and lots of other societies since, including ours—has never been easy. No matter what the society, human beings often are greedy and interested in holding on to whatever power they can get— even in the church. We say that the church is "the body of Christ," yet that body is often broken because the church is also a human institution. It's sad to admit, Raymond, but throughout history the church frequently has supported injustice in the service of maintaining the status quo—the way things are.

Apartheid means apartness in Afrikaans, the language of the white minority in South Africa. It names a system of racial injustice that controlled that country from 1948 to 1994.

I grew up in the segregated South, where the message preached by many all-white churches sounded more like "don't rock the boat" than "all of you are one in Christ Jesus" (Galatians 3:28). It would have been bad enough—but at least honest—if those church people had simply said, "We've decided to be a social club instead of a church, and we just don't want to associate with black folks." But instead they tried to convince themselves that *God* wanted it to be that way, that *God* preferred racial injustice. These same worn-out arguments were used to support apartheid in South Africa during your own lifetime, Raymond.

The God I worship is not a God of "the way things are" but a God who "is making all things new." As a teenager I held fast to my faith in God even though some of the churches in my hometown were treating me and other persons of color unjustly. Because my own congregation was very supportive, I was blessed with a positive experience of church alongside these negative ones. The black church tradition in this country was born during the days of slavery, so it's been strengthening me and other members to resist oppression for a long time. Those slaveholders didn't realize what a revolutionary book they were giving my ancestors when they gave them the Bible!

Justice is not for "just us"; it means fairness for others as well.

Raymond, I don't want to leave you discouraged about the church. Lots of folks have had a change of heart, and today I could walk into almost any church in my hometown and be welcomed with open arms. That's how much has changed during my lifetime. God is "making all things new," and I've seen it happen again and again.

OCTOBER 15

Evelyn, I've been thinking about what you said, how people can use their religion to put others down. Seems like that's happened over and over again throughout history. It's bad enough when life is unfair, but then people come along and say, "God made it this way," or "God wants it to be this way." That must really make God mad!

OCTOBER 16

Yes, Raymond, I think that does make God mad. Do you know about the Hebrew prophets in the Old Testament? A whole section of the Bible called "the Prophets" talks about how angry God gets when people use religion to support injustice. In the time of the prophets, political leaders— usually kings—were backed up by royal priests who used their religious authority to justify the kings' actions. You could consider these royal priests as the kings' "spin doctors." They interpreted Israel's history in a way that made the kings look good, sometimes even telling people that the king was like a god and describing God as a king not so different from the human king. These priests hoped the people would think that God had put the king in charge and that everything was just the way God wanted it to be.

But then along came these crazy folks who totally challenged the royal story. These "prophets" weren't predicting the future exactly; they were telling anyone who would listen how *furious* God was about the way things were going. The prophets directly confronted the kings and the royal priests by preaching that God doesn't side with the people who sit on thrones but with poor people and widows and orphans, who have no rights and no one to care for them. Ignoring people such as these is unjust, the prophets proclaimed—and God is ANGRY!

When the prophet Amos speaks the word of the Lord, we hear moving descriptions of injustice. He addresses this word to the powerful people who "sell the righteous for silver, and the needy for a pair of sandals—they who trample the head of the poor into the dust of the earth, and push the afflicted out of the way" (Amos 2:6-7). These people "turn justice to wormwood, and bring righteousness to the ground!" (5:7). What especially angers God, Amos says, is that they do all this *and also* love to participate in religious festivals and praying and fasting. God hates this behavior and is very clear about the alternative: "Let justice roll down like waters, and righteousness like an everflowing stream" (5:24).

The prophet Isaiah also proclaims that the Lord does not desire for us to go around acting religious but rather for us to practice basic kindness toward others. When you share your bread with hungry people or give homeless people a house and poor people clothing to wear, *then* "the LORD will guide you continually, and satisfy your needs in parched places, and make your bones strong; and you shall be like a watered garden, like a spring of water, whose waters never fail" (Isaiah 58:11).

We still have prophets today, Raymond. You could call anyone who is a troublemaker for the sake of God's justice a prophet. You will rarely find them hanging out with the rich and famous. Usually they're living among people who are poor, in the slums and barrios.

What I've learned from prophets—ancient and modern—is that God is *passionate*, full of anguish about the way human beings mistreat one another. Prophets don't give us a specific game plan for fixing things though. They usually speak in poetic images. Isaiah's images of justice as a healthy garden and an abundant water supply are good examples.

Living through the hot dry summers in Dallas, you can see why I'm drawn to the image of a healthy garden with plenty of water! I think God is happy when all of us are *flourishing* instead of shriveling up because of injustice.

NOVEMBER 20

Hi, Evelyn. I like the garden image for justice. This past spring I helped my mom plant some rosebushes in the backyard. We watered them every day, and they looked great until those 100-degree days in July and August. Then they all turned brown and died. Mom was pretty upset, but we learned that you just can't grow roses in some climates. I guess it's like that with people too. When you look around, there seem to be lots of places in the world where people just wither up and die—sometimes literally because of lack of water, even though wealthy countries could help them with this need.

Speaking of plants, in my U.S. History class today we learned about César Chávez, a Mexican-American like me who stood up for migrant farmworkers. I signed up to do my report on Dolores Huerta, who started the United Farm Workers union with Chávez. Together they dedicated their lives to helping farmworkers get a living wage, clean drinking water and toilets in the fields, decent housing, health benefits, and the freedom to work without sexual harassment and assault. Would you consider these two modern-day prophets?

DECEMBER 1

Hi, Raymond. From everything I know about Chávez and Huerta, they would certainly qualify as prophetic figures. I'm so glad you're learning about them. Just think about the difference these two leaders were able to make in the lives of so many people! That kind of change can happen when we join together with others to work for social justice. This is not work we can do on our own.

Do you recall meeting Thomas, the son of one of my faculty colleagues? Although Thomas is only 17, he's already working for economic justice around the world. During his junior year,

Thomas drove with a friend from Texas to Washington, D.C., to participate in the justice movement called Jubilee 2000. This national gathering protested the enormous debt that developing countries in South America, Asia, and Africa owe the World Bank.

Thomas believes that greed is the greatest cause of poverty around the world and the reason economic injustice persists, so he was urging the wealthy nations who run the World Bank to give the poor nations a break on their loans and interest payments. Thomas joined with thousands of others in a nonviolent march in which they chanted and sang their support for debtor nations. Some of the protesters who formed a human chain across an entranceway were arrested. Thomas was one of 24 young people, ages 13 to 18, who had to spend the night in jail as a result of this witness.

Thomas feels proud of his stand on behalf of people who are poor. And fortunately, Thomas feels supported by his family and friends. The support of a community makes all the difference in how much you are able to risk in these situations.

Raymond, what made the civil rights movement happen in this country was the broad support of communities—especially *faith communities*—for leaders such as Rosa Parks and Martin Luther King Jr. And young people were right at the heart of this movement.

For instance, 15-year-old Joyce Ladner and her big sister Dorie became civil rights activists in Mississippi. Their parents let them join the youth chapter of the National Association for the Advancement of Colored People. Two years later, as college students, they joined the Student Nonviolent Coordinating Committee. Joyce and Dorie worked in the voter registration campaign during the summer of 1964. These sisters joined others in protest

239

marches, sit-ins, boycotts, rallies, and mass meetings. They knew the potential dangers they might face, but they also knew a caring community stood behind them every step of the way.

Whenever I get discouraged, Raymond, I read about women like Huerta, Parks, and the Ladner sisters. Working on behalf of justice is hard work, and sometimes we don't see results during our own lifetime. What inspires me is seeing the extraordinary accomplishments of ordinary people when they are supported by strong communities of faith. I hope their stories will inspire you too.

MARCH 1

Evelyn, I need to tell you something—something that happened at school. Last week I was kinda roughhousing with this guy named Peter. We got carried away and he started calling me names. First he called me a "Border-hopper." I told him to shut up and turned to leave. Then he called me a series of names: "Beaner, Wet Back, Taco Mouse." I couldn't hold back—I ran after him and hit him hard. The soccer coach grabbed us just in time and pulled us apart. I told the coach what had happened, and he really got on Peter's case. Afterward I felt brave because of how I stood up for myself, but I also felt ashamed about the whole thing and didn't tell my mom until today. Can you help me make sense of this?

MARCH 4

Raymond, you've heard the saying "Sticks and stones may break my bones but words can never hurt me." Well, that's not true, is it? Words *can* hurt, and racial slurs are like a slap in the face. They make us feel small and exposed. They make us feel *shame*. Even feeling justified in hitting back doesn't help us deal with our shame.

Revenge is *bitter*sweet—after the sweetness wears off, the bitter taste remains in your mouth. In place of revenge, civil rights leaders taught *non-violent* ways of confronting people who are putting you down. Your *first* response to humiliating treatment needs to be claiming your own dignity as a person created in the image of God. This awareness sets you free to respond to injustice in creative rather than violent ways.

Leaders such as Gandhi and King realized the power of using non-violence to protest injustice. It takes great courage, but it also involves practical skills that ordinary people can learn. During the sixties, civil rights

An eye for an eye only ends up making
the whole world blind. . . .
For myself, I've always found that
we're all such sinners, we should leave
punishment to God. . . . I want to
change their minds, not kill them for
weaknesses we all possess.

—attributed to Mohandas K. Gandhi

demonstrators practiced keeping their cool while instructors role-played insulting and threatening them. This practice prepared them to respond to humiliating treatment calmly when they were assaulted while demonstrating on buses or at lunch counters. Rosa Parks had such training—it was not just a spur-of-the-moment decision when she refused to go to the back of the bus!

Raymond, I pray that in every circumstance you will have the strength to act and react out of your God-given human dignity. Life will be unfair at times, and ethnic insults will continue to sting. But you can always hold on to the truth that you are precious in the sight of God. No one can take that away from you.

APRIL 3

Hi, Evelyn. I like what you said about claiming my dignity and respecting myself. Fighting back feels like the thing to do when somebody puts me down, but I want to try to find other ways to stand up for myself—and for others.

I'm thinking about what all this means for the way we treat girls at school. I think this is a justice issue too. When we're in the lunchroom, some of the guys play a type of rating game. Guys will pass around a paper with 10 girls' names down the side and categories across the top. We don't even know some of these girls very well. They are rated mostly by their looks. Sometimes girls find these charts and really get their feelings hurt.

It's awkward for me because some of the guys who like this game are my friends. I don't like playing the rating game, but I don't want to lose my friends either. What do you think?

APRIL 7

Raymond, do you remember the idea of justice as *human flourishing*? Justice is like a plant that needs ongoing care and attention. When you notice a situation that's unjust, it's like seeing weeds in the garden. Those weeds are always growing, and a good gardener stays alert and roots them out day after day, one at a time.

You've noticed an unjust situation that many high-school girls have to put up with on a daily basis. They may face a "rating game," verbal harassment, or even a slap on the bottom when they walk down the school hallway. This kind of treatment makes girls feel humiliated and exposed, powerless and insecure. We know this is not good soil for human flourishing—for any of us.

Confronting any situation of injustice takes courage, Raymond. It's especially tough when friends are involved, as in your case. Sometimes we're called to stand up and speak the truth in front of a whole group. Other times, we can work one-on-one with people to change their hearts and actions. That might be the wise way to go with your lunchroom buddies. Begin by talking privately with a friend—someone you suspect shares your discomfort. Then recruit at least one more friend. You'll feel a lot more confident bringing up the matter before the whole group when you have a few other guys who agree and support you. Make sense?

APRIL 29
Evelyn, I'll talk one-on-one with some of my friends, as you suggested. I hope it works. Thanks for the advice.

We had quite a discussion in history class today about the death penalty. I guess it was on everyone's mind since Texas executed another person last night. Most of the students said that this guy was getting what he deserved and that the state is obligated to put such persons to death. "Justice, pure and simple," they said.

But it doesn't seem that simple to me. I guess I don't like the idea of my home state executing somebody almost every week. Doesn't Texas lead the nation in capital punishment? I also wonder how Christians can justify killing people, even people who have done terrible things. Maybe it's the *fair* thing to do, but it doesn't seem like the *right* thing to do. Didn't Jesus tell us to love and pray for our enemies?

MAY 2
Raymond, you've raised some great questions. Discussing the issue of capital punishment really does force us to think hard about matters of justice.

Justice can feel like a burden. It's my life, my passion, my direction . . . , but sometimes it feels like such hard work. I can only work for justice when I've got a community with me. And even then, it helps to know that our little community doesn't have to do it all, because there are others around the world. ■■■■■■■■■■■■■■

—EMILY, 17

A person who's helped me understand this from a faith perspective is Bryan Stevenson, founder of an organization called the Equal Justice Initiative in Montgomery, Alabama (www.eji.org). Bryan helps death-row prisoners appeal their death sentences. This is not work that a lot of folks care to do. They assume that the law has been followed and that these prisoners are simply getting what they deserve "to balance the scales of justice." But Bryan is a lawyer, and he knows that people who are poor and people of color don't always get good legal representation in our country. So Bryan and his colleagues do what they can to make the legal system *fair for all—even for those who do bad things and treat others unjustly.* That's a real challenge, Raymond, because our gut instincts tell us that folks who act unjustly don't deserve just treatment themselves.

As a Christian, Bryan knows that *God always works through grace and mercy.* One way of thinking about justice is to see it as a balancing scale: If you do something bad, you should get an equal amount of punishment. But Bryan knows that Christians are called to do more than balance an equation. We're called to be agents of God's mercy in this world. We believe that people's hearts and minds can change and that a constant circle of "getting even" will not produce the flourishing-garden world Isaiah described.

Constantly trying to keep the scales in balance—making sure everyone gets paid back for everything they do wrong—would be a tense, mean way to live. That way *shows no mercy* to anyone. On the other hand, understanding that God is merciful—even to people like you and me, who do some wrong every day even though we don't commit capital crimes—frees us up for a better way to live. If we are grateful for God's mercy to us, we can move beyond asking, *What's fair for me?* and *What's fair for my group?* and begin asking, *What's fair for everyone?* When we make that shift, we can see that justice is not a form of payback but instead a *new thing* God is doing for the whole world.

This change has been evolving in South Africa during recent years, Raymond. Archbishop Desmond Tutu describes this amazing experiment in his book *No Future Without Forgiveness.* When the apartheid government was dismantled and a democratic government elected, South Africa chose to be guided by a vision of *merciful* justice rather than by a notion of justice that emphasized revenge. Tutu and other leaders were appointed to a Truth and Reconciliation Commission (TRC) to hear testimony about politically motivated crimes committed by all sides during the apartheid era. Applicants for amnesty were required to make a full confession of guilt, which was often heart-wrenching to hear. Many horrible stories of brutality and violence came to light. This way did *not* sweep injustice under the rug!

The TRC trusted that God's mercy and forgiveness would enable South Africans to begin the long process of healing without resorting to continued violence, including the violence of executing people who had committed wrongs. This unprecedented process seems to be working. It has become a model for other countries to follow in their attempts to move beyond long-standing ethnic feuds. When *justice for all* is the goal, mercy is a way of getting from here to there. It's the refreshing rain that waters the parched earth and makes human flourishing possible.

Raymond, I'm inspired by the way young people have often had a passion for seeking justice. And I believe you have the power and ability to stand for justice today just as others have historically. I want you to flourish in the grace of God like a well-watered rose stretching its petals toward the rays of the sun. God wants *all people* to blossom and flourish, and the prophet Micah (6:8) proclaimed what God requires of each of us to make this happen: "Do justice, . . . love kindness, and . . . walk humbly with your God."

That's the "good life"—a way to live that's good for everyone. ∎

|||Grieving

People die. Kids die. And their deaths lead to a lot of confusion, pain, frustration, and sometimes a loss of faith. This chapter helps teens draw upon the practice of lament to deal with death, as we learn to share our pain with God and our community. ■ ■ ■ ■ ■ ■ ■

—Tatiana Wilson, 14

I just read a story that reminded me of the pain I experienced when my best friend died. The story was about Nkosi Johnson, a 12-year-old boy who inherited AIDS from his mother and who has come to symbolize the epidemic for the entire country of South Africa. South Africa has a fast-growing AIDS problem; millions are now infected with the virus that causes the disease. In July 2000, Nkosi begged South Africa to stop rejecting people with HIV/AIDS and to begin caring for the hundreds of thousands of children whose parents have died of this disease. Did you know that many South Africans now attend one or two funerals every weekend? Tragically, many funerals are for children who have died of AIDS. Brave, emaciated Nkosi spoke out and shamed his country's leadership. And then he died.

Why, God?

Why all these deaths? Why Nkosi? And why my best friend? Why did God let my wonderful, smart, and really cool best friend die in a car accident?

Sometimes broken things can be repaired—some tape here, a little glue there. But sometimes things can't be fixed. Death is so permanent. Hearts, bodies, and spirits can be broken by disease or catastrophic events. When my best friend died, I knew this couldn't be "fixed" with a bit of glue

GRIEVING

Do you remember the first time someone you knew died? How did you feel? What did you do to cope?

■■■■■■■■■■■■■■■■■■■■■■■

or a special surgical procedure. When I heard the news, I was shocked. I felt like I was trapped in the middle of a storm. Why her, God? Why me?

I wanted someone to hold me, but I was too embarrassed to sit on my mom's lap and cry. I thought I was losing my mind. I would hide in my room and hold on to my old teddy bear. Hiding out in my bedroom was easier than trying to find a place to hide at school when I could feel tears coming. My stomach hurt; it was tied up in knots. My heart beat so hard during those first hours after learning about the accident, I thought it would burst. I was just 13, way too young to know about obituaries and funerals. I hadn't planned on writing a will until I was at least 40!

Do you remember the first time someone you knew died? How did you feel? What did you do to cope?

Loved ones die

Of all the losses we have to face as human beings, death is the most mysterious, and the most powerful. Death doesn't make sense and seems so unfair, especially when it claims the lives of young people like my friend or Nkosi Johnson.

Just as we're surrounded by life, we're also surrounded by death. Dealing with death can be confusing when you're young and still figuring out how you're supposed to live. I think of Amy, a 14-year-old from New York, one of the thousands of children who lost parents in the attacks on the World Trade Center and the Pentagon. Amy's mother was 42 years old and raising her daughters, Amy and Jasmine (age three), as a single parent. She also was helping care for Amy's six-month-old daughter, Marilyn. Amy's parents were divorced, but her father has stayed in touch and been supportive of Amy, Jasmine, and Marilyn. Amy says, "I'm OK. I just hold on to my family and my friends. They have been helping me."

No one knows the actual number of children who lost parents on September 11, 2001. Every one of these children will have to grow up too soon. These terrible events also affected everyone in the United States as well as in communities all around the world. There was and continues to

■ ■ ■ ■ ■ Why Me?
Why do I always feel pain?
Why is it that my day always rains?
Why am I so lonely,
With no one to talk to, or no one to hold me?
Why is it that my tears always flow?
To end the sadness, what do I do? Where do I go?
No one to protect me when I'm in fear;
I am so lonely 'cause no one's near.
Why is it that sadness and loneliness and fear
Are constant company?
I don't know. But why me? ■ ■ ■ ■ ■
—TATIANA, 14

GRIEVING

be a sense of profound global public grief. Weighed down by shock and grief over the amount of death and destruction, all of us ask, "Why?"

Have you lost someone close to you and found yourself asking the question "Why me?" At this moment you may not be grieving someone's death. Yet in every high school there are people like Amy who are dealing with deep personal loss. It's important to know how to support others in their time of grief. And it's important for you to know how to grieve *yourself* when you lose someone dear to you—a friend, a grandparent, a brother or sister, your mother or father.

The death of a loved one comes crashing in like a sudden storm, full of sound and fury. No matter how young, strong, wealthy, or smart you may be, without any warning you find yourself standing all alone in the cold pouring rain, wondering where in the world to run for cover and comfort.

Coping with storms

Experiencing grief over the storms of personal loss is natural. But giving yourself the time and space to grieve fully is hard, especially in our society where everyone is so busy and so eager to "fix" things. Even well-meaning friends will tell you, "Hurry up and get over it already!" Or with a sympathetic tone of voice: "You know, all the tears in the world won't bring him back. So dry your eyes and get on with your life." Or the clinical approach: "I know a good therapist who can help you deal with your loss." Sometimes the storm clouds are so dark and menacing that professional therapy, including a responsible use of medication, is necessary.

Therapy—*healing*—is especially important when confusion and unresolved issues accompany death. Grief can be intensified by other emotions we have when someone dies. When 18-year-old Tom died after slamming his car into a tree on the way home from a drinking party, his friends were grief-stricken. But they also felt anger at him for being irresponsible, guilt that they had not stopped him from driving that night, and relief that

■ ■ ■ ■ ■ ■ ■ ■ ■ ■ ■ ■ ■
Death is heavy and painful—a shock to our system. Lament is a practice in which, by God's grace, we can hold the hurt and share our grief in a healthy way. ■ ■ ■ ■ ■ ■ ■ ■ ■ ■

the same thing had not happened to them. Even more complex feelings emerged for Donna, whose father died after leaving the family. At age 16, she was devastated to think that she would never see him again—but also angry that he had seen her so little when he could have. Sorting out these feelings was not easy for the teens in these situations. Grief grows even more complicated than usual in troubling circumstances, including death that comes by a person's own hand or death that ends an important but broken relationship before we have time to mend it.

Jews and Christians have a practice that provides "therapy" when the storm clouds roll in and we're grieving loss beyond repair. This practice is called *lament*. To lament means to *express sorrow* or *to mourn out loud*. The practice of lament gives you time and permission to vent your pent-up anger, your deep sadness, and your self-blame. You allow yourself to grieve in a way that leads to healing and renewal. As you pour out your grief, loss, pain, and anger in the presence of God, you discover that God hears your cries of anguish and comforts you. While you can't remove the storms, quiet the thunder, or stop the lightning from striking, you can trust your tears to be the raindrops that release the clouds, allowing rays of sunlight to shine through. Before catching a glimpse of the rainbow, though, you have to brace yourself for the raging storm within.

Arguing with God

Most of us have been taught that it's not polite to argue—and we figure arguing with God is especially impolite. The first step in learning to lament, however, is to realize that arguing with God is OK. God is big enough to handle our complaints and our anger. God is loving and gracious enough to hang in there with us. As the apostle Paul claimed centuries ago, nothing will be able to "separate us from the love of God" (see Romans 8:38-39). *Nothing* you can say to God will keep God from loving you.

I learned this lesson when my friend died. "If you're so good and powerful, God, how could you allow a thing like this to happen?" I was furious. I wanted to throw things and lash out at somebody—especially at God: "Maybe you *don't* care . . . maybe you're not even listening. . . . And you expect *me* to worship *you*? What kind of loving Parent sits back and lets a son die? You could have rescued him, but you didn't even try!"

I didn't just think those words; I said them! I ran and ran on the jogging track in the middle of the night and yelled them. A little voice in my head was saying, *You know you shouldn't be talking this way. Nice girls control their anger.* But I ignored that voice, because it was lying. Instead I stood there raging in the rain, arguing with God Almighty.

> **God is our refuge and strength, a very present ■ ■ ■ ■ help in ■ ■ trouble.**
>
> —PSALM 46:1

When I was young, I learned it was OK to be angry with God. Now I know that my anger can be a real gift. Your anger can be a wake-up call, a reminder to feel your feelings. The feelings we experience are not good or bad; they just *are*. What will we do with that energy? How can we use anger *creatively*, for identifying where we've been hurt or for spurring us to right a wrong? Paying attention to anger doesn't mean we need to act out our impulses and hurt somebody. Nor does it mean that we need to deny our feelings. Paying attention to anger means taking our relationship with self, with others, and with God seriously.

The power of lament

I was still trapped in a storm, bitter and raw from my friend's death, when I made an amazing discovery: Parts of the Bible describe people arguing and getting angry with God. When I read Psalm 77, for instance, I could see and hear myself in the words of this ancient song: crying aloud to God, my soul refusing to be comforted, forgotten promises, sleepless nights ("You keep my eyelids from closing"). How could God have created a world that allows this kind of pain? I wasn't letting God off the hook for the bad, nasty things that happened to my community or to me. Had God forgotten to be gracious? forgotten me? forgotten my best friend?

Reading those words of lament in the Bible opened up my deep pain and grief. I became sad and got a little scared. I wondered if God really existed, if God really cared. Had "God in anger shut up [God's] compassion?" One day, I had a strong longing to be able to say with the psalmist, "It is my grief that the right hand of the Most High has changed" (verses 9-10). Right then, my doubt seemed like a raging storm. I prayed for strength and read on.

As I read Psalm 77, I learned that others have gone to God when they were in trouble, for comfort amid fatigue. I remembered my grannie's teaching me that "even if confusion and chaos are all around, God is still here with us." As my tears fell, I read about the clouds pouring out water at the dawn of creation. And I read about God's leading the Hebrew slaves out of Egypt and through the Red Sea to freedom (see verses 16-20, and compare Exodus 12:31–14:31). I gradually came to sense that Someone was there, listening to my complaints. And that Someone cared for me in the midst of my sorrow. I was not ready to sing and dance like Miriam (see Exodus 15:20), but I knew deep in my soul that I could trust God and that I could be made whole again.

An entire book of the Bible—the Book of Lamentations—is devoted to lament, as are about 50 of the 150 psalms. A lament is like a play in three acts:

Act I: People get mad at God and pour out their raw emotions.

Act II: Gradually those who complained to God remember God's help in the past and know that God has heard them.

Act III: Those who lament realize they can trust God with their lives and they tell God, "Thanks!"

The movement from *arguing with God* to *remembering God's goodness* to *praising God* is not a process we can rush for ourselves or for others. The

Has God forgotten to be gracious? Has God in anger shut up all compassion?

—PSALM 77:9 *(An Inclusive Version)*

GRIEVING

practice of lament gives us the time to be with our own pain and with other people in their pain. There's real power in this gift.

A few years ago, a half dozen teens in Louisville, Kentucky, organized an alternative Sunday school class. These young people brought their electric guitars, drums, microphones and amplifiers and set up a recording studio in the church basement. For inspiration, they discussed the biblical experience of exile and read psalms of lament, especially Psalms 6, 22, 28, 42, 43, and 69. In these psalms they discovered a range of images for expressing their own feelings of anger and disappointment about life. One of their original recordings—called "How Long?"—picked up on the impatience expressed in Psalms 74 and 79. When they poured out their pain before God and in the company of one another, the storms did not trouble them as much as before. Through the driving rhythms of drum and guitar, these young musicians began to feel a more powerful and healing presence moving among them.

But these teens did not stop with Act I. They also wrote songs based upon psalms of thanksgiving and trust, especially Psalms 18, 30, 40, 66, 116, 100, and 118. They *remembered* that God is good, that God is for us, that God cares for us as a shepherd cares for sheep. The memory of God's goodness and care for us is Act II, a passageway from lament to hope and renewal. In Act II it's important to name *specific* ways God has provided for us, in our own lives and throughout human history. We can't move directly from complaint to praise.

Psalm 23 lists specific reasons for trusting God to care for us. Think about all the aspects of God's activity this psalm describes: providing rest, food, water, guidance, protection, comfort, healing, shelter. During periods of grief, suffering often isolates us, makes us feel frightened and alone. Yet the psalmist proclaims that God is with us, even as we "walk through the valley of the shadow of death." During our most difficult times, we can trust that God is with us and cares for us.

■■■■■■■■■■■■■■■■■■■■■■■■■

I will call to mind the deeds of God; I will remember your wonders of old.
—PSALM 77:11 (*An Inclusive Version*)

Psalm 6

Psalm 22

Psalm 42

Psalm 43

Psalm 28

Psalm 69

For Christians, memory is an amazing thing. We not only remember the past; we also remember *the future*. We remember a promised time when death will be no more and when God will wipe away every tear from our eyes. A time when I'll run and play with my friend again instead of staring at her cold grave. A time when Amy and her mother will share laughter and stories and a delicious meal. And though we only catch glimpses of that promised time in this present life, we praise God for the wonderful new life that awaits us.

"Bless the Lord, O my soul, and all that is within me, bless [God's] holy name." These opening words of Psalm 103 are at the heart of Act III, our praise of God. In this third movement, we express deep gratitude for all God has done and will do. We trust that God will be faithful to God's promises—in this life and beyond this life. And we dare to thank and praise God even when we're still spinning from grief, when all we see is a glimmer of rainbow peaking out from behind the storm clouds.

■■■■■■■■■■■■■■■■■■■■■■■■

God is my shepherd, I shall not want.
　God makes me lie down in green pastures,
and leads me beside still waters;
　God restores my soul.
God leads me in paths of righteousness
　　for the sake of God's name.
Even though I walk through the
　　valley of the shadow of death,
　I fear no evil
for you are with me;
　your rod and your staff—
　they comfort me.
You prepare a table before me
　in the presence of my enemies;
you anoint my head with oil,
　my cup overflows.
Surely goodness and mercy shall follow me
　all the days of my life,
and I shall dwell in the house of God
　my whole life long.
—PSALM 23 *(An Inclusive Version)*

GRIEVING

Are you grieving over the death of a good friend or relative? Begin writing letters to that person, sharing your pain and grief over his or her death as you honor the individual's life.

Yes, there's healing power in lament. But there is no way to tap into this power except to go through the eye of the storm. The good news is this: We don't have to face the storm alone. God is always with us, to guide and protect, to listen to the cries of our hearts.

Punching pillows and planting roses

Arguing with God and singing songs of lament are powerful ways to deal with the loss of a loved one. Just as tears provide relief, your whole body can *let go* of grief. You can

- punch pillows,
- help an older adult do chores,
- beat on a drum,
- clean out all your closets, even when it's not springtime,
- put on an old shirt and then rip it to shreds,
- kick-box,
- run five miles,
- play loud music and shout.

A wise woman once told me that if someone does something cruel, you should plant a tree. When someone dies, you can plant a tree in that person's memory. Or you can plant a rose garden. When my grandmother died, all her grandchildren decided to plant a rose garden in her memory. Grannie's rose garden had always been special. Her rose beds were beautiful, and below them she planted string beans. Those were the sweetest beans, and the green leaves and stalks made a beautiful contrast to the pink, yellow, white, and red roses. Today many people enjoy the rose garden we planted at Grannie's church, and the colorful flowers remind us of our grandmother's remarkable, faithful life.

When a member of our church youth group died, we needed a ritual to help us cope with her death. We created a special service which featured all her favorite music and a liturgical dance performed against a backdrop

GRIEVING

of slides showing our friend at church camp. Our youth group made a pact to meet for prayer every day for two weeks before school. During those two weeks, many of us also abstained from meat and spent an hour each evening in total silence: no talking, no music, no TV, no computers. We also collected money that we usually spent on junk food and started a fund to help kids in trouble. Together, these activities put us on the path to healing.

Lamenting together

For the family and congregation, a funeral or memorial service offers a time for communal lament. Go to these services if you possibly can. They'll help you grieve your loss and stand in solidarity with other mourners. In some communities, people have a wake for the deceased prior to burial. At a wake, friends and family gather to share memories of the person who has died. A wake may have a festive atmosphere, which can feel odd when you're not in a party mood. But being present for those who are mourning the loss of a loved one doesn't mean denying your own sadness and discomfort.

Death is a mystery, so when someone dies, we don't need to explain it by saying, "It must have been God's will." The truth is, we don't know God's will. Death and God's will are both mysteries. Do you remember what Jesus did when he learned that his good friend Lazarus had died? He didn't tell Mary and Martha, "Oh, don't fret; it must have been God's will for your brother to die." Instead, Jesus wept (John 11:35). He openly grieved the loss of his friend before calling him back to life. Jesus didn't try to explain death, and we don't need to either.

We don't need to console mourners by reminding them that "God never gives us more than we can bear." As a Presbyterian minister proclaimed following the death of this wife in an SUV rollover, "That's bullhockey! We can't bear this. There is plenty of stuff in this world we

GRIEVING

cannot bear. The verse means that God will never give us more than God can bear. God will bear it and bear us up, in and through it."

Persons in grief don't need a lecture; they need us to be present with compassion. When grieving the loss of a loved one, our friends need to know that they are not facing the world alone. And they need to know that others can *keep the faith* for them even when they may find it difficult themselves. When their lips are frozen, their hearts and minds numbed by the storm of sadness, we can pray on their behalf. When their voices catch and their hearts have no melody, we can lift our voices in song. And when our friends find themselves surrounded by the dark storm clouds of despair, we can hold on to the hope expressed in an African-American spiritual: "When it looked like the sun wasn't gonna shine anymore, God put a rainbow in the clouds."

Glimpsing the rainbow

Christians grieve but not as those "who have no hope" (1 Thessalonians 4:13). Our hope is anchored in the death and resurrection of Jesus Christ. Indeed, the risen Lord is the lighthouse beam that guides us through all the storms of life. Being Christian doesn't enable us to avoid the storms but provides the beacon of light we need to see in the midst of blowing wind and driving rain. When the storm clouds begin to lift, we see that this ray of light appears as a rainbow, bringing color and hope to our gray world even as raindrops continue to fall.

Have you ever sung or heard "Precious Lord, Take My Hand" by Thomas A. Dorsey? Dorsey composed this song during a period of intense grief after his wife and baby boy died. He buried them both in the same casket. Then he fell apart.

At that moment I came closest to rejecting God. It didn't seem fair for God to make it a double loss. I had tried to live by God's will. Was this my reward?

Dorsey didn't "get over" the death of his dear family, but he didn't let anger and grief consume him either. A week later he went to visit a friend,

GRIEVING

and together they walked over to a neighborhood music school. It was late evening as Dorsey sat down at the piano, his hands rambling over the keys. In the midst of great sorrow, Dorsey felt God's consoling presence. And he found his fingers composing a new melody.

The words—like drops of water from the crevice of a rock above— seemed to drop in line with me on the piano:

Precious Lord, take my hand,
lead me on, let me stand,
I am tired, I am weak, I am worn;
through the storm, through the night
lead me on to the light:
Take my hand, precious Lord,
lead me home.

Thomas Dorsey saw a glimpse of the rainbow, a sure sign of God's love and care for him in the midst of the storm. He knew God had healed his spirit and that in our deepest grief, God is closest to us. Dorsey offered his song of lament to God and received a blessing. The blessing came not only to Dorsey but to the millions of people who have been comforted and inspired by "Precious Lord" since that song was penned in 1932.

Perhaps you are grieving a personal loss as you read these words. Perhaps you are standing with others who are mourning the death of a loved one. The grief and other emotions you are experiencing are natural and inevitable. But when you glimpse a rainbow amid the storm, know that you are not alone. God is with you, and God can handle all the anger and cursing and complaints that your grief provokes. You are surrounded by fellow sufferers who are also grieving loss; they will open their hearts to you and hold you up as you try to get your bearings again. Give yourself— and others—time and space to grieve in a way that leads to healing and renewal. That's what the practice of lament is all about. ∎

EMILY SALIERS
DON SALIERS
MARK MONK WINSTANLEY
LIZ MARSHBURN

‖‖‖Music

Music isn't some shrink-wrapped product you buy at the store. Music is a human thing, a body thing, and a spirit thing. You don't have to play a musical instrument to join in the practice of making music. Simply listening to music or singing along with your friends is a way of sounding your life. Music is an incredible universal language, truly a gift from God. Sometimes when I'm moving to music, it's as if time stands still. I'm so focused, so caught in the moment that the stresses of life and school just seem to disappear. I literally feel one with the universe.

■ ■ ■ ■ ■ ■ ■ ■ ■ ■ ■ —Liz Marshburn, 17

In the center of the big room stood a table covered with drums and tambourines, rainsticks and finger cymbals, maracas and bells. The team who wrote this chapter had brought them from Atlanta to the North Carolina camp where the authors of this book had our first meeting. There were enough instruments for everyone, something different for each. When it was time to start, Mark waved his hands across the table, inviting folks to gaze on each instrument in turn. "Choose one that seems right for you," he coaxed in his lovely British accent.

Liz, who had been in Mark's ninth-grade class the year before, knew exactly what to do. She lifted a rainstick almost as tall as she was, holding it high with the physical grace of an accomplished gymnast. Many others thumped or rattled a few instruments before finding one that pleased them. Emily seemed to be at home with them all; most had been sent to her by fans who wanted to thank her for the gift of her music as a member of the Indigo Girls, a Grammy Award–winning duo. She chose a drum from South Africa and settled onto a chair, the drum between her legs. All eyes turned to her. *Yes, we're ready*, the group seemed to be thinking. *Show us what to do.*

But Emily did not strike her drum. Instead, she handed Tim a bigger drum and asked, "Would you get us started?"

After only a moment's hesitation, Tim struck the taut skin of the drumhead with the sharp heel and branching fingers of his young brown hands. *Thum, tum-tum. Thum, tum-tum. Thum, tum-tum. Thum, tum-tum.* The beat was sure and steady, slow but not too slow. It was a beat everyone could catch and join. And join we did, one by one, until the beat belonged to all of us and we belonged to it. Alexx, on a small drum of higher pitch, added syncopation. Betsy had a low-pitched bell she rang in a regular pattern, slower than Tim's beat but still in rhythmic harmony. The music grew more and more complicated as our many instruments embellished it with beautiful, surprising clunks and swooshes and tings— loud for a while, then softer, then loud again, over and over.

The music seemed to rise up from our very souls and bodies to take on a life of its own. After a while, it started to fade. One by one we dropped out of the circle, until only three people were playing. Tim remained focused on the deep rhythmic *Thum, tum-tum, thum* of his large drum. Emily echoed with a *thum* and a *tum* on her smaller drum. And Liz added the occasional *whoosh* of a rainstick. The music subsided into a single drumbeat that finally faded into the damp night air. We all sat motionless, enveloped by the silence for several minutes. Not a word was spoken, yet somehow making music together had drawn us mysteriously closer.

When the silence felt finished, we talked for a while, and then we made more music, music of all different kinds. Several folks shared their talents on piano, guitar, or violin. Some sang songs both serious and humorous. We sang "Amazing Grace," which all of us knew even though we came from many different churches. Another sing-along involved us all in a rousing chorus to celebrate a new year for Matt, who turned 15 that day, and Tim, who would turn 14 the next. Even after part of the group went to bed, others stayed up for hours, playing their favorite CDs.

This chapter is about the Christian practice of making music. That statement might make you think of a church choir or church members singing from a hymnal. And those images are indeed part of this practice. All the authors of this chapter have enjoyed singing in church and

in choirs at some point in our lives. Making music together in worship weaves individuals together into a flexible, rhythmic, physical whole like our drum circle; everyone has a part, and the resulting sound is bigger than any one of the participants.

In this chapter we want to show you how the practice of making music also takes shape beyond the walls of church buildings. Music is God's gift to all people and to all creation. We want to explore three features of this practice:

- the way music opens us to be in community with others
- the way music rises up from our physical selves and also from the physics of the universe
- the way music gets us in tune with God and with the peace and justice God intends for all people

A community woven from rhythm and sound

Singing together brings people together with more than their voices. It creates shared memories and meaning. For Don and Emily (who are father and daughter), this happened in a special way on family vacations. Emily remembers, "We had a big old ugly green station wagon, with room enough for us four sisters in the back with Mom and Dad up front. To pass the time, we often sang songs together, picking as many harmony parts as we possibly could. We sang rounds from camp and church like 'White Coral Bells' and 'My Paddle's Keen and Bright,' right along with sacred music by Bach. We would improvise on our favorite songs from tapes and the radio. I will forever remember the feeling of how the songs joined us together in the growing darkness, as we were hurling through time and space, the

Do you have a favorite song that you used to sing ■ ■ ■ ■ ■ ■ ■ ■ ■ in the car with your family or friends? What memories does it bring back for you now?

car speeding through Ohio cornfields and Pennsylvania hills and past the dimly lit roadside stations."

Singing almost always brings us into community with one another, even when we're singing "Take Me Out to the Ball Game" at a stadium. You may have a similar experience at a live concert. Although you're surrounded by people you've never seen before and will never see again in this life, somehow you sense a kinship with those next to you and an instant bond with the whole audience. Looking back on that warm spring night in North Carolina, our writing group remembers the Way to Live drum circle as a key step toward our becoming a community. That event was especially powerful because all of us were invited to be musicians that night—even the ones of us who can't carry a tune.

Sharing music with someone else can create a special bond between you. Or it can express a bond that already exists. Emily remembers bonding this way as a teenager: "When I was in high school I discovered Joni Mitchell. Actually a friend introduced me to her music. That's the way most music gets passed around. We shared those songs in our struggles and little triumphs. When my friend Denise moved to France, we soothed the ache of separation by writing long letters peppered, colored, and accented by lyrics from our favorite songs. Those songs could say things just right in ways we couldn't say on our own. I signed my yearbook for Amy (who is now the other lead member of the Indigo Girls) with a Joni Mitchell quote. This seemed the only way to capture our friendship."

Another wonderful characteristic of music is its ability to unite us even across long distances, as happened for Emily and Denise. This connection is not just for friends. In making music, we join larger, invisible communities, some of which stretch across years and generations. Emily

Is there a particular song or a piece of music that goes straight to your heart?

shares a memory from her early traveling days: "Amy and I were driving in a car with Joan Baez across deep-South backroads, murky with dripping Spanish moss. Joan began to sing old spirituals, folk songs, anything that came to mind. I had the distinct sense of being surrounded by the beauty and depth of her voice and these songs. We drove through the dark night, fully present to one another in those moments the power of music gave us. It was as if all of the people who sang these songs long before us were there. The people whose names we don't remember who sang slave songs and chain-gang songs and the blues, and also Billie Holiday, Woody Guthrie, Bob Dylan—they were all there. I felt God was close, and I knew that the music was a divine gift."

Music even goes beyond life, linking us with people we've loved and lost. A family sang "For All the Saints" in church one day and suddenly found themselves moved to tears for a beloved sister and daughter who had died. And one boy told us that the song "That's What Friends Are For" took on special significance for him after his best friend was killed in a car accident and a group sang that song at his funeral. "Every time I hear that, he's there, and he's still my friend!"

Music is a body thing!

Have you ever had the feeling that your whole body can recognize certain songs? You hear a note or two and start to sway back and forth and mouth the words, while the memory that accompanies the song races through your being. The body can give itself over to music more deeply than the mind alone can do. The rhythms of our bodies are ready to hear the beat and feel the pulse. Maybe that's because our bodies—centered in the rhythms of heart and breath—make a certain kind of music themselves.

Music helps me express emotions I didn't even know I had. —JESSICA, 16

It's natural for our bodies to pulse with energy, blow air in and out, and erupt in sneezes, coughs, and burps. When we make music deliberately, our bodies are fully engaged. Singers breathe deeply, and drummers use their hands. Some of us also learn to move our fingers rapidly across a keyboard, draw our lips tightly across a mouthpiece, or drag a bow across a quivering string to create music.

A woman in Don's church tells a story that illustrates how deeply music can enter our bodies—how music can actually become a part of us, whether we know it or not: "My husband had been gradually going downhill with Alzheimer's. At first we didn't know what was happening, just that he kept forgetting things, but eventually he was diagnosed. The kids and I decided that he should stay at home as long as possible. But we rarely took him out, even to church. This was a relief, in a sense, because going out always made him confused, and all of us were embarrassed for him around old church friends he could no longer name.

"Then one Sunday when our daughter and son were home from college, we just decided to go to church together. By this time, my husband had almost stopped speaking, and he usually could not even recognize his own children. So we were nervous about this outing, and we made sure to sit in a pew toward the back of the church. My husband sat silently through much of the service. Then suddenly, when the congregation rose to sing after the offering, he too stood up, straight as could be, and joined in: 'Praise God from whom all blessings flow.' He didn't miss a single word! We were dumbfounded, and tears streamed down our faces. It was like a little miracle. For a glorious moment, he was alive to us and to something outside himself—all because this song and these words were imprinted so deep inside him."

I fall asleep to the Dave Matthews Band every night because it brings me peace. Music is a whole experience and I couldn't live without it. —SEAN, 17

Music takes deep root in us partly because it works in and on us in multiple ways. Sometimes music's *rhythm* grabs us, practically forcing our feet to move to the beat. The pulse of the beat echoes with our heartbeat, and we feel united with the music.

Sometimes the *melody* won't let us go—like sentences in a language we know but cannot speak. The notes curve up and down, rising and falling. High notes, low notes, running up, falling down, all put together in a pattern we take into ourselves. (Does a melody ever get stuck in your head so that you find yourself humming it over and over again?)

Sometimes we notice the *harmony*. Harmony intensifies both the melody and the words. Thanks to harmony, we can move through various emotional spaces in different kinds of music. We may want simple, comforting harmonies, like those in folk songs or ballads. Or we may want the wild, wailing harmonies of B-rock or fusion, with startling mixtures of instruments and voices.

Sometimes we relate to the *words*, the poetry. Song lyrics offer us a way of communicating with others and a way of putting our own unformed feelings into words. Stitching words together with melody, rhythm, and harmony makes them easier to remember and more expressive. The heartbreak, wisdom, or comfort conveyed by words and music together are greater than what either can do alone.

All these aspects of music—rhythm, melody, harmony, words—work together. The practice of making music not only leads us into community with one another; it also enables us to experience our own thoughts and feelings in a way that is beyond words. And because music is so powerful and so deeply rooted in body memory, people often encounter God while sharing in the practice of making music. The songs we sing in Christian

Let the heavens be glad, and

Let the sea roar, and all that fills it;

Let the field exult,

Then shall all the trees of the forest

worship—whether printed in a hymnbook or projected on a screen—are pathways to community with others and to unity with God. The North African bishop Saint Augustine is said to have commented many centuries ago, "Whoever sings, prays twice" (or rather, *"Qui cantat, bis orat"*).

The universal language of music

Mark—a man of many interests who is fascinated by religion and music and science—suggests that music tells us something about the unity of the universe itself. "Music is not just a human thing," he says. "In some ways it is truly a universal language. To quote the Rodgers and Hammerstein classic, 'The hills are alive with the sound of music!' But so are the trees and the planets, the rivers and the fields. Indeed, the entire universe is alive with the sound of music!"

Whether you live near the beach or in the heart of the city, whether your home is on the hot plains of Texas or in the hills of Tennessee, music is there. Its sounds vary—the crash of surf on the beach, the rumble of buses in the city streets, the electric whirring of cicadas, the rustle of leaves on an autumn day—but rhythm and harmony are everywhere. The whole of creation seems caught up in a fantastic symphony.

Scientists once believed the smallest particles in the universe were atoms. Then they discovered electrons and protons. Then came quarks. Now scientists have discovered components they call strings. Strings are like tiny pieces of spaghetti but millions of times smaller. They vibrate like strings on a violin or guitar but at a fantastically high frequency. If the scientists are right, the most fundamental particle in the universe is a vibrating string! Think of it! This discovery offers a new way of understanding a very old idea: The whole creation is singing to God.

let the earth rejoice; and everything in it. sing for joy before the LORD. —PSALM 96:11-12

In an ancient sacred story from India, God is said to "dance creation." God is depicted as a great dancer, and the whole world is God's dance. If the dancer were to stop dancing, the dance itself—the world—would cease to be. According to this story, we can hear music everywhere because all that exists is caught up in a single great cosmic dance, from the rhythmic swirl of galaxies to the vibration of tiny subatomic particles, from choruses of birds at sunrise to the gurgle of water cascading over the face of a mountain. God is dancing it all.

Christians and Jews tell the story of God's speaking everything into existence (see Genesis 1). But there is something quite harmonious and musical about the way creation responds to God's voice. Our vision of the world and our sacred scriptures, the Bible, are full of music. "O sing to the LORD a new song; sing to the LORD, all the earth!" It's as if all of creation can't help but sing out God's praise! This exclamation is from Psalm 96, one of 150 songs, expressing every human emotion, that are gathered in the Bible's Book of Psalms. Although we don't know the exact melodies and harmonies the ancient Israelites used when they sang these songs, those who read them aloud in Hebrew hear beautiful rhythms in the verses. Many Christian communities around the world sing psalms every day to new melodies that reflect their own musical tastes, and many popular hymns and songs are also creative adaptations of specific psalms.

Making music: getting in tune with God's justice and God's peace

Most teenagers listen to 20 or 30 hours of music each week, usually alone. Yet music can exert its greatest power when we listen, play, or sing together. Whether we are in a car, on a bus, around a campfire, in the streets, in church, or in a choir, band, or orchestra, the union of our sounds enhances our appreciation of the sacredness in this practice and the sense of God's holy presence through it.

Some say it's possible to listen to music that demeans women

During the American civil rights movement, people sang in churches and in the streets. "We shall overcome, we shall overcome. . . ." Making this music together signaled a step into community and a step toward freedom. Music played a crucial role also when people in South Africa were struggling against the system of racial oppression called apartheid. The song "We Are Marching in the Light of God" moved both body and soul during those times. Songs like these express some of our deepest human yearnings. Today people all over the world sing both these freedom songs.

Music has ignited and sustained the work of peace and justice throughout human history. In 1989 Emily witnessed that connection in Germany. She remembers: "Thousands of teens and others helped bring down the Berlin Wall. The Indigo Girls were there. On a bitter-cold day, I took a chisel to that huge symbol of division between people. Amy and I physically took a crack at that thick gray wall. Film footage of our hammering was later released on a video for the song 'Get Together.' Money from that single went to Habitat for Humanity. Music bridged the space between construction that divided and construction that united people."

Stories of how sharing music motivates people to take action for a better world also come from individuals. Emily receives many letters from fans who say that her songs have been important to them. One girl wrote to say that the words and rhythms of "Prince of Darkness" gave her hope to overcome the power of drug addiction and live in the Light. A neighbor of Emily's in Atlanta was inspired by the song "Shame on You" to assist Latin American women organize for better health care. And many gay youth thank Emily for songs like "Trouble," "It's Alright," and "Philosophy of Loss," because the words and music express what it's like to be gay and accepted. For all these fans, sharing music offers strength and courage.

Music has that kind of power. If it's true that "you are what you eat," it's also true that you become what you hear and take to heart. Songs shape our souls. That's why it's important to ask whether some music and some or glorifies violence and screen out those parts. What do you think?

words are good for us. Listening to words that hurt or demean other people may be like eating toxic substances. Music with such words may not serve us or our community well. How music is used also matters. The Nazis used beautiful music for evil purposes when they made Jewish musicians play Mozart in the shadow of Holocaust gas chambers.

A sad but inspiring story reported by survivors of a mass rape and murder in 1981, during El Salvador's civil war, illustrates how the music we know by heart can shape us. One of the youngest victims did not scream or cry out as she was assaulted. Instead, she began to sing hymns and simple songs from her childhood. She stopped only when she had breathed her last breath. At first the soldiers responsible for the violence were astounded, but soon they became afraid and ashamed of what they had done. The simple songs of faith—her culture's version of "Jesus Loves Me," learned in a village church—became a powerful witness against unspeakable evil.

A gift from God, an offering to God

Music has always been a fundamental part of human life. And from the beginning of time, it has been a powerful way to worship God. Some oldies—the psalms especially—have been (and will continue to be) sung for centuries. But music is alive and therefore develops new expressions as times change. Every year musicians compose hundreds of new melodies and translations for singing the psalms in their attempt to allow more people to enjoy and understand them. A similar creative process shapes all our music.

In 1940, for example, a 25-year-old man moved from his home in Switzerland to establish a Christian community of prayer, song, and out-

I love singing in the school choir. The chorus room is unlike any other room. I simply love to make the sound with the whole group. Not everybody has a great voice. But when we really get into the words and the music, it's like I'm part of a huge instrument. Besides, we have more fun in that room than in any other class in high school. —TAMIKA, 16

reach in the small village of Taizé in eastern France. Brother Roger, as he came to be known, gathered an ecumenical community of brothers even as Europe was being torn apart by war. Meditative singing formed the core of their common worship, and now the "songs of Taizé" are being sung all over the world. The Taizé community attracts thousands of teen and young adult pilgrims each week, going there to sing and pray. (Learn these songs at www.taize.fr)

Each of us will need many songs as we find a way to live. And we will need communities in which to learn these songs and folks with whom to share them. We'll discover music at concerts or on CDs, and we'll find music at church, at camps, or at youth gatherings.

Making music can help us to become what God intends us to be— fully human, fully alive! Some of us recently experienced a fulfillment of this potential in a college chapel when a 90-voice African-American gospel choir filled every corner of the space with rocking, vibrant sound. Their music started quietly, gradually growing in strength and picking up new ranges of harmony until it finally burst out in glory. Then, very slowly, the music became quiet again; "Jesus, Jesus . . . ," the voices sang. All were hushed in the room as the music seemed to end. But then—like a fire of glowing embers—it burst into flame once more. The music would not end. The members of the choir were praying as they poured out their faith, their yearning, and their hope through their strong young voices. They prayed not just for themselves but for the whole congregation. And not just for the whole congregation, either, but for the whole living world! Those who heard their song couldn't tell the music from the prayer, couldn't tell the dancers from the dance.

Music is the language of the soul that we can hear, share, and pray together. Will you join us in the music? ■

Music for the tough times. Music for the party times. Music for in-love and out-of-love. Music for when you've got the blues. Music for joyful times. Music for lonely times Music that heals. Music that brings it all back. . . .

III**Prayer**

Praying is about opening yourself up to God. People pray in some form when they have wants or are thankful, but this chapter says that prayer can also be a way of life. If we can see and practice prayer everywhere in our lives, we can be constantly in touch with God and always feel God's love.

■ ■ ■ ■ ■ ■ ■ ■ ■ ■ ■ ■ —Alexx Campbell, 15

In a Siskiyou County juvenile detention center a 16-year-old-boy is locked up for assault and robbery. After three months of confinement, he takes a staple out of the sole of his shoe and carefully scratches "HELP ME!" in the floor of his damp cell.

He's praying.

Just after midnight a great-grandmother sneaks out of the vacation cabin, slips off her nightgown, and swims out into the middle of the lake. She floats on her back, looking at the glittering stars, listening to crickets. Slowly, she starts to sing.

She's praying.

In the waiting area of the hospital emergency center a teenage girl lies on a gurney. Her clothes are torn and bloodied, her left arm and shoulder wrapped in gauze and bandages. Around her stand three of her friends, their hands placed on their injured classmate. With eyes closed they stand very still, seeking to send healing love and peace through their bodies.

They're praying.

Back behind the football stands of his high-school campus, a freshman boy receives his first kiss from his girlfriend. He runs home whooping and hollering. Coming to a grove of oak trees, he jumps, swatting leaves and yelling at the sky, "Yes! Yes! Yes!"

He's praying.

Anxious from listening to her parents' vicious arguing, a 13-year-old girl pops the latch on her bedroom window, grabs her skateboard, and lowers herself down to the blacktop alley. Within minutes she is gliding on her board through the city park. She breathes in the elms and maples, the grass and ferns. She listens to the rhythm of the skateboard wheels clicking across the cement grooves. She feels the cool air flowing over her body.

She's praying.

Everybody prays

Atheist, Buddhist, Hindu, agnostic, Christian, Muslim, or none of the above—everybody prays. Walk inside a classroom on the first day of finals and you'll see kids taking out pencils, looking up, and saying, "Please let me pass this test." Walk down the maternity ward at the local hospital and you'll find parents rocking their babies, whispering, "Thank you, thank you." The five-year-old lying on her back in the grass staring at the clouds, the junior-high boy in the tract home writing in his journal at 2:00 A.M., the college buddies singing around the beach bonfire, the single father passing out coffee to homeless men—they're all praying.

Prayer isn't reserved for churchgoers, devout people, ministers, and monks. Prayer isn't limited to words, churches, or religious objects. Prayer is a relationship that everyone has with the mysterious Power of Life. Prayer is a basic human activity. But what makes an experience "prayer"? Is every peaceful feeling, every cry for help, every hopeful desire considered prayer?

Heart's desire

Human *beings* could almost be called human *wantings*. Sometimes it feels like we all are born with a tiny Cookie Monster in our brain who continually cries: "Me want candy." "Me want new shoes." "Me want drive car."

Have you ever experienced being "nudged" to pray? Maybe it's a feeling inside or a thought that comes to you. Christians believe that often the Spirit of God stirs within us, nudging us to pray. Take a walk or go sit outside. After a few minutes of quiet, say to Jesus, "Teach me to pray." See what thoughts, images, scriptures, feelings, or situations come to you. Pray as Jesus leads you to pray.

"Me want sexy girl." Desires for pleasure, possessions, entertainment, and other distracting stuff bombard us every day. If we look beneath these wants, we find more basic desires for food, warmth, and companionship. If we're willing to look further, we'll discover even deeper desires that reside way down in the center of our beings. We long for unconditional love, freedom, and joy.

These human longings can't be satisfied by a person or material object. Yet when we notice these longings, our hearts open and our attention is drawn out, beyond ourselves toward a deeper Power. Opening our hearts and releasing our longings out toward the Power of Life makes an experience "prayer."

Often prayer begins as a longing in the heart, a longing for love, a longing for connection, a longing to make contact with a Power greater than ourselves. Sometimes it begins as a desperate need for help, peace, strength, or comfort. Other times prayer's beginning is a deep hope for others—an ache for suffering to stop, for the earth's healing, for care of the poor. Sometimes prayer begins in fear. We reach out for something to save us, to protect us, to let us know that we'll be OK. Sometimes prayer feels like a longing that's been met, like a deep spring of peace welling up within our hearts, spilling over and filling us with gratitude and love.

Look over the stories of prayer at the beginning of this chapter. Each person expresses a longing for help, healing, connection, gratitude, love, or peace. Some of the individuals are longing through words ("Help me!"), others through their bodies (the girls with their hands on an injured friend). Some experience their longing burning within them, while others feel their longing is being met (the woman singing). Everybody prays because everybody longs.

Giving it to God

What makes a prayer *Christian* is directing our longings to God rather than to an anonymous "Power." Christian prayer is opening our hearts for God to receive and address our longings. Christians experience God as the Presence of Love in the world that welcomes our wants and desires. We know this love most directly through the life and companionship of Jesus Christ.

Throughout the New Testament, people open their hearts to Jesus and offer him their raw desire: "Heal my eyes." "Make my friend well."

When was the last time you felt a deep longing? After reading this paragraph, place your hand over your heart. Close your eyes, sit for a few minutes, and notice your breathing. ■ When you feel ready, imagine a long winding staircase that goes from the top of your head down into the depths of your heart. ■ Imagine walking down that staircase slowly, from your head down into your heart. ■ As you come near your heart, what do you notice? Is there fear, boredom, anger, or love? ■ Imagine yourself reaching the end of the staircase in the very center of your heart. What does it look like? Is it warm or cold? Is it dark or light? ■ When you're ready, ask your heart this question: "What do I *really* long for?" ■ Spend the next few minutes repeating this question. Notice what images, feelings, and thoughts arise.

■■■■■■■■■■■■■■■■■■■■■■■■■■■■■■■■

"Teach me." "Change me." Jesus encouraged people to bring him their desires. Again and again he asked people, "What do you want?" In response, people brought despair, doubts, hope, and anger. They wept at his feet, held his hand, or touched his clothes. Others just simply longed to be with him. They sat, listened, walked, or ate with him.

Another way to see the variety of Christian prayer is to observe how Jesus prayed. For Christians, Jesus was not only the Presence of God in the world, he was also the presence of a regular human being. Jesus experienced many of the same sorrows, desires, feelings, and thoughts that we have. "Teach us to pray," Jesus' friends said to him one day. So Jesus did. He told them stories—of a person who went to a friend's house in the middle of the night to borrow food. The friend was asleep in bed, but after persistent knocking he rose from bed and came to the door to help. "Keep praying even when it seems like nothing is happening," his message seemed to be; "God is responding."

Other times Jesus told them how to pray: "Pray in secret, in your room, with the door shut." Often he showed his friends how to pray by his own example. He prayed in nature. He prayed on mountaintops, by lakes, and in deserted places. He prayed with his friends and with hurting people. He prayed with his body—lifting his arms, laying his face down on the ground, lifting his eyes toward the sky. He told his friends what to pray for:

"Pray for your enemies." "Pray for food." "Pray that you won't be tempted." "Pray that God's way of life will happen all over the world." "Pray for forgiveness." Christians all over the world have memorized some of Jesus' words of prayer and pray them each Sunday as the Lord's Prayer.

We see that for Christians prayer can take forms as diverse as any human relationship: talking, listening, acting, being. Prayer may be physical only (lifting arms to the sky, kneeling, curling up on a bed); prayer may be listening (noticing the words, images, feelings that God gives you); prayer may be action (helping a friend); or prayer may be just being (sitting and enjoying God's presence in the world).

Polite words and magic wishes

As a child I thought that prayer concerned only my wants. Every night at bedtime I would present God with a long list. "Dear Lord, please let it snow tomorrow. Let Dad come home early from work. Please don't let me have too much homework. And please smite Jeff and all his future offspring for breaking my bike. In Jesus' name, amen."

I seemed to think God was a giant genie in the sky and prayers were magic wishes. By observing my parents and others at church, I learned some of the tricks to make the magic work: You had to close your eyes and not peek. You couldn't smile or giggle. You had to start with "Dear Lord," and you had to end with "In Jesus' name." I learned that God could be touchy. Prayers had to be polite and formal. You had to say "thank you" and give lots of compliments ("God, you're looking so *mighty* today!"). You had to use all the right titles—Jehovah, Creator, Your Royal Godness.

You also had to be careful not to get too pushy. It was best to pretend like what you really wanted didn't matter. The trick was to ask first for all the things *God* wanted before mentioning what *you* really wanted: "God, help me to be good. Help me to be kind. Help me to be loving—and—oh yeah *(as if you didn't care),* please find some way to get me the new Starmaster III Video Laser Adapter—not the generic laser adapter but the really cool Starmaster III—and let there be peace on earth. In Jesus' name, amen."

Clearly the best prayers were by people with deep voices who spoke God's special and unique "ith" language: "O God of Zion, thankith thee forith thisith dayith. Grantith that we mayith be worthy of thy . . ." (this is the part where I usually fell asleep).

Strolling Prayer ■

One way to experience your relationship with God is to take a walk with Jesus. ■ Go outside and prayerfully ask Jesus to walk with you. ■ As you walk, notice what it's like to invite Jesus to be with you. Share any thoughts, worries, or concerns that come to you as if you are telling them to a friend. ■ What do you see around you as you walk with Jesus? Where is your attention drawn? ■ You might close this time by thanking Jesus for his companionship.

Unfortunately I could never get the magic to work. Many of my prayers were not answered (God never smote my neighbor Jeff, who grew up, got married, and has lots of children). I couldn't understand why I should pray. What was the point of bringing my wants to God if God never met them?

Being in love

Listen to prayers in church on a Sunday morning, and you can understand why as a child I believed that prayer was about trying to get what you want (or want what you get). Most prayers in church are a long list of wants: "Help Doug feel better." "Let the Giants win on Saturday." "Give us rain for the crops." Although our longings and desires bring us to prayer, the purpose of prayer is not to get what we want. (Then God would be Santa Claus.) The purpose of prayer is to open our hearts to God. Like any loving relationship, the greatest pleasure is just being with the one you love. "God is love," writes John in the New Testament, and for Christians, prayer is being in this love, having a relationship with the Presence of Love as encountered in Jesus Christ. Prayer, then, is an experience of opening our hearts to God's love and allowing God's love to enter all the worries, concerns, longings, and joys that we carry.

I have two boys, Noah, age five, and Joseph, age three. I spend a big part of my time with them responding to their wants and desires: They need a glass of water, they're cold from splashing their feet in the toilet, their eyes are stuck together with peanut butter and they can't see. Each time they bring me a need or desire, I try to respond. Some desires are fleeting: "I want gum." Others are deeper desires: *"I want gum."* Sometimes their needs are unspoken. They cry and lift their arms; they tug on my leg to dance with them; they climb on my lap and want me to hold them. Like prayer, many of their interactions with me begin as a want. "I want to be with you." "I want help." "I want a hug."

Often I meet their desires: I bring them water when they're thirsty or hold them when they're sad. Other times their desires go unmet: They want a skinned elbow to stop hurting; they want me to stay home from work; they want to keep horses in their room. If you were to watch all the inter-actions between my sons and me, however, I don't think you would say that the relationship revolves around asking and receiving. I hope you would see a dad and his kids loving each other. For the truth is that my sons bring their desires to me because they love me, and I respond to their needs because I love them. With every desire they bring to me, we have an opportunity to deepen our relationship. I love them by giving them a glass of water. They love me by asking for warm socks or crying on my lap.

Like my relationship with my sons, prayer is ultimately about being in love. Prayer is the practice of giving and receiving love. This is what our longings lead us toward—a loving relationship with God. For this reason, prayer often involves the same activities found in any loving rela-tionship. We may talk, or we may listen; we may pour out our heart, we may feel hurt and argue. We may be together without words—we take walks, work, play, or just sit together, our hearts full and open, just enjoying the presence of the one we love.

Be yourself

It's Sunday morning at First Friendly Church. The members are seated in their pews as the pastor ascends the lectern: "Good morning, everyone. Let us begin our service today with prayer. Please bow your heads. Dear

Being with God
When do you feel most alive and open to God? Is it when you are walking, writing, being with friends, singing? ■ Next time you engage in an activity you enjoy, ask God to be with you. ■ See what it's like to do this activity as a prayer, noticing God with you as you write, play, sing, or whatever. ■ How do you feel when you share something you love with God? How could this activity become a regular time of prayer?

God, you do nothing to stop the suffering in the world. You're a liar and your promises sicken me. I'm filled with anger toward you. In Jesus' name. Amen. Now, does anyone have any announcements?"

This scene is difficult to imagine, yet it should not be an uncommon experience in church or in any praying community. Any real loving relationship naturally includes times when you are hurt or angry. Real love means being real honest. It means not hiding doubts, sadness, questions, or disappointment. Any prayer life that involves only happy feelings is a surface relationship.

Remember Dan Taylor in the movie *Forrest Gump*? Taylor was a lieutenant in the Vietnam War. Wounded during a difficult battle, he ends up losing both his legs. Years later, still angry about the loss of his legs, he is working with Forrest on a fishing boat. On Sundays he goes to church with Forrest but sits in the back, too angry with God to participate in the service. One night while fishing, they're hit by a horrific storm with crashing waves and swirling winds. The legless Taylor straps himself to the topmast of the boat, shakes his fist at the sky, and lets God have it. Screaming and cursing at God, he yells, "Come on! You call this a storm? You'll never sink this boat!" Forrest Gump later comments that after this night of yelling at God, Taylor is able to find peace and gratitude toward God for his own life.

> ■ ■ ■ ■ ■ ■ ■ ■ ■ ■ ■
>
> **He was praying in a certain place, and after he had finished, one of his disciples said to him, "Lord, teach us to pray, as John taught his disciples."**
>
> —LUKE 11:1

When we feel God is absent from us, perhaps we are absent from ourselves. God is present in our hearts, but we are afraid to be with ourselves. We have too much anger or hurt, so we stay distracted, busy with friends, and we stop praying—anything besides just being with ourselves.

Praying our hearts implies praying all that is inside of us—the good, the bad, and the ugly. Only then are we truly in a loving relationship with God, a relationship where we can be honest about ourselves. Only then can God's love penetrate the depths of our being.

Even Jesus prayed, "My God, my God, why have you forsaken me?" (quoting Psalm 22:1). In the Book of Psalms we find this prayer: "Why, O LORD, do you stand far off? Why do you hide yourself in times of trouble?" (Psalm 10:1). Real prayer invites us to be ourselves, even when our parents, friends, or society can't accept who we are. This invitation is the gift of prayer—to stay in touch with who we are. Praying keeps us connected to our own heart, and soon we discover that to be with God is to practice being with the truest part of ourselves.

Finding our prayer

Every morning in our home my wife calls my two sons over to the couch, puts her arms around them and holds them. She talks softly to them, strokes their hair, and rubs their backs. I often noticed this morning ritual but never asked her why she did it. One recent morning we were late to an appointment. Just as we were about to go out the door, Jill called the boys over to the couch and began her normal routine of slowly holding them and stroking them. I quickly became upset and

Oh my toenail's long, everyone's wrong, mash potatoes for supper . . .

began to complain, emphasizing how important it was for us to get out the door. My wife stopped me in midsentence and said, "Listen, if these boys don't start the day being held and loved, they won't be able to be themselves the rest of the day."

If we are going to be truly ourselves, then we need to spend regular time being held and loved by God. To find that nurture, we need to give time to prayer. As we pray, our longings can surface and our hearts can open to receive God's love. The best way to begin praying is to discover the ways in which you already pray.

Usually, when I come home from work, I pick up my guitar from its stand in the living room, sit on our frumpy green couch, and begin to pluck out various chord progressions. Sometimes I play the same three or four chords over and over like a broken CD player. Other times I play little tunes and sing whatever words come into my head ("Oh my toenail's long, everyone's wrong, mash potatoes for supper . . .").

This time of rather aimless music playing makes me feel like myself. I no longer have to wear the Project Director mask that I present at work. I can relax, be myself, and enjoy being alive through the music. Sadness, silliness, thoughts of love and beauty all swirl in and around me as I play. I often feel like I'm playing my own heart, the mixture of feelings and desires that reside there. Over the years, I've realized that this is a time of prayer for me. It's a time when I am open and available to God. So each time I pick up the guitar, I simply say this little prayer, "Be with me, Lord," and then as I play I'm aware of God's being with and close to me. God is listening to the music, dancing on the strings, laughing at the idiotic words, joining

The great thing is prayer. Prayer itself. If you want a life of prayer, the way to get it is by praying. . . . You start where you are and you deepen what you already have. —THOMAS MERTON

me when longings for peace or sadness for a friend arise. My guitar time has become a time of prayer and enjoying God.

In what activity, place, or situation do you feel most alive and present? Could this possibly be your prayer time? Chances are, your heart already is open to God at those moments.

Becoming prayer

Throughout Christian history people have tried to understand prayer not as something you *do* but as something you *be*. Paul encourages us in 1 Thessalonians to "pray without ceasing," and many Christians have been inspired to try to live their life as a prayer. One such person was Brother Lawrence, a 17th-century monk who converted to Christianity at age 18. Brother Lawrence wasn't a good preacher; he wasn't a visible leader or eloquent writer; in fact, he spent most of his life as a dishwasher and cook's helper in a monastery. Although Brother Lawrence wasn't a great leader, he was a great pray-er. Brother Lawrence believed that all of life should be prayer. Instead of reserving prayer for chapel or other set times, he tried to live with the awareness that he was always in the presence of God. He tried to notice and acknowledge God's presence in all places and in all activities. He believed washing dishes or cleaning floors was just as prayerful as kneeling in the sanctuary.

> **Lord of all pots and pans and things . . .** Make me a saint by getting meals And washing up the plates!
>
> —BROTHER LAWRENCE

He called this "practicing the presence of God." The way he practiced was simple. Throughout the day he would just turn his heart's attention to God's presence, as if noticing a loving friend in the room. He then would work, eat, talk, or engage in other activities with the awareness that God was present and loving him. In this way, all of his actions became prayer. He could engage in all activities with a heart open to God. He could see God present and loving him in the food he ate, the sunshine through the windows, the dirty dishwater, and any other ordinary experience.

This state of being is the final hope of prayer—that we might become prayer. Whether we are with our friends, playing sports, mowing the lawn,

Setting a Regular Time of Prayer

You may feel drawn to develop a more formal prayer time. Here are a few suggestions to consider:

1. Find a space that helps you pray, perhaps a space of beauty but not full of distractions. Your space might be a chair in the backyard, a darkened room with a candle, a comfy chair next to the fireplace, a bed in your room, a chapel in your church.

2. Once you have chosen the space, set a time. Start with a small amount of time, like 10 to 30 minutes.

3. Take a few moments to just sit in silence. Allow your body and mind to settle a little. When you first sit down to pray, your insides are like a muddy pond. To clear the pond, sit and wait. Eventually the mud settles to the bottom, and the water becomes clearer. Usually it helps to find a simple word or phrase to repeat: "Jesus Christ"; "Into your hands I commit my spirit"; "Abba, I belong to you"; "Peace"; or some other phrase. Simply say this phrase over and over within you as though you're listening to the rhythm of the ocean. As interesting thoughts arise, don't try to stop them or latch on to them. Just keep saying your phrase.

4. After five minutes or so, begin to do what you love to do with God. That may be writing your thoughts in a journal, painting, reading scripture, or continuing to sit in silence. It may be lying on your back, singing, dancing, or whatever helps you open your heart to God.

5. At the end of your set time, offer thanks to God and close with a simple prayer for the day—something like "Lord, help me to be loving this day" or "Help me to see you in every person I meet."

6. Keep at it. Jesus taught that the most important part of prayer is being persistent (see Luke 18:1-8). The more we continue to pray, the more our heart opens for receiving and giving love. Try to continue the same prayer practice even when you get bored or tired of it. Praying is a little like playing an instrument or being an athlete: It takes practice. Over time you'll discover that your prayer time will begin to transform you. You may notice a greater sense of peace, a deeper longing to help others, a greater hunger to be with God, a stronger sense of who you are. These are natural fruits of spending time with God. ▪▪▪▪▪▪▪▪▪▪▪▪

studying, or riding in the car, we are aware of God's loving us. As we practice noticing God's love, we begin to engage in all of our relationships and activities with an open heart, bringing loving attention to all we meet and all we do.

Jesus' prayer

One summer I had the privilege of spending a week with 60 high-school students from around the country at a conference on prayer and spiritual growth. After learning and practicing many different forms of prayer, we decided to spend one of our final days in the poorest area of nearby San Francisco. We arrived early in the day and walked around the neighborhoods, shelters, medical centers, and distribution centers that served the homeless population. We stood in line and ate lunch with over 2,000 homeless people at a Catholic kitchen and shelter.

At the end of the day, we walked into an old cathedral in the middle of this poverty-stricken neighborhood. We were stunned. Marble floors, high arched ceilings, passionate paintings in gold and red, dark oak pews, polished brass, and a striking crucifix at the front of the sanctuary. Our group of young people and adults spent a few minutes just walking around, hushed and reverent in the midst of the beautiful architecture and sacred art. After a while we gathered at the front of the sanctuary and began to talk about our day, about the hungry people, the children and families who were living in cars, the similarity between their lives and our own. Suddenly one girl said, "But they're not really homeless. They have this cathedral— this is their home, and in truth it's our only real home too." As she spoke, she pointed to the pews, and for the first time we noticed all the people—men and women asleep in the pews, street children sitting and playing in the back of the cathedral, small groups of weathered men drinking

Practicing the Presence ■ ■ ■ ■ ■ ■ ■ ■ ■ ■ ■ ■ ■ ■ ■ ■ ■

Think of something that will remind you of God's presence with you. It could be hearing school bells, noticing your watch, or seeing children. ■ Every time you come across your reminder, turn your heart to God. Become aware of God's presence as you continue to go through your day. ■ What is it like to notice God? What are you like when you are aware of God's presence with you?

288

coffee and enjoying the quiet, women in worn shoes and layered jackets kneeling and praying.

We realized then, in an inexpressible way, that despite the pain and hopelessness we had witnessed, despite the shock of so much suffering, somehow all of us, street people and suburban people, rich and poor, drug addicts and high-school students, were all under God's cathedral of love. Somehow in the silence of that moment we knew that the whole screwed-up, unjust, heartbreaking mess of humanity was covered in the nurturing acceptance, freeing love, and uncontrollable joy of God. Unexpectedly one young girl stood up and took off her shoes and socks. We looked at her, paused, then one by one, without saying a word, the rest of us began slipping off our footwear until we all stood barefoot, our skin pressing against the cool marble. Like Moses on Mount Sinai, we were on holy ground. There was an awkward silence. Someone began singing a blessing. The rest of us joined in and spontaneously we began to spread out, walking among our brothers and sisters in the cathedral, singing love and blessings to them while at the same time receiving love and blessings in return.

For those few moments we were no longer praying for God's justice, longing for the suffering to stop, we simply were prayer. Fully awake, fully transparent to God, allowing God's love to flow in and through us toward everyone we were seeing. As I walked, barefoot, tears in my eyes, I realized one of the deep mysteries of prayer. God was praying to us. God was asking me and others to answer Jesus' prayer for unity and peace among all people. God was crying out to me to share Christ's hope and work for love and peace to bloom in the world.

I stopped. Stood silent. Listening and opening to God's prayer. Then I answered, responding with the only response I could give to such a sweet and beautiful desire. I prayed the prayer Jesus taught us, the prayer that has held the longing of so many people over the centuries, the prayer that held my own longing. The prayer that Jesus himself prayed:

Our Father in heaven, hallowed be your name, your kingdom come, your will be done, on earth as in heaven. Give us today our daily bread. Forgive us our sins as we forgive those who sin against us. Save us from the time of trial and deliver us from evil. For the kingdom, the power, and the glory are yours, now and for ever. Amen. (ICET)

Becoming prayer means praying with Jesus, praying as Jesus prayed. It means praying for the despised and the broken-hearted. It means praying for the end of violence and environmental destruction. It means praying for the hungry, the lonely, and the abused. As we become prayer, we begin to get in touch with Jesus' prayer, with the very spirit of Jesus praying within us, "with sighs too deep for words." We notice that our longing and our prayer actually are shared with God. And that our longing and our prayer are shared with other people. When Christians gather together, we know that Jesus' spirit is with us. We support one another in opening our hearts before God. We remind one another that God is as close as our next breath. We encourage one another to listen for God's prayer. We join Jesus in praying for bread and for-giveness, for everyone's longings—even the earth's—to be met and held by the One who loves us. With Jesus and through Jesus we return thanks and love for all that we are given, for all the moments when we notice we're alive.

> ■ ■ ■ ■ ■ ■ ■ ■
> **Likewise the Spirit helps us in our weakness; for we do not know how to pray as we ought, but that very Spirit intercedes with sighs too deep for words.**
> —ROMANS 8:26

We love God by praying with God—our eyes stuck with peanut butter, our elbows skinned, our minds filled with cookie-monster desires—we bring it all to God. "Amen," we say to God. Then, nearer than our own heartbeat, we hear God whisper within us, *Yes, my beloved. Amen. And one more thing, I love you too.* ■

DOROTHY C. BASS
WITH JOHN SCHWEHN
AND MARTHA SCHWEHN

‖‖Practice

During the two years it took to write **Way to Live** and prepare it for publication, the 18 teenagers and 18 adults who were involved learned a lot. We've put as much of what we learned into this book as we could. We are proud to send it out into the world. We hope that it will help you learn about a way to live. ■ ■ ■ ■ ■ ■ ■ ■ ■ ■ ■ ■

> **But we also need to issue a warning:**
> Reading this book is
> only a small part of your journey into
> the abundant life God offers.

The authors of this book learned a lot—and discovered the truth of this warning—by experience! We are real people, longing for good lives and a better world just as you do. So in this last chapter we want to tell you some insights we've had during our two years together.

Practice doesn't make perfect. And that's OK. Alexx makes this point well as he reflects back on our process. "In giving away 40 items from my room for Lent, I realized how difficult it can be to make a change in your life, even if you really want to make it," he says. "After becoming attached to material things, it was really hard to give away some of the stuff that I had for a long time. I even kept some of the better things I own, not willing to give away all my CDs or my stereo. People might think I am being hypocritical. However, it is important to understand that none of us will ever attain true perfection or a perfect sense of what God wants us to do with ourselves."

Many of the teenagers in our group were intrigued by the "Stuff" chapter—and so were the adults—because it challenged our own obsession with material possessions. This practice was inspiring, both in the way Alexx and Mark lived it and in the examples they shared from the early church and history. Some of us did our own Lenten giveaways the next year. But Alexx remained realistic and modest about how hard this practice is.

Some people would say that it's not worth doing a practice at all if others can find flaws in your performance. We don't agree. First of all, as Christians we don't claim to have reached a state of perfection or even a state of moral superiority to others. Instead, we live in the promise that God loves us even when we fail. That knowledge sets us free to risk living in new ways rather than staying stuck in old ones. And besides, we don't see practices as finished performances; that's why we say we are just *practicing* them. "A practice is what you do to get better at something like playing the cello or basketball," says Clinton, who worked on the "Bodies" chapter. "With enough practice you become a musician or an athlete." With practice, you also become a more welcoming person, a better friend, a stronger advocate for justice, and a more caring part of creation—not all at once, perhaps, and never perfectly. But through a practice, you become a little more involved in the loving, challenging life of God.

Emily, who wrote about "The Story" and "Food," says that doing the practice as a member of the community with Jesus at its heart gives her extra freedom to make mistakes. She is a vegetarian—not the normal thing in Spokane, Washington. "Sometimes at school," she says, "I feel like people are trying to trip me in my practice and that it's my personal responsibility to be a model and show it can be done. In my Christian community, however, I have a place to let down, even when the other members aren't vegetarians. I don't feel so alone and scrutinized. I don't have to pretend the practice is always easy. I can talk about the hard parts."

We know that some Christian communities can get pretty judgmental. Church is not always a place where we feel like we can "let down," as Emily put it. Emily speaks of belonging to supportive Christian communities. The community of people who wrote this book together is one, but let's be honest: Our group wasn't perfect.

Small steps can make a big difference. Sometimes it may seem that saying you're a Christian means you have to be a Mother Teresa: Give away *all* your stuff and devote your *entire* life to showing compassion for those who are suffering. Some people are indeed called to this kind of heroic service. Most of us, however, need to figure out how to make meaningful changes in our everyday lives within the places and the roles we already occupy.

That approach might sound wimpy, but it's not. Making these types of changes can be a significant way of resisting pressures to conform that are present in your school or neighborhood. After reading the "Stuff" chapter for example, John (who worked on the "Time" chapter) became disgusted with certain labels on his clothing. He didn't like being transformed into a walking billboard, and he had learned about working conditions in some of the factories where his clothes were manufactured. Now he has cut the label patches off his pants, and he wears his brand-logo T-shirts inside out. When he has outgrown these clothes, he'll be careful about what he buys next time. By making this choice, he is resisting the status-symbol system in his high school and becoming freer than he was before—more independent from peer pressure and more aware of his connection to the people who make his clothes.

Maggie (who wrote about "The Story" and "Food") speaks of other ways in which trying to live the practices more intentionally has changed her. "I am naturally a shy person," she says, "but this process has helped me to see the importance of reaching out and welcoming others. Being able to do that in one community—this group of authors—has helped me to do it in other places too." Perhaps the small step for you is not resistance to peer pressure but to a tendency in your own personality or habits. For Maggie this tendency was shyness; for Alexx it was attachment to his stuff.

Tim ("Creation") and Jack ("Play") report that deciding to devote small but regular amounts of time to prayer and Bible reading made a difference. "It is so cool when you begin to notice that God is present," says Jack. "After being more intentional in my practice of prayer, now the realization that God is with me sometimes sneaks up on me at other times of the day too. This is a wonderful, peaceful feeling." Tim speaks of how the practice of Bible reading is taking root deeper in him. "When I first started, I was the one always telling other people what they should know about the Bible. But now, something in the Bible can hit me in the face, and I realize it's directed right at me. I read something, and I feel like tearing out a verse and putting it up on the refrigerator."

In all these cases, small steps have led to deeper involvement.

Growing into a way to live is not like having to do your chores before you can have dessert. You can have dessert along the way. Writing this book was not a chore, though it was hard work. For each of our three meetings, everyone read the entire rough draft, turned in comment sheets, and spent several hours in small groups going over the chapters. But before, between, and after all this work, we had *fun*. We played incredibly dumb games to introduce ourselves to one another. We rode the Ferris wheel in Chicago and the cable cars in San Francisco. We ate—boy, did we eat! We busted a piñata after Nancy told us about its Christian symbolism as part of a worship service. The fact that it was a worship service did *not* inhibit anyone when it came time to dive for the candy.

But the best dessert of all—the sweetest part of each gathering for many of us—was an ongoing game of capture the flag. It started innocently enough in the mountains of North Carolina, when Frank Rogers and Mark

Yaconelli recruited players to their teams. (These guys are from California and look real easygoing in their jeans and longish hair, but do not be deceived! They are *fierce!*) The rivalry continued *inside* the hallways of a huge hotel in Chicago, with floors 35 and 37 as Frank's territory, 36 and 38 as Mark's, and elevators and stairwells as safe zones. The parking garage of our San Francisco hotel provided the third venue.

As you start exploring the practices in this book, don't forget to have dessert along the way. Don't become obsessed with the practice of work and neglect the practice of play. Let the good that God gives through each practice be yours, not only something you hope will benefit others. Treasure your own body as made in God's image. Experience the satisfaction of living truthfully. Allow other people to welcome you, even as you go around welcoming others. See how God is caring for you through the beauty of creation, even as you struggle to develop a way to care more responsibly for the earth.

Having a community is important. Remember how Martha felt after the mission trip (see "Life")? She had glimpsed a way to live that seemed right, but she was worried about how to continue it once she was back in the regular world. Coming home from each authors' gathering, Martha felt the same way. But now she knew that what she needed was a community—right in her own town. On the Sunday evening after our Chicago meeting, she got home exhausted after staying up until 2:00 A.M. playing capture the flag. She had homework to do, but she refused to miss the meeting of her church youth group because she was keenly aware of that need for a community within which to live her way into God's promises. She carried this awareness to school. Because reading the "Creation" chapter had drawn out her own profound caring for the environment, she dropped one of her musical activities and joined the Earth Awareness Club.

Whenever we human beings make an important commitment, we long for a face-to-face community to support us in it. That's why we invite all our friends and relatives to our weddings and find workout partners to encourage our fitness routines. Face-to-face communities can be difficult to find, but we urge you to seek good ones wherever you can—at a church, at your school, and among your families and friends. Share your growth in practices with others who understand and want to grow in similar ways.

Sometimes you may feel that no one is listening when you speak. This is painful. We trust you won't experience that kind of pain too often in your life, but we do need to tell you that life in the Holy Spirit will include loneliness and longing. When you have a vision of *life abundant*, you can also see more clearly all the ways in which this world blocks *life*. The more you let yourself feel your longing for justice, the more the injustice you witness every day will break your heart. When you go against the flow in your high school by refusing to belittle an unpopular student, somebody probably will belittle you as a result. When teenagers and adults have been together in a way that is fun and mutually appreciative, you will be angered even more by the walls that so often go up between these two groups.

To fully embrace this way to live, you need to know that you are yourself embraced by God, and so is the whole world, even though the vision of abundant life has not yet been fulfilled. Within a community that trusts God's embrace, we help one another to live as the prophet Micah said—doing justice, loving kindness, and walking humbly with God.

This is a long book! How does it all hang together?
Yes, this book is long. If it had fewer pages, it would be easier to fit in a pocket and perhaps less intimidating for some people to start reading. The fact is that it could be much longer than it is—*much* longer. We could give countless other examples of how the community with Jesus at its heart has practiced these practices over the centuries and in cultures all over the world. And we could add other practices. Health. Nonviolence. Science. Family. And many more.

We have done what we could, and we are grateful to God that we are not required to be perfect. Now we are turning this book, and this way to live, over to you. What will *you* do with it?

We hope you will

• **Listen carefully.** Which practice calls you to greater involvement in what God is doing in you and in the world around you? Find a community of people with whom to practice the practice you identify.

• **Explore a practice not included in this book** and develop your own "chapter" about it. Explore in teams of adults and teenagers. Share what you have learned in a report or guided experience for a larger group or on our Web site (www.waytolive.org).

• **Get a "serious" group to which you belong to play capture the flag** or another crazy game. Convince a goofy group you're in to take on some hard work together.

• **Become more aware of the practices you are already living** and the places where you already experience God's presence. When you realize that you have overcome an obstacle that used to drag you down into a hole of fear, celebrate! When you find a life-giving community or experience the presence of God or realize that you are growing into the person God wants you to be, rejoice! Write it down, speak it out loud, and give thanks!

• **Take the first step that's right for you**, and then the next, and then the next.

But we still haven't said how this way to live all hangs together. It all hangs together in God. In, with, and under all these practices is the very source of life, the God who made you and everything else, the same God who is always at work to renew and heal all creation, including you. As you explore this way to live, we pray that you will come to know and love God, your neighbor, yourself, and all creation ever more fully. ∎

MORE WAYS TO LEARN ABOUT CHRISTIAN PRACTICES

The authors of *Way to Live* have prepared two resources to help readers get more involved with the ideas in this book:

> www.waytolive.org (a Web site for teens)
> *Way to Live: Ideas for Growing in Christian Practices with Teens*
> (a guide prepared by the authors of *Way To Live* for group leaders, which is available for free download at the Web site)

This book, the Web site, and the guide were developed by the Valparaiso Project on the Education and Formation of People in Faith, a project of Lilly Endowment, Inc., based at Valparaiso University in Valparaiso, Indiana. The Valparaiso Project has also developed other books and resources. To learn more about these, visit the Valparaiso Project Web site www.practicingourfaith.org

This Web site is named for the project's first book on Christian practices, *Practicing Our Faith: A Way of Life for a Searching People*, edited by Dorothy C. Bass (San Francisco: Jossey-Bass, 1997). Check the Web site for an up-to-date list of project publications!

THE AUTHORS

Eighteen adults joined by 18 teenagers collaborated in writing *Way to Live*. We enjoyed the 50/50 balance and recommend it as a great way for adults and teens to work together! We planned the book and shared drafts of the chapters at meetings in San Antonio, Texas; Montreat, North Carolina; Chicago, Illinois; and San Francisco, California. At each meeting, chapter teams got feedback on drafts of their chapters; later, authors worked with the editors to prepare the final version of each chapter. It took one year to write the chapters and another year to design and produce the book.

The authors come from many parts of the United States and from several Christian denominations.

Dorothy Bass is director of the Valparaiso Project on the Education and Formation of People in Faith, a Lilly Endowment project based at Valparaiso University. Dorothy and her twins, **John** and **Martha,** write about *life, time*, and *practice*.

Susan Briehl is a Lutheran pastor (ELCA) and a writing associate with the Valparaiso Project. Susan and her daughters, **Emily** and **Maggie,** write about joining *the story* and about *food*.

Alexx Campbell is a high-school sophomore living in San Anselmo, California. He is a member of Sleepy Hollow Presbyterian Church (their motto is "we're neither"). Alexx enjoys running and has made close friends on his high-school track team.

Betsy Crowe "I was born in Austin, Texas, but moved to Atlanta when I was 10 so that my mom could attend Emory's Candler School of Theology. In Texas, my family and I went to church at University United Methodist Church where I was baptized. For the first few years in Atlanta, we didn't join a church, but ever since eighth grade, my dad and I have been members of Decatur (Georgia) First United Methodist Church. I am currently in the 10th grade. I am involved in and really care about my church youth group. I like going there for the fellowship and because we sing so much. Also, when I am there, I know I am in a moral setting, where I am cared about. Most of my best friends are in my youth group."

Jack DePaolo is a sophomore at Asheville High School (North Carolina). He plays tennis tournaments year-round, so when he's not in school, he's probably on a tennis court somewhere.

Angela Fernández is a sophomore at Loretto Academy in El Paso, Texas. Angela enjoys drawing, writing poetry, and playing tennis. She helps with the confirmation program and assists in leading retreats at her local Catholic parish.

Kaitlyn Filar "I am from the tiny town of Davidson, North Carolina. I'm currently finishing up my junior year at North Mecklenburg High School. I play volleyball for my school and am on a Junior Olympics team. I attend Saint Mark Catholic Church and was confirmed as a Catholic, but I consider myself somewhat of a wandering Christian. I haven't found the one church that I enjoy most, but I'm loving the experiences I gain in searching for my place. One thing that does feel right is Young Life. I was first introduced to it through my older brothers, and now I try to go to the weekly meeting every chance I can. College students lead each meeting, trying to share and spread Christianity for all who are interested. These leaders have become great friends, along with the other high-school students who I never would have gotten to know outside of Young Life."

Timothy Frazier is a ninth-grade honors student at Rancho Cucamonga High School (California). An accomplished pianist, Tim is a cell-group leader at the Cucamonga Christian Fellowship.

Carol Lakey Hess is a Presbyterian minister (PCUSA), practical theologian, and novelist. Carol and her daughter **Marie** write about *creativity*.

Marie Hess is a senior at Haddon Heights High School (New Jersey). She plays soccer and runs track and is an aspiring songwriter and guitarist.

Joyce Hollyday is associate conference minister for the Southeast Conference of the United Church of Christ. Joyce and her niece **Kaitlyn** write about *welcome*.

Cheryl A. Kirk-Duggan, a minister in the Christian Methodist Episcopal Church, is director of the Center for Women and Religion and assistant professor of theology and womanist studies in the Graduate Theological Union (California). Cheryl and her niece **Tatiana** write about *grieving*.

Judy Kuo is a senior at Alan C. Pope High School in Marietta, Georgia. Along with fellow youth group members from the Atlanta Taiwanese Presbyterian Church, Judy participated in a monthlong mission trip to teach English and Bible stories to orphaned children in Taichung, Taiwan. She is an accomplished violinist and performs with the Atlanta Youth Orchestra.

Carol Lytch, a Presbyterian minister (PCUSA), coordinates the Theological School Programs for Strengthening Congregational Leadership for the Fund for Theological Education. Carol and her daughter **Katie** write about *friends*.

Katie Lytch is a sophomore at Saint Francis High School in Louisville, Kentucky. She plays basketball, tennis, and volleyball for her school and sings in the Louisville Youth Choir. Most important to her is attending the church—Second Presbyterian—where her father is the pastor. There Katie participates in the youth group and the Cantate Choir and teaches Sunday school for three-year-olds.

Liz Marshburn is a junior at Saint Pius High School in Atlanta. A second-year USGA level-10 gymnast, Liz was chosen as a member of the Georgia All-Star Cheerleader Squad. She participates regularly in mission trips sponsored by the Cathedral of Christ the King.

Matthew Mistal is from Brandon, Mississippi. "I am a member of Pine Lake Baptist Church. I am currently in the 10th grade at Jackson Preparatory High School. The one activity that I care about probably more than everything is taking care of my 1997 Honda Civic. I wash it every day and wax it at least once a week. I work to buy things for my car such as a CD player. It is the first thing that has ever been just mine, and I work hard to take care of it."

Rodger Nishioka is associate professor of Christian Education and Youth Ministry at Columbia Theological Seminary in Georgia. Rodger and **Judy** write about *forgiveness*.

Kay Bessler Northcutt is a Disciples of Christ pastor and retreat leader. She teaches at Phillips Divinity School in Oklahoma. Kay and her nephew **Clinton** write about *bodies*.

Evelyn Parker is assistant professor of Christian Education at Perkins School of Theology, Southern Methodist University. Evelyn and **Raymond** write about *justice*.

Nancy Pineda-Madrid is a Roman Catholic lay leader and a doctoral student in systematic theology at the Graduate Theological Union (California). Nancy and her niece **Angela** write about *work*.

Don Richter, a Christian educator and Presbyterian minister (PCUSA), is project associate for the Valparaiso Project. Don and **Jack** write about *play*.

Raymond Rivera is a ninth-grader from Mesquite, Texas. He is United Methodist and enjoys attending a Bible study at church with his sister and friends.

Frank Rogers is a Roman Catholic lay leader, an actor and storyteller, and a professor of religious education at the Claremont School of Theology (California). Frank and **Tim** write about *creation*.

Don Saliers is the Franklin N. Parker Chair of Theology and Worship and director of the Master of Sacred Music Program at Emory University (Georgia). A United Methodist minister, Don composes choral church music and serves as organist/choirmaster for Emory's University Worship community. Don collaborates with daughter **Emily** Saliers, **Mark** Winstanley, and **Liz** to write about *music*.

Emily Saliers is one-half of the Indigo Girls, a Grammy Award–winning singer-songwriter duo, whose acclaimed recordings and performances are complemented by their commitment to social justice and humanitarian concerns. When not on tour, Emily resides in Decatur, Georgia, where she also owns a restaurant. Emily joins her dad (**Don**), **Mark** Winstanley, and **Liz** to write about *music*.

John Schwehn lives in Valparaiso, Indiana. He is in the ninth grade at Valparaiso High School and belongs to Christ Lutheran Church (ELCA), where he is active in the youth group. Every summer he and his family go to Holden Village, an ecumenical Christian retreat center in the Cascade Mountains, where he can get away from pressures and reflect on the important things in life.

Martha Schwehn is one and a half minutes older than her brother, John. She is also in ninth grade, a member of Christ Lutheran Church, and a member of the extended Holden Village community. She sings in the youth choir at church and plays the oboe at church and in the school band and orchestra. She is also learning to play the guitar.

Clinton Trench "Currently I am playing lots of music. I am expanding my CD collection and playing cello, double-bass, and bass guitar. My friend Paul also plays cello and guitar. I play everything from rock to funk to blues to classical." Clinton, a ninth-grader, lives in Stillwater, Oklahoma.

Magdalena Briehl Wells is a freshman at Lewis and Clark High School in Spokane, Washington. She is part of a four-year advanced placement studio art program and drew the pictures of books that represent the three authors in "The Story" and the foods that represent the authors in "Food." Along with other members of her youth group at Saint Mark's Lutheran Church, Maggie enjoys tutoring elementary-school kids.

Mary Emily Briehl Wells, a senior at Lewis and Clark High School in Spokane, is passionate about our care for creation, especially wilderness areas where she loves to hike. She and others involved in 20/20 Vision, an organization promoting peace and protecting the environment, are campaigning to pass the Young American Worker's Bill of Rights.

David White, a United Methodist minister, is director of the Youth Discipleship Project at the Claremont School of Theology (California). David and his nephew **Matthew** write about *choices.*

Melissa Wiginton serves on the staff of the Fund for Theological Education, directing the Partnership for Excellence and providing administrative leadership. Melissa and her daughter, **Betsy,** write about *truth.*

Tatiana Wilson "I live in Bay Point, California. I attend Phillips Temple CME Church in Berkeley. I've been attending church since I was two years of age. I am an usher, I sing in the choir, and I am a member of the Praise Dance team in my church. My current grade point average is 3.6. I am in eighth grade. What I really care about is keeping my grades up and being successful in school. My grandmother encourages me to accomplish this goal. She is the reason I keep my head up and keep going."

Mark Monk Winstanley is director of Emory University's Youth Theological Initiative, a summer program for rising high-school seniors. A native of England and a Roman Catholic lay leader and choral director, Mark collaborates with **Don** and **Emily** Saliers and **Liz** to write about *music.*

Mark Yaconelli is director of the Youth Ministry and Spirituality Project at San Francisco Theological Seminary. Mark and **Alexx** write about *stuff* and about *prayer.*

REFERENCES

Life

The Teresa of Avila quotation is in the public domain. The quotation from Augustine of Hippo is from Book I, Chapter 1, of his *Confessions*, available in many editions. The quotation "Preach the Gospel at all times. If necessary use words" is widely attributed to Saint Francis of Assisi and is based on instructions he gave to friars who had not been authorized to preach: "Let all the brothers, however, preach by their deeds" (chapter 17 of Francis's Rule of 1221).

The Story

"Sarah and her husband had had plenty of hard knocks in their time, and there were plenty more of them still to come, but at that moment when the angel told them they'd better start dipping into their old age pensions for cash to build a nursery, the reason they laughed was that it suddenly dawned on them that the wildest dreams they'd ever had hadn't been half wild enough." Frederick Buechner, *Peculiar Treasures: A Biblical Who's Who* (San Francisco: HarperSanFrancisco, 1979), 153.

Suggested Reading: *Manna and Mercy: A Brief History of God's Unfolding Promise to Mend the Entire Universe,* by Daniel Erlander (1992) is a wonderful, whimsical, hand-illustrated introduction to the biblical story. Order from Daniel Erlander, P.O. Box 1059, Freeland, WA 98249; (360) 331-4066. Rolf E. Aaseng, *A Beginner's Guide to Studying the Bible* (Minneapolis, Minn.: Augsburg Fortress Publishers, 1991), which provides basic steps for studying short passages or whole books of the Bible; Craig R. Koester, *A Beginner's Guide to Reading the Bible* (Minneapolis, Minn.: Augsburg Fortress Publishers, 1991); and Diane L. Jacobson and Robert Kysar, *A Beginner's Guide to the Books of the Bible* (Minneapolis, Minn.: Augsburg Fortress Publishers, 1991), which gives a concise, easy-to-understand introduction to each of the 39 books of the Old Testament and the 27 books of the New Testament.

Bodies

The definition of *compassion* is from *Merriam-Webster's Collegiate Dictionary, Tenth Edition* (1993), 234.

Stuff

For historical background on the Pacific Northwest see "The Makah Tribe: People of the Sea and the Forest," by Ann M. Renker at http://content.lib.washington. edu/aipnw/renker/. Learn more about Saint Anthony (and lots of other interesting folks) in Robert Ellsberg, *All Saints: Daily Reflections on Saints, Prophets, and Witnesses for Our Time* (New York: Crossroad Publishing, 1997).

Food

All the Gospel stories in this chapter are from Luke, for whom meal sharing, or "breaking bread," is a central sign of the reign of God and the way of Jesus. Stories of giving thanks: feeding the five thousand (Luke 9:12-17); the Last Supper (Luke 22:14-20); and the meal at Emmaus (Luke 24:28-35). Stories about Jesus and his unlikely companions: Zacchaeus (Luke 19:1-10); Mary and Martha (Luke 10:38-42); the five thousand (Luke 9:10-17); eating with sinners (Luke 7:36-50) and with "religious" people (Luke 11:37-54). The parables: the banquet story (Luke 14:15-24) and the lost son (Luke 15:22-24).

The phrase "the breaking of bread" is used in the Acts of the Apostles in a description of early Christian worship: "They devoted themselves to the apostles' teaching and fellowship, to the breaking of bread and the prayers" (Acts 2:42). See also Luke 24:35; Acts 2:46-47; 20:7, 1 Corinthians 10:16-17.

"If the only prayer . . ." is from *Meditations with Meister Eckhart*, ed. Matthew Fox (Santa Fe, N.M.: Bear & Company, Inc., 1982), 34.

Thomas Merton, a 20th-century Trappist monk, devoted much of his study to the connections between Christianity and Buddhism. In his final talk, delivered a couple of hours before his accidental death, Merton said this about compassion: "The whole idea of compassion, which is central to Mahayana Buddhism, is based on a keen awareness of the interdependence of all these living beings, which are all part of one another and all involved in one another." Thomas Merton, "Marxism and Monastic Perspectives" in *A New Charter for Monasticism: Meeting of the Monastic Superiors in the Far East*, ed. John Moffitt (Notre Dame, Ind.: University of Notre Dame Press, 1970), 80.

"I Want a Fast" is by Jan L. Richardson, *Sacred Journeys: A Woman's Book of Daily Prayer* (Nashville, Tenn.: Upper Room Books, 1995), 108–9.

Creation

Children's Letters to God was compiled by Stuart Hample and Eric Marshall (New York: Workman Publishing, 1991). Food from the 'Hood is a student-owned and operated business that began in 1992 when students at Crenshaw High School planted a garden in urban Los Angeles. In addition to selling produce at a farmers' market, they created their own salad dressings, which are available at local markets or by mail. The profits from this business provide college scholarships for the student owners. For more information on Food from the 'Hood, check out their Web page at www.foodfromthehood.com or call 888/601-FOOD. The quotation from David W. Orr is in *Earth in Mind: On Education, Environment, and the Human Prospect* (Washington, D.C.: Island Press, 1994), 46.

Creativity

"The Creation," by James Weldon Johnson, is from *God's Trombones: Seven Negro Sermons in Verse* (New York: Viking Press, 1927), 20. The quotation by Hildegard is from Gabriele Uhlein, *Meditations with Hildegard of Bingen* (Santa Fe, N.M.: Bear & Company, 1983), 35. The quotation from Katherine Paterson is from her book *A Sense of Wonder: On Reading and Writing Books for Children* (Reprint ed., New York: Plume, 1995), 70-71. The quotation by Emily Dickinson is cited in Richard B. Sewall, *The Life of Emily Dickinson* (New York: Farrar, Straus and Giroux, 1980), 23. The quotation by Ed Kowalczyk comes from "The Beauty of Gray," a song on the 1991 album *Mental Jewelry* by the band Live. The Meister

Eckhart quotation is from *Meditations with Meister Eckhart*, ed. Matthew Fox (Sante Fe, N.M.: Bear & Company, 1982), 107.

Work

The quotation by Frederick Buechner is from *Wishful Thinking: A Theological ABC* (New York: Harper & Row, 1973), 95. The José Hobday quotation is from "Neither Late Nor Working," *Creation Spirituality* (May/June 1992): 20. Omar Gil's statement is from "A Maquiladora Worker Tells His Story," as told to David Bacon, dated September 14, 2000, at www.pacificnews.org/jinn/stories/6.18/000914-a.html. The quotation by Alice Koller is from her book *The Stations of Solitude* (New York: Morrow, 1990).

Play

A classic book on the practice of play is Johan Huizinga, *Homo Ludens: A Study of the Play-Element in Culture* (Boston: Beacon Press, 1950). The quotation by Michael Jordan is from *For the Love of the Game*, ed. Mark Vancil (New York: Crown Publishers, 1998), 46. The Michael Joseph quotation is from *Play Therapy* (St. Meinrad, Ind.: Abbey Press, 1990). The "Turning Things Upside Down" section was inspired by Walter Wink's discussion of Jesus' Third Way in *Engaging the Powers: Discernment and Resistance in a World of Domination* (Minneapolis, Minn.: Augsburg Fortress Publishers, 1992), 175–93.

Time

The story of the creation of day and night is in Genesis 1:1-5.

Here is the full quotation about the rise in SAT scores after Edina, Minnesota, schools delayed the beginning of the school day: "Preliminary results of research at the University of Minnesota indicate there might be a link between a school's starting time and grades. Dr. Wahlstrom found that the top 10th of Edina's senior class scored 580 to 600 on the SATs, both math and verbal, before the time change. In the three years after, the range was 720 to 760" (Douglas Martin, "Late to Bed, Early to Rise Makes a Teen-Ager Tired," *New York Times*, August 1, 1999, sec. 4A, p. 26). This issue of the *Times* is also the source of Dr. Mary Carskadon's information about teen sleep needs.

Statistics on teen time use are from www.medialifemagazine.com/features/researchpages/researchpgarchive/research.htm and the Barna Research Group (1999 and 2000 figures). For further reading on this subject, see Dorothy C. Bass, *Receiving the Day: Christian Practices for Opening the Gift of Time* (San Francisco: Jossey-Bass, 2000).

Truth

John K. Ryan, trans., *The Confessions of Saint Augustine* (Garden City, New York: Image Books), 70, 74.

Choices

In preparing this chapter, Matthew and David interviewed friends about how they make choices; read about the history of the spiritual practice of "discernment"; and for several months kept journals about their own choices, using the processes described here. This process afforded a great opportunity for an uncle and a nephew to learn more about each other, this difficult and delightful world and God's work in it, and the generous resources our faith communities offer for fullness of life.

The Thomas Merton quotation is from *New Seeds of Contemplation* (New York: New Directions Publishing, 1972), 29. We found these resources helpful: *The Imitation of Christ* by Thomas à Kempis (written sometime between 1390 and 1440)—you can browse it at http://www.leaderu.com/cyber/books/imitation/imitation.html); Dennis Linn, Sheila Fabricant Linn, Matthew Linn, *Sleeping with Bread: Holding What Gives You Life* (Mahway, N.J.: Paulist Press, 1995); and, on Quaker decision making, Parker J. Palmer, *Let Your Life Speak: Listening for the Voice of Vocation* (San Francisco: Jossey-Bass, 1999).

Friends

Carol and Katie prepared this chapter by inviting a group of teens from Louisville, Kentucky, where they live, to get together to talk about friendship. Half of the teens are African-American, and half are white. They come from different parts of the city and different economic backgrounds; from public, private, and parochial schools; and from Catholic, Protestant, black, white, and racially mixed churches. The stories woven into this chapter come from this group of teens. See *The Four Loves,* by C. S. Lewis (San Diego: Harcourt, Brace, & Company, 1971) for more about ancient Greek concepts of love. The section on spiritual friends was inspired by Kenda Creasy Dean and Ron Foster, *The Godbearing Life: The Art of Soul Tending for Youth Ministry* (Nashville, Tenn.: Upper Room Books, 1998). Direct quotations from an online interview with Beverly Daniel Tatum may be found at http://teachers.net/archive/tatum111099.html.

Welcome

Learn more about the Sojourners ministry and magazine at www.sojo.net. "With Arms Wide Open," written by Tremonti/Stapp, is on the Creed album

Human Clay. The story of Le Chambon is told in the book *Lest Innocent Blood Be Shed,* by Philip Hallie (Harper & Row, 1985) and in the video *Weapons of the Spirit* (Friends of the Le Chambon Foundation, 1989).

Forgiveness

Some books on forgiveness are Bob Libby, *The Forgiveness Book* (Boston, Mass.: Cowley Publications, 1992); Dennis Linn, Sheila Fabricant Linn, and Matthew Linn, *Don't Forgive Too Soon: Extending the Two Hands that Heal* (Mahwah, N.J.: Paulist Press, 1997); Lewis B. Smedes, The *Art of Forgiving: When you Need to Forgive and Don't Know How* (New York: Ballantine, 1997); Simon Wiesenthal, ed., *The Sunflower: On the Possibilities and Limits of Forgiveness* (New York: Shocken Books, 1998); Oscar Hijuelos, *Mr. Ives' Christmas* (New York: HarperCollins, 1995); L. Gregory Jones, *Embodying Forgiveness: A Theological Analysis* (Grand Rapids: Eerdmans, 1995); and Donald W. Shriver Jr., *An Ethic for Enemies* (New York: Oxford University Press, 1998).

Justice

Learn about Joyce A. Ladner in her book *The Ties That Bind: Timeless Values for African American Families* (New York: John Wiley & Sons, 1999). Paul Tillich's sermon "You Are Accepted" is in *The Shaking of the Foundations* (New York: Charles Scribner's Sons, 1948).

On flourishing, see Thomas Hurka, "Three Faces of Flourishing" and Thomas E. Hill Jr., "Happiness and Human Flourishing in Kant's Ethics," in *Social Philosophy and Policy Journal* 2 (1999): 44–72. On the prophets, see Walter Brueggemann, *The Prophetic Imagination* (Philadelphia: Fortress Press, 1978). Desmond M. Tutu, *No Future Without Forgiveness* (New York: Doubleday, 1999), tells about the Truth and Reconciliation process in South Africa.

Grieving

Amy's story appeared in "Orphaned by terrorism—an agonizing road for kids of Sept. 11" by Charisse Jones in *USA Today* (October 19, 2001). The poem "Why Me?" is by Tatiana Wilson (Baypoint, Calif.: 2000). The translation of Psalms 77 and 23 is from *The New Testament and the Psalms: An Inclusive Version* (Oxford: Oxford University Press, 1995). The Thomas A. Dorsey story is drawn from an article in *Guideposts,* "From Bawdy Songs to Hymns" (December 1, 1950) and a 1973 interview with Thomas Dorsey on National Public Radio (transcribed at www.npr.org/programs/specials/vote/100List.html "Take My Hand, Precious Lord"). Stephen Goyer's sermon is used by permission of the author. On Jewish grieving practice, see "The Shivah Call: Comforting the Mourner," http://www.beingjewish.com/ cycle/nichum.html

Music

Don Saliers wrote the chapter "Singing Our Lives" in *Practicing Our Faith*, ed. Dorothy C. Bass (San Francisco: Jossey-Bass, 1997). The story of the young martyr of El Mozote also appears there on page 191. The original story may be found in Mark Danner, "A Reporter at Large: The Truth of El Mozote," in the *New Yorker* (December 6, 1993).

Prayer

"The great thing is prayer" are words spoken by Thomas Merton on the eve of his final trip to Asia at the end of his life. See M. Basil Pennington, *Centering Prayer* (New York: Image Books, 1982), 56. The "Kitchen Prayer" attributed to Brother Lawrence is cited in the preface to his book *Practicing the Presence of God* (Old Tappan, N.J.: Spire Books, 1967), 8.

ACKNOWLEDGMENTS

This book was made possible by the support of Lilly Endowment, Inc., a private family foundation in Indianapolis. We are especially grateful to Craig Dykstra, vice president for religion, for his encouragement. It was Craig who taught us to think about a way to live that takes shape as we participate in Christian practices. He has been a good friend and wise adviser to both editors for many years.

As the editors began to plan this book, they gained helpful advice from Tom Beaudoin, Kenda Creasy Dean, Ron Foster, Patricia Hersch, Carol Lytch, Robert McCarty, Evelyn Parker, Julia Speller, David White, and Mark Yaconelli during a consultation at Valparaiso University. During the writing phase, authors were welcomed into lovely meeting space at the Montreat Conference Center (North Carolina), Fourth Presbyterian Church (Chicago), Old First Presbyterian Church (San Francisco), and San Francisco Theological Seminary. Later several leaders in youth ministry reviewed the manuscript: Tom Bergler, Kenda Creasy Dean, Mike Fellin, Steve Gerali, Frank Santoni, Lani Wright, Karen-Marie Yust. Our editor at Upper Room Books, Robin Pippin, participated in this review and was helpful at every stage of the process. Others who contributed insights include Doug Magnuson, Lynn Schofield Clark, Jennifer Schmidt, Di Herald, Bonnie Kunzel, Teri Lesesne, John McClure, Fred Niedner Jr., Jeremy Myers, Tracie Myers, Fred Hofheinz, Jim Still-Pepper, Thomas Davis, and Jonathan Richter. We are grateful to all for their insight and encouragement.

The work for this book was coordinated from the office of the Valparaiso Project on the Education and Formation of People in Faith. This project has a wonderful home at Valparaiso University; the editors are grateful to the university for its support. We also thank Anne Spurgeon, the Valparaiso Project office manager, for her work on the many details associated with author meetings and manuscript preparation.